AF328763

The Digital Asset
Technology Guidebook

The Digital Asset Technology Guidebook

Deciphering the Keys to Crypto, Blockchain, and Decentralized Finance

David Utzke, PhD, MSc, MBA

WILEY

Library of Congress Cataloging-in-Publication Data:

Names: Utzke, David author
Title: The digital asset technology guidebook : deciphering the keys to
    crypto, blockchain, and decentralized finance / David Utzke.
Description: Hoboken, NJ : John Wiley & Sons Inc, 2026. | Includes
    bibliographical references and index.
Identifiers: LCCN 2025027025 | ISBN 9781394319596 hardback | ISBN
    9781394319602 adobe pdf | ISBN 9781394319619 epub
Subjects: LCSH: Cryptocurrencies | Blockchains (Databases) | Finance
Classification: LCC HG1710.3 .U76 2026
LC record available at https://lccn.loc.gov/2025027025

Cover Design: Wiley
Cover Image: © Sergey Nivens/stock.adobe.com
Printed and bound by CPI Group (UK) Ltd, Croydon, CR0 4YY

C9781394319596_270925

Contents

Foreword   ix
Preface – Author's Insights   xv

Introduction   **1**

Chapter 1   Distributed Ledger Architectural Primitives with
                a Historical Perspective   9
                Distributed Ledger: The Beginning   11
                The First Distributed Ledger   13
                The Contribution of the Merkle Cryptographic
                    Hash to DLT   14
                Cryptographic Digital Signatures in DLT   15
                Consensus in DLT   17
                Consensus Protocols vs. Consensus Algorithms   18
                Distributed Network Architecture and Topology   25
                Nodes and Clients in Distributed Networks   29
                Messaging Protocols in Distributed Networking   31

Chapter 2   Distributed Ledger Transparency: Types of
                Network Design   39
                Permissioned vs. Permissionless Design   41

| | Private vs. Public Network Design | 44 |
| | Federated Network Design | 47 |

Chapter 3 Distribute Network Secure Data Ledger
	Architectural Design Typologies	51
	Distributed Computing	54
	Distributed Networking	55
	Data Ledger Structures in DLT	56
	Data Ledger Structures: Block Ledgers	58
	Data Ledger Technology Structures: Blockless Ledger Architecture	65
	Hybrid Ledger Architecture	72

Chapter 4 Alternative Ledger Frameworks — 81
| | Relay-Parachain Model | 82 |
| | Hub-zone Model and App-chains | 86 |

Chapter 5 The Distributed Ledger Stack — 91
	Layer-0 (L0)—TCP/IP Layer	95
	Layer-1 (L1)—Mainnet (Main Network) Layer	96
	Layer-2 (L2)—Developer Layer	102
	L2 Contracts in General	102
	L1-to-L2 Contracts	107
	State Channels	110
	Roll-ups	114
	Bridges	118
	Oracles	121
	Side Chains and Child Chains	124
	Side Chains	125
	Child Chains	127
	Layer-3 (L3)—Distributed Applications Layer	128

Chapter 6 Digital Currency in the Context of Currency and Money Systems — 131
	Money vs. Currency	132
	Money	133
	Currency	134
	Digital Currency	137

Digital Asset Taxonomy, Typology, and Topology
    Insights 146
Taxonomy 148
Typology 150
Topology 151

Chapter 7 Governance Tenets of Distribution,
Democratization, and Decentralization ($G=D^3$) 153
Tenet 1: Governance in Distributed Systems 158
Tenet 2: Governance in Democratized Systems 161
Tenet 3: Governance in Decentralization 164

Chapter 8 Trends in Use Cases and Convergence with
Other Technologies 173
Digital Asset Reserve Funds 174
Tokenization of Real-World Assets (RWA)/
    In Real-Life Assets (IRLA) 187
Synthetic Fiat 188
Synthetic Securities 201
Layer-2 Contract Meme Tokens and Layer-3
    Project Development 208
DeComm, DePIN, DeREN, DeWiFi, and DeVS 214
Quantum Cryptography & Quantum
    Entanglement Distributed Networks 216

Conclusion 221
Index 225

Foreword

In the rapidly evolving world of distributed ledger technology (DLT), few individuals bring as much diverse expertise and real-world experience to the table as Dr. David Utzke. Dr. Utzke's journey into the world of DLT, digital currencies, and blockchain technologies is one marked by a unique blend of academic excellence, military service, forensic investigation, and a deep commitment to education and knowledge-sharing.

Dr. Utzke's academic journey began with a bachelor's in agri-business and preveterinary medicine, followed by a master's in forensic accounting and international finance. His passion for computer science led him to complete a doctorate in financial economics, along with several postdoctoral degrees, including work in cryptoeconomics at MIT and an MSc in blockchain engineering and digital currency. His academic pursuits were complemented by practical experience, working with the Cyber Crimes Unit at the US Treasury—Internal Revenue Service Criminal Investigations. For more than a decade, Dr. Utzke has served as a forensic and heuristic expert in DLT, digital currencies, and alternative payment systems, contributing to high-profile investigations that have brought criminals to justice in areas such as money laundering, trafficking, and cybercrimes. During this time, I personally relied on the insights and knowledge of Dr. Utzke to help guide and inform our team during the most influential period of digital asset development. We saw unprecedented investigations involving billions of dollars and sophisticated transactions all over the world that brought creative solutions for the first time in law enforcement. These solutions were a direct result of the work performed by Dr. Utzke.

The rapid evolution of digital assets has reshaped the global financial landscape, offering new opportunities for innovation, efficiency, and financial inclusion. These technologies have enabled responsible financial advancements, expanded access to secure and affordable financial services, and reduced the cost of cross-border transactions. However, alongside these benefits, digital assets also present significant risks—serving as potential tools for tax evasion, money laundering, cybercrime, and other illicit financial activities.

Recognizing these challenges, IRS Criminal Investigation (IRS-CI) has emerged as a leader in combating digital asset-related crimes. This specialized unit focuses on investigating cyber-enabled financial crimes, enforcing tax compliance, and disrupting illicit financial networks that exploit blockchain technology, alternative payment systems, and the dark web. Through the deployment of cutting-edge investigative tools such as blockchain analytics and open-source intelligence (OSINT), IRS-CI has strengthened its ability to trace, investigate, and prosecute those who seek to misuse digital assets. This commanding department didn't miraculously form overnight; it took years of experimenting, training, and educating personnel on the technology surrounding digital assets and cybercrime. Early on it became apparent that our investigators and analysts needed more development and education around the tools, technology, and tactics that criminals utilize to exploit this ever-evolving area. In conjunction with Dr. Utzke, IRS-CI revolutionized the way government attacked this problem. We focused on public private partnerships and leveraged relationships in industry to learn from those who truly were engrossed in the environment and deploy cutting-edge tools. We engaged law enforcement partners across the globe to force-multiple efforts against the criminals who quickly deployed a Cybercrime-as-a-Service (CaaS) model. We, in turn, needed to effectively incorporate Enforcement-as-a-Service (EaaS)—a coined term that highlights the collective power of law enforcement coming together, similar to that of the Marvel Avengers.

Lastly, leaning on academia to help drive the core education and foundation of digital assets, DLT, and all things that would morph into this ecosystem, we find ourselves at the beginning, as a student of the world around us.

IRS-CI's impact is evident in several high-profile cases where digital assets were exploited for criminal purposes:

- Bitfinex Hack (2016): IRS-CI seized $3.6 billion in stolen cryptocurrency tied to the 2016 hack of the Bitfinex exchange. Special agents traced the stolen bitcoin through a complex blockchain trail to a New York couple, Ilya Lichtenstein and Heather Morgan, who attempted to launder 119,754 bitcoin. The case resulted in the largest government cryptocurrency seizure to date.
- xDedic Marketplace: A notorious online marketplace that sold access to compromised computers and personal data was dismantled through an international effort led by IRS-CI. The platform facilitated more than $68 million in fraud and impacted victims across industries, including hospitals, emergency services, and government infrastructure. Seventeen individuals have been charged or extradited in connection with the operation.
- BTC-e Exchange: From 2011 to 2017, BTC-e operated as a cryptocurrency exchange that laundered billions of dollars. Russian national Alexander Vinnik, a key figure in the operation, was arrested and pleaded guilty to crimes including identity theft, drug trafficking, and laundering criminal proceeds.
- OneCoin Ponzi Scheme: OneCoin defrauded investors out of more than $4 billion under the guise of a legitimate cryptocurrency. However, it was neither actively traded nor usable for purchases. Cofounder Sebastian Greenwood was sentenced to 20 years in prison in 2023, while the other cofounder, Ruja Ignatova, remains a fugitive and is listed on the FBI's Most Wanted List.
- Welcome to Video: The largest child exploitation market by volume of content, Welcome to Video used bitcoin to monetize illegal materials. IRS-CI helped dismantle the platform, rescuing at least 23 victims and leading to the arrest of more than 300 individuals worldwide. The investigation revealed the site had more than one million bitcoin addresses, indicating an extensive global network of users.

- North Korean Exchange Hack: North Korean hackers allegedly infiltrated virtual currency exchanges, stealing millions of dollars and laundering the funds through Chinese over-the-counter traders. One such attack saw $272,000 stolen and "chain-hopped" through various cryptocurrencies to obfuscate the transactions. A related hack in 2019 resulted in the theft of $2.5 million, which was funneled through more than 100 accounts at another exchange.
- Terrorism Financing: IRS-CI played a critical role in dismantling three cyber-enabled financing campaigns that supported terrorist organizations, including al-Qaeda, Hamas's military wing, and ISIS. This operation resulted in the largest-ever seizure of cryptocurrency tied to terrorism, leading to the confiscation of millions of dollars, 300 cryptocurrency accounts, and various online platforms used for fundraising.

As of early 2025, IRS-CI holds billions of dollars in seized digital assets, approximately half of which is tied to restitution for victims. With hundreds of ongoing investigations, the agency has maintained an impressive conviction rate of 90% to 95% in prosecuted cases. These figures underscore the unit's effectiveness in identifying, investigating, and bringing cybercriminals to justice.

As the digital economy continues to evolve, so too must the efforts to ensure its integrity. This book explores the intersection of digital finance and the technology that supports it, offering a deeper understanding of these capabilities. Through detailed insights and real-world experience, Dr. Utzke will walk through the critical components that create both the positive and negative impacts of this space.

Dr. Utzke's approach to DLT and digital currency is both technical and humanistic, shaped by his extensive background in data science and his first-hand experiences working with complex data to solve critical cases. His deep understanding of blockchain technologies, DeFi (decentralized finance), and the wider implications of DLT across various industries is reflected in his passion for teaching and knowledge-sharing. His focus on education and fostering the next generation of digital currency experts led him to the University of Advancing Technology (UAT), where he has become a vital part of the faculty, offering students an insider's perspective on the rapidly advancing world of DLT.

In this book, Dr. Utzke brings that wealth of knowledge to the page, offering readers a comprehensive exploration of DLT, digital currencies, and the vast ecosystem of technologies that are converging to shape the future of our financial systems, communication networks, and more. From the historical roots of distributed ledgers to the cutting-edge advancements in DeFi, blockchain architecture, and the intersection of emerging technologies like AI and quantum computing, this book provides both theoretical depth and practical insights.

Whether you are an investigator, analyst, student, professional, or an enthusiast of the technology that is transforming society, you will find in these pages the expertise of someone who has lived and breathed these innovations, shaped them through his work, and is now dedicated to sharing them with the world. Dr. Utzke's contributions to DLT have not only been technical but deeply impactful, helping to bring justice in high-stakes investigations, and making a difference in the lives of countless individuals.

As you embark on this journey through the world of distributed ledger technology, you will be guided by the wisdom of an individual whose expertise, experience, and values are as multifaceted as the technology he explores.

—Jarod Koopman
Exec. Director Cyber and Forensic Services,
US Dept. of Treasury-IRS Criminal Investigation Division

Preface – Author's Insights

For many, reading what I concentrate on concerning the technologies of distributed computing, distributed networking, and data ledger structures in this book is going to be like the interaction in the movie *The Matrix* where Neo (played by Keanu Reeves) had to make a choice. Morpheus (played by Laurence Fishburne) presented Neo with the choice of taking the red pill or the blue pill. Morpheus asks Neo, "Do you want to know what IT is?" referring to the Matrix. Morpheus explains that the Matrix is the system of control that operates in your mind to blind your eyes from the "truth." Neo asks, "What truth?" Morpheus replies to Neo that his mind has been imprisoned. Matrix theory in reality is based on the idea that the world is an algorithmic computer program with rules that determine how things work. The movie suggests that individuals have the power to choose their own destiny and break free from the illusions that have been created. I suggest as an academic, developer, and researcher that many interacting in the distributed network ledger environment, like the Matrix, have had their minds imprisoned by group-think that is preventing them from clearly understanding the true flaws, vulnerabilities, and realistic benefits of the convergence of the technologies that comprise distributed network ledger technology.

So, as Morpheus to Neo, I offer you a choice. A choice to accept the blue pill and the story ends: You don't read the content of this book, and your understanding of the convergence of data ledger structures, distributed networking, and distributed computing continues to be all about what you know as the Matrix, or "blockchain" in this context. But by choosing to accept the red pill, you read the book, and I take you down the rabbit hole and open your mind as to how deep the rabbit hole goes. And just as Neo makes his move and reaches for a pill, Morpheus says, "Remember, all I'm offering is the truth, nothing more." And so, I leave you with the choice knowing that all I am offering is the truth. If you've chosen the red pill, please read on.

I'm beginning with a quote from the 1905 work of George Santayana, a psychology professor at Harvard, *The Life of Reason: Reason in Common Sense*. The following quote is at the center of my rationale and decision on why I agreed to write this book:

> Progress, far from consisting in change, depends on retentiveness. When change is absolute there remains no being to improve and no direction is set for possible improvement: and when experience is not retained, as among savages, infancy is perpetual. *Those who cannot remember the past are condemned to repeat it.*
>
> In the first stage of life the mind is frivolous and easily distracted; it misses progress by failing in consecutiveness and persistence. This is the condition of children and barbarians, in whom instinct has learned nothing from experience.

I have over four decades of involvement with digital assets and converging technologies of cryptography, distributed computing, distributed networking, and data ledger structures under what is presumptuously called "blockchain." And in the name of blockchain, there are so many different renderings of what it is when in fact it includes the convergence of several technologies that had existed for decades. And it is with these existing technologies that are involved in the development of an architectural design that distributes an encrypted data ledger across a distributed computing network utilizing the contrived term blockchain that has resulted in a significant amount of incorrect thinking. But take note, distributed network ledger architectures were around long before the term blockchain was architected to describe technologies many did not take the time to learn about. There is so much more to learn about these technologies that will assist professionals in making decisions on whether to adopt a digital asset for use, or how it was used by a bad actor, or proactively determining how it can be used by a bad actor.

Over the decades I have witnessed the good, the bad, and the ugly in my academic study, research, and development of investigative techniques. There is a rich historical background of incredible and brilliant individuals who paved the way many, many decades before I began my academic studies. And I now find that the teaching of this history is lacking in the current culture. As such, I have been provided the opportunity to present what seems to be a lost history involving these technologies behind what is called the blockchain (i.e., The Matrix).

Individuals reading this book who have entered this area of technology with little to no experience or formal education in DLT, computer science, cryptography, or digital asset algorithms have not received the benefit of learning about the past that brought us to the present age of digital assets and the underpinning technologies. Other individuals reading this book may only know about the technologies of distribution from what they have learned from work experience, articles on websites written by contributors such as attorneys, tech journalists, bloggers, podcasters, or web developers working in the distributed Layer-3 DApp space who typically know little more about the underlying technology than the general reader and even less about the historical roots of the technology. Many who write or speak on the topic describe their expertise on LinkedIn as "crypto" or "blockchain" experts either because they completed a short-course from a company that provides a technology service, a developer of a popular platform or company, or because of their position as a regulator at a federal entity or consulting company. So many frauds emanate from claims of expertise. Don't fall for the hype behind the term expert. A person is determined to be an expert through a combination of deep knowledge, extensive experience, and proven skills in a specific field. This expertise is typically gained through education, training, and dedicated effort. Expertise is often recognized through achievements, publications, or contributions that demonstrate a high level of proficiency—the accolade of expert is bestowed by peers, not a self-proclamation.

What I want to bring to the discussion by writing this book is to add depth to the conversation by providing a superlative technological overview with a historical perspective given to those who introduced these technologies with the objective of benefiting those who want to gain a deeper appreciation for these technologies and perspective on realistic future development.

In this book I draw attention to the often unrecognized historical experts who spent a lifetime developing and evolving technologies that brought us what we have today. These are individuals like Dr. Shannon, Leslie Lamport, David Chaum, Ralph Merkle, and others who have been recognized by their peers and attained the title of expert. Through this insight into the historic development of a technology and about how these early experts were thinking about the technology will allow us to responsibly develop these technologies well into the future and pass it on to the next generation. Those who evolve current day technology contribute by standing on the shoulders of those who came before.

The historical accounts of the technology revolutionaries of the past have been lost for many different reasons, but, without going down that path, it is this lack of historical perspective that allows present mistakes to be recreated by unenlightened entrants into a technology who have not learned the past and are now repeating the mistakes of the past. This is an increasingly recognized problem with AI LLM agent assisted coding, called "vibe coding," that has led to the introduction of code from those who have not learned the principles of cybersecurity and DevSecOps. While this may be presented in a more intuitive way for people to code without having to learn anything about what they are doing, it is amplifying mistakes of the past of not paying attention to vulnerabilities leading to bad actors who do know what they are doing committing crimes against society. As I frequently share with students, those that do not know the history do not have a perspective on the future, which highlights the importance of understanding the past to inform future decisions. It suggests that by learning from history, we gain insights into societal patterns, trends, and potential pitfalls, allowing us to make more informed choices about the future. Essentially, history provides a framework for understanding the present and making better choices for the future.

Writing this book comes from a desire to pay forward what has been given to me by imparting a portion of the academic learning, research, and development experience I have received from so many professors and mentors who invested their time and effort to give me a solid foundational education. And not just an education, but to share their gained knowledge and what they learned from those who came before them. I will sum up why I am writing this book by adapting a biblical principle from a portion of Romans 10:14 regarding my motive to share a portion of what I have learned over the past four decades: "…and how shall they hear without a teacher?"

Introduction

In the Preface, I shared a few paragraphs from George Santayana's 1905 work that contains a familiar and often misquoted truism. However, the overarching context is what I wish to accomplish in this book: Educate to ensure the responsible progress of DLT. As Santayana wrote, "Progress, far from consisting in change, depends on retentiveness. When change is absolute there remains no being to improve and no direction is set for possible improvement: and when experience is not retained, as among savages, infancy is perpetual."

In this book, I am attempting to present the content in a conversational lecture format rather than in a formal textbook or research format that I was required to use in my doctoral dissertation, masters theses, and other formal documents that I wrote when working in the federal government. I am also providing select pieces of my many years of economic and technology research such as the "Distributed Ledger Digital Asset Taxonomy" model for risk assessment of distributed ledger digital assets, a model that I developed years ago in one of my postdoctoral projects that has withstood the test of time. In addition, I share a number of abridged versions of my graduate course architectural diagrams portraying various project frameworks that have been developed in the distributed ledger technology stack over the past 16 years. And I present the content with the historical building blocks of how these technologies arrived and the role they are playing at the time of this writing. I will also introduce a knowledge reset by "going logically and concisely into the complexity" of the technologies of distributed networking, distributed computing, cryptography, and data ledgers to expose the errors of oversimplification of the complex components of distributed network ledger technologies, the digital asset taxonomy, topology, and typology, to be able to present a risk-based analysis to encompass the unique attributes of the digital assets created in the DLT technology stack. It is through understanding the complexities laid out in this book that I provide the information for professionals to become better investigators, policymakers, educators, compliance regulators, etc. And by understanding what goes on under the hood, those that interact with distributed ledger assets will understand in more depth how a criminal exploits L2 contracts containing bad code, how a money launder can move a L2 digital asset with less transparency than a L1 digital asset, why only a fraction of L2 digital asset transactions are discoverable on-ledger, and the list goes on.

The lack of precise instruction on technology of distributed ledger and digital assets has led to a significant amount of heuristic analytic and research error that is misunderstood as a forensic science in the cohort of people who construct transaction narratives involving the distributed network and data ledger technology when evaluating cybercrime, cybersecurity, and transparent on-ledger activity and missing much of the off-ledger transaction activity. And as the Layer-2 (L2) and Layer-3 (L3) technology stack structure on the Ethereum platform has developed beyond that of the rudimentary infrastructure of the Bitcoin blockchain, it has increased the opportunities for L2 contract exploits to abscond digital assets owned by other people, cybersecurity vulnerabilities through web interfacing, creating new opportunities for schemes and scams, and most obvious is the loss of transparency in transaction activity within the L2|L3 substructure outside of the algorithms developed for Layer-1 (L1) designed decades ago for transparency.

And this goes to my point, from the historical perspective of technological evolution, distributed ledger parameters were developed with specific objectives such as providing privacy, security, and transparency—this is the true distributed network ledger trifecta. However, the present state of development focus has disregarded the previously established objects, which have not been followed because historical technology development ethical parameters have been forgotten (or ignored) and traded for the perceived greater goal of monetizing. Exploits in the millions to billions of dollars are growing, aggregate transaction volumes in L2|L3 projects have now exceeded $3 trillion, and reported revenues by these L2|L3 projects are more than $1 billion in just the first quarter of 2025.

Developers ignoring the historic guardrails have resulted in thousands of people being taken advantage of through hype and misinformation led by people engaging in developing what was meant to provide security through cryptographic algorithms and sound architecturally engineered designs. The current developments introduced are significantly less secure without the cryptographic protections but continue to call it "crypto" or even quantum proof. Rectifying the neglect of research and formal academic learning involving the historical development of technology primitives is necessary to become fully educated in technology development ethics, accessibility parameters for all people, and grasp the social implications of introducing certain technologies that lead to degen trading and new fraud techniques or methods (i.e., Method: a comprehensive, structured process or system used to achieve a specific goal. Technique: refers to a specific skill or way of doing something, often within a broader method.) A haphazard development of distributed ledgers and minting of digital assets using L2 contracts and interfacing them as L3 Distributed Applications (DApps) webpages adds an additional level of vulnerability for people and digital assets.

I read and hear so much daily misinformation about digital assets and associated technologies disseminated by marketers, developers, enthusiasts, evangelists, bloggers, podcasters, and others. Many developers have come to the distributed ledger Layer-2|Layer-3 enterprise environment from the traditional webpage programming and internet TCP/IP infrastructure space without a formal education in cryptography, cybersecurity standards, or a background in DLT architectural engineering. My interactions with developers have occured over nearly 20 years of working in federal international investigations, analyzing digital code from transactions of exploited Layer-2 contracts, and conducting security reviews of Layer-2 contracts and Layer-3 Distributed Applications (DApp) analysis. It comes as no surprise why cybercriminals, and other bad actors, are so drawn to using these technologies to take advantage of vulnerable individuals.

Professional enforcement around the technology has been led down the path of classifying all digital assets under a singular risk ranking and giving it the incorrect title of "crypto." Thus, cybercriminals easily exploit these non-crypto DeFi contracts and apps. And therein lies the danger; people believe there is some cryptographic protection and that all digital assets are safe because of cryptography and cryptanalysis.

To this day, I continue to convey to students and attendees at lectures that people will eventually (through education) realize that what they believe to be "crypto" protected assets are not protected by cryptography and will begin to litigate those who associate the term "crypto" with digital assets. Having spent 20 years educating government entities, graduate students, and CPE participants on this fact, I will make the same prediction in this book: Someone will eventually litigate the use of the term "crypto" as an allusive synonymous reference to digital assets while the cryptography is in the transaction data ledger, and keys which has nothing to do with the actual asset. And with that context, I use the phrase "digital assets" in lieu of "crypto" to make this significant distinction. The taxonomy and typology of digital assets will be covered in a later chapter, and these distinctions will be discussed for greater clarification as well as to increase the understanding of these assets and their uniqueness.

I have been involved with digital assets and the technologies that have converged with digital assets for 40 plus years at the time of this writing. And with that perspective, there has been an increasing amount of misinformation about many of these technologies and their convergence. For instance, architectural components such as distributed computing, distributed networking, data structures (the four basic data structure types are linear data structures, tree data structures, hash data structures, and graph data structures), and type of encryption methods are frequently excluded in the white papers of development projects, if a white paper is even provided, and yet there is often a claim of open source code with no indication of having components of the preceding. In fact, many of the projects introduced over the past eight years have nothing to do with what they call "blockchain" but are essentially using mainnet platforms for app development just like they use the Apple or Google app stores to introduce their "killer" app to the public. Of course, then it is up to the public to determine if it is a legitimate app and not an attempt to commit fraud.

This leads to additional concerns over additional technologies converging with distributed network ledger. Artificial intelligence and quantum computing, often described as emerging technologies even though they have been sciences in their own right prior to the 1950s, are now converging with digital assets inside and outside of DLT environments. For example, AI, an umbrella of technologies that will be addressed later, is now engaging with the Layer-2 stack of the DLT. There are questions about AI technologies introducing negative outcomes generally, but few in DLT development are questioning whether AI technologies should be integrated with DLT architecture or what guardrails should be put in place given the potential for negative convergence outcomes. This is a topic that I would love to cover, but space is limited in this book to take it on.

Another technology garnering attention, other than its impact on current cryptographic models, is the recent developments of quantum entanglement creating a framework for a quantum internet. Synthesize this with the 2010 paper describing a method to create a quantum currency; it surprises me that people are spending so much time contemplating the demise of today's cryptography when they should be looking at the demise of what they call "the blockchain." And I do take up this topic in the last chapter.

Other topics I elaborate on in this book include the rapid pace of development of L2 contract tokens in the DLT technology stack. This should be a primary concern given the Degen Casino Model development that began emerging in 2019, and yet, project foundations and legitimate developer communities are not self-regulating developers entering their platforms in an effort to preempt government regulators from stepping in and taking over and to reduce fraudulent behaviors.

There are many jurisdictions involved in attempting to regulate the DLT space. But global community stakeholders can, and should, come together to introduce a self-regulated environment for introducing independent third-party intermediaries to develop standards and security conventions. Intermediaries are so deeply ingrained in the framework of digital assets by the DLT community in the form of massive corporations and foundations that are frequently driving the conversation in government with a self-interest in mind, so introducing another third-party around responsible development should not present a challenge. Ask the question: Are regulators better positioned to set standards for the community, to understand the technology used by the community, to be community centric?

Responsible development is extremely important and cannot happen if much of what is known about the technology is persistently identified as nascent. Researching and learning about what is perceived as nascent takes work. It necessitates doing the hard work of learning about the complexity of the technology. Without learning the complexities, one does not have the knowledge to critically analyze the complexity to communicate the simplicity. Currently, the trend is to short-circuit the hard work and go directly to simplicity, which is rationalized as a necessity to drive adoption. However, I have found over two decades of working in federal cybercrime investigations that the individuals most vulnerable are those who have been educated with the technological simplicity presented by evangelists, enthusiasts, and developers who provide everything about a converged technology in a contrived notion of the term blockchain.

My concerns of simplification for the sake of adoption are summed up in a core principle frequently articulated by Steve Jobs: "It takes a lot of hard work to make something simple, to truly understand the underlying challenges and come up with elegant solutions. [...] It's not just minimalism or the absence of clutter. It involves digging through the depth of complexity. To be truly simple, you have to go really deep."

I trust there is an excitement for moving forward in the journey of learning the history of today's distributed ledger technology, digital asset taxonomy and topology, and about the architectural components underpinning DLT. In order to truly appreciate the order and purpose of these technologies, it means acquiring an understanding of the complexity. And to do that, it requires adopting a critical thinking mindset that drives us to ask questions and move past the passivity of acceptance.

This book is written for any individual who wants to move past the hype and misinformation found on the web. To accomplish this, one needs to be able to think critically about the historical underpinning and evolution of these technologies. If this can be accomplished, it is with a new mindset that we can better understand how technologies can be converged while moving into the future.

It is appropriate to mention in the introduction that the intended audience of this book are professionals in the areas of investigation, regulatory compliance, regulatory policymaking, law enforcement, investment advisory, and academia. However, it is also beneficial to any reader wanting to learn more about digital assets and the associated technologies.

For investigators, compliance personnel, regulators, and law enforcement, this book provides a much deeper insight into all of what happens in digital asset movement in ways that emphasize the limitations tracing services have, and don't catagorically disclose, that the majority of ledger transactions across all platform stacks can't observe off-ledger transactions that are bundled and hashed then moved from L2 to the L1 mainnet but categorized as on-ledger reporting. In addition, most services do not properly teach the difference in the sciences of forensics and heuristics. Heuristics technique used in ledger analytics is an approach that employs a pragmatic method that is not fully optimized or perfected to fully account for the full scope of possible transaction conduits but is nevertheless "good enough" as an approximation or attribute substitution involving cryptographic key exchange of digital assets. This falls short of the forensics necessary for the admission of evidence. Related, and just as significant, is the lack of proper training and education of the distributed network ledger technologies in the methods necessary for forensic attribution. Forensic attribution involves using forensic science in intelligence gathering, and legal analysis to determine who or what was responsible for a particular event. This process helps in understanding the nature of the incident, classifying it, and potentially deterring future similar actions.

Investment professionals will get insight into the DLT stack that demonstrates that technical analysis of price movement is not the entire picture of value. Supplementary aspects presented in this book is that DeFi (Decentralized Finance) actually has only a distributed network architecture and is in reality a Democratized Finance space within the DLT stack and not in fact decentralized (i.e., management and control spread across the community). This is because developers of L2 contracts, who, in totality, own the contract and collect the proceeds from the contract (i.e., centralization). And when it comes to due diligence, some of the tasks that should be included are the ? translation of the L2 contract code to discover the transaction fees going to the contract creator, which is over-and-above the gas fees that are paid; the date of the last contract security review conducted;[1] the developer's history of transparency and how many of its contracts have been exploited due to security flaws or other exploits; and if the developer is being transparent with its contract users/customers and tax authorities in the developer's jurisdiction and disclosing the accounting of revenues from their contract(s). Overall, a deeper discrimination of the taxonomy of digital assets risk and distributed ledger architecture associated with specific layers within the DLT stack is warranted, if not mandatory, for investment professionals.

And last, but not least, academia, in which I wrap up with this: "Simple can be harder than complex because you have to work hard to get your thinking clean around the complex in order to make it simple. But it's worth it in the end because once you get there, you can move mountains." This is a lesson I teach to all learners I speak with.

---

[1] NOTE: just like annual accounting audits, cybersecurity contract reviews are not a once and done exercise.

Chapter 1

Distributed Ledger Architectural Primitives with a Historical Perspective

Richelle Mead, urban fantasy author, wrote, "History is important because it teaches us about the past. And by learning about the past, you come to understand the present, so that you may make educated decisions about the future."

This quote is exceedingly apropos to this chapter as I unmask the primitives of distributed ledger technologies (DLTs) and combine them with the rarely taught historical perspective that provides a necessary appreciation for the evolution of what these technologies have become today. I trust providing this historical prospective will offer enlightenment and knowledge to chart an intelligent path forward through the lens of information rather than misplaced enthusiastic hype for professionals working in the areas of development, investment, compliance, regulation, and other activities surrounding these convergent technologies. And it is with a history perspective that provides context for understanding future trends in the context for how they will evolve over time. And on that topic of history, Nathan Rosenberg is credited with first using the term "convergence" in the context of technology in his 1963 work "Technological Change in the Machine Tool Industry," which signified the union of at least two distinct fields within science, technology, markets, or industries.

One of the benefits of studying historical events and information from various perspectives is that it allows individuals to develop the ability to critically analyze information, recognize patterns, evaluate different viewpoints, and form well-supported conclusions. For example, when I ask graduate students in their first course on distributed ledger, or conference attendees attending one of my speaking engagements, "Who was the first to introduce a blockchain model," the answer is constantly unanimously incorrect.

Currently, the examination of the evolutionary history of distributed ledger, distributed computing, data ledgers, and cryptography surrounding digital assets that have code is most commonly denoted as beginning with the 2009 deployment of the Bitcoin payment network and its embedded digital asset bitcoin (BTC). What eludes the masses, however, is that the historic ushering in of these technologies commenced many decades prior to the mainstream thinking that is commonly communicated by many who are touted as experts. Why do they get it wrong? It is a lack of historical context.

The myth of what I see taught in many certificate and education programs by many legitimate and well-known organizations is unfortunate. In addition, public trust government officials are also the messengers of misinformation that lead people down the wrong path in their knowledge about the technical aspects of distributed network ledger technologies. What follows is objective and factual documented information with the only purpose of correcting many of the false narratives that have been propagated and passed on by those who are parroting others who have told the story or whose primary objective is to encourage adoption of the digital asset space in an effort to sell an asset or a related service under the guise of fabricated information.

At the outset, it is important to grasp that digital asset code is coupled with other technologies, and each will be covered separately to ensure that digital assets are not conflated as being a component of distributed network and data ledger technology. So, given that data ledgers, distributed networks, and distributed computing were the first to be historically presented, that is where I will begin.

Distributed Ledger: The Beginning

The history of distributed ledger primitives is a fascinating study, and an important exercise, to fully appreciate the technologies being uncovered. It is also out of recognition and respect to those who developed what we have today. Developers today wrangle over ensuring they are recognized for their achievements, and my commitment in this book is dedicated to sharing about as many of the predecessors as I possibly can who built the foundational technologies we use today in the distributed network ledger technology stack, but who are infrequently recognized for their contributions.

The history of distributed ledgers begins with the "Father of the Information Age," Dr. Claude Shannon. Perhaps to the dismay of many, the concept of a distributed ledger did not begin with the Satoshi Nakamoto team—I use "team" because the Bitcoin white paper is written as "we." The concept actually started with Dr. Claude Shannon (1916–2001) in his 1949 Bell Labs published paper titled "Communication Theory of Secrecy Systems," the foundation of information theory.[1] This paper is the basis for the dismantling of classical cryptography and introduced the underpinning of modern secret-key cryptography, which is elaborated upon in far more detail in "Development of Cryptography since Shannon" by Koc and Ozdemir.

The modern design of block ciphers is based on the concept of an iterated product cipher in Shannon's 1949 publication, which analyzed product ciphers and suggested them as a means of effectively improving security by combining simple operations such as substitutions and permutations.

---

[1] Shannon, C. (1949). Communication theory of secrecy systems. *Bell System Technical Journal*, 28(4), 656–715. https://typeset.io/papers/communication-theory-of-secrecy-systems-2y1h3cz20a.

Shannon describes a block cipher as blocks with a constant transformation, and a secure block cipher is suitable for the encryption of a single block of data at a time, using a fixed key. Many other realizations of block ciphers include Advance Encryption Standard (AES), which are classified as substitution–permutation networks. Shannon even introduced the conception of a "bit" (a portmanteau of binary digit).

After completing an undergraduate degree at the University of Michigan, Shannon started graduate studies at MIT, where he wrote his master's thesis in 1937 titled, "A Symbolic Analysis of Relay and Switching Circuits," that applied a mathematical discipline called Boolean algebra to the analysis and synthesis of switching circuits that turned circuit design from an art into a science; the paper is now considered as the starting point of modern-day digital circuit design.

Shannon's contribution to war cryptography can be found in a 1945 report (declassified in 1957) titled "A Mathematical Theory of Cryptography," which outlined the first theory, relying on both algebraic and probabilistic theories. It is for this reason that Dr. Shannon is often recognized as the "father of mathematical cryptography." Shannon explained that he was interested in discrete information consisting of sequences of discrete symbols chosen from a finite set. He gave definitions of redundancy, equivocation, and information.

Shannon's work impacted nearly every aspect of modern life today, having influenced such diverse fields as communication, computing, cryptography, neuroscience, artificial intelligence, cosmology, linguistics, quantum physics, and genetics. A short video on YouTube (https://youtu.be/0wlmzvf8_gI?si=b8Do2c3EUOvW0i12) provides a respectable overview of Shannon's contributions.

With all his contributions to the modern information age and cryptography, the world does not know this man. Especially those who should, such as people who work in DLT. Solomon Golomb, a mathematician, engineer, and professor of electrical engineering at the University of Southern California, wrote, "It is no exaggeration to refer to Claude Shannon as the 'father of the information age,' and his intellectual achievement as one of the greatest of the twentieth century."[2]

---

[2] Siegfried, T. (2016). Claude Shannon's information theory built the foundation for the digital era. *Science News.* https://www.sciencenews.org/blog/context/claude-shannon-information-theory-digital-era.

In his day, Dr. Shannon's insights were not comprehended nor what his contributions would bring, in large part because his work was so far ahead of his time. But it is in this book that Dr. Shannon's work is recognized for his conceptualization, which would give the world underpinning of DLT well before there was a Satoshi Nakamoto. In fact, without the contribution of Dr. Shannon's information theory, one could theoretically point out that there would have been no internet, which provides the DLT Layer-0. At a minimum, it may have taken many additional decades before realizing the existence of an internet.

With the leadoff of the primer of Dr. Shannon's introductory concept of block ciphers as a primitive to block ledger architecture, we'll move on to the next DLT development—the introduction of the first distributed block ledger.

The First Distributed Ledger

Putting DLT history into a timeline, it is notable that the first distributed sequential linear block architecture was deployed in 1995, which is intellectualized in the 1991 white paper, "How to Time-stamp a Digital Document," by Drs. Haber and Stornetta. This occurred 14 years before the Bitcoin payment network distributed ledger architecture that was deployed in 2009 (conceptualized in the Bitcoin white paper released in 2008), which was builds from many of the concepts of Haber and Stornetta's distributed sequential linear block architecture, which builds on Dr. Shannon's concept of block ciphers from 43 years earlier and David Chaum's 1982 doctoral dissertation "Computer systems established, maintained and trusted by mutually suspicious groups."

When I lecture and accept speaking requests on distributed systems, digital assets, and cybersecurity/cybercrimes, discussions frequently gravitate toward historical viewpoints, and few are aware of the fascinating history of DLT. Of the few who are aware, a majority have never read the white papers to truly understand the use case or the Bitcoin network architecture. In fact, I have not found anyone who knows that the Haber-Stornetta distributed ledger continues to operate to this day. Anyone in the world can examine the *Sunday New York Times* classified section under the heading "Notices & Lost and Found" for the new unique hash. Instead of publishing individual hashes to a public digital distributed ledger, they are added to the weekly *Times* circulation making it impossible for anyone to backdate timestamps or validate electronic records that were not exact copies of the original. The three papers written by Haber and Stornetta articulating their work are (in order of publishing):

- "How to Time-stamp a Digital Document" (1991)
- "Improving the Efficiency and Reliability of Digital Time-stamping" (1992)
- "Secure Names for Bit-strings" (1997)

It is important to learn about the architecture of this first cryptographically secured distributed block data ledger, but that will be covered later, so now let's move on to one of the key architectural primitive components used in all current variations of distributed data ledgers: the Merkle Tree.

The Contribution of the Merkle Cryptographic Hash to DLT

Merkle trees are named after Ralph Merkle, who made the proposition in his 1987 paper titled "A Digital Signature Based on a Conventional Encryption Function." In 1980, Merkle published a paper titled "Protocols for Public Key Cryptosystems," and he is one of the developers of public-key cryptography (aka asymmetric cryptography), the inventor of cryptographic hashing, and more recently a researcher and speaker on cryonics.

Merkle is a renowned cryptographer, known for devising Merkle's Puzzles, co-inventing the Merkle–Hellman knapsack cryptosystem, inventing Merkle-Damgård cryptographic hashing, and, as noted previously, Merkle trees.

And so, 30 years after Ralph Merkle's introduction of the Merkle tree, it became essential as an architectural component to the development of the Bitcoin payment network. In section 7 of the Bitcoin white paper, before discarding spent transactions to save disk space, they will be captured in a Merkle tree hash and prevent the breaking of a block's hash, and only the root will be included in the block's hash so "old blocks can then be compacted by stubbing off branches of the tree." Thus, the interior hashes have no need to be stored.

As the Bitcoin paper describes, the formation of this infinite tree structure, it is the result of information being sent through a cryptographic hashing function, which converts the data into a sequence of alphanumeric characters of a specific length that is determined by the hashing algorithm utilized. So, without the architectural component of the Merkle tree, the Bitcoin block ledger would be far more burdened with transaction storage issues, and the Bitcoin network would likely have disintegrated many years ago by needing to destroy past transaction data. However, because of the integration of the Merkle tree, the future transaction verification and the immutability of block validation are courtesy of cryptographic hashing and the Merkle tree. However, this is not the only cryptographic contribution.

Cryptographic Digital Signatures in DLT

Cryptographic hashing with the Merkle tree is used in DLT architecture to provide a way to efficiently verify the integrity of large datasets but; the digital signature algorithm (DSA) is another necessary component to DLT architecture to help ensure that a transaction has not been tampered with. And this leads to the development of elliptic curve cryptography (ECC). Introduced in 1985, Victor Miller and Neal Koblitz both independently developed the idea of using elliptic curves.[3]

At this point it is sufficient to understand that ECC is a key-based technique for encrypting with a focus on asymmetric cryptography (i.e., key pairs: private and public keys). ECC is relevant because it led to the conceptual introduction of Elliptic Curve Digital Signature Algorithm (ECDSA) in 1992 by Scott Vanstone ("Responses to NIST's Proposal") in response to NIST's (National Institute of Standards and Technology) request for public comments on its first proposal for Digital Signature Standard (DSS). ECDSA was not accepted as an ANSI (American National Standards Institute) standard until 1999 and was then accepted in 2000 as an Institute of Electrical and Electronics Engineers (IEEE) and NIST standard. (NOTE: a discussion on Post-Quantum Cryptography (PQC) will be taken up in a later chapter.) It is notable that ECC generates smaller keys than other digital signature methods; however, each serves different purposes.

---

[3] Neal Koblitz, N. (1987). Elliptic curve cryptosystems. *Mathematics of Computation,* *48*(177), 203–209; Miller, V. (1985) Use of elliptic curves in cryptography. *Lecture Notes in Computer Science,* 218.

In the first introduction of a distributed network ledger, the Haber and Stornetta time-stamping service maintained under the company Surety is the original design of a distributed ledger but was never associated with the terminology of blockchain or distributed ledger. It was simply intended to be a system that geographically spreads (i.e., distributed) synchronized and sequenced digital data (i.e., a ledger) that is verified and cryptographically secured. Many of the modern distributed ledger architectural designs have become exceedingly complex, of which there are more than 850 Layer-1 projects to date, and incorporate the use of emerging technologies that stretch the limits of convergence to create a more robust system. However, with the nuance of each new project being introduced, development has moved to Layer-2 where the security components of Layer-1 are largely lost and have introduced all new cybersecurity vulnerabilities and financial cybercrime avenues for bad actors to take advantage of.

So, as the Bitcoin payment network architecture was in development, it was being designed by incorporating technologies available at the time to create something technologically advanced system relative to previously developed systems from the 1990s. The Bitcoin developers wanted a platform that could independently maintain a record of digital asset transactions (i.e., data ledger) and message each new version of the transaction ledger across a network of nodes (i.e., distributed network). And they wanted a secure network validation algorithm, but it also needed to converged a digital asset component in a way that permitted the digital asset element to be a transfer of value between participants in the network—i.e., peer-to-peer (P2P) value transfer. This was made possible through the incorporation of ECDSA Secp256k1 in addition to the other components discussed later in this chapter. Secp256k1 is the label for just one of the specific elliptic curves used in cryptography. The "Sec" portion is short for Standard for Efficient Cryptography, which is a consortium that develops commercial standards for cryptography.

ECDSA Secp256k1 made it possible to contractually agree to a digital asset transaction with a cryptographic digital signature that immutably establishes the date and time of a digital asset transaction. This aspect of ECDSA contributes to solving the double-spend issue that was unresolved in the early cryptographically secured digital currencies of the 1990s. And on the point of DSAs, there is not enough emphasis and articulation on the fact that the cryptography of a DSA is not a transferable characteristic to the underlying digital asset. To unambiguously express it another way, there is no cryptography in digital assets such as bitcoin, or any other distributed ledger asset for that matter. Therefore, referring to a digital asset as crypto is not only a misleading statement suggesting security that doesn't exist, but is also technically incorrect. Only the cryptographically created key pair, the transaction signing DSA, and the recorded transaction hash, all the stuff that happens around the digital asset, involve cryptography. It is a requisite to ensure this is abundantly clear. I fully anticipate future litigation against professionals by those who those that experience a loss of their distributed ledger assets because of the "crypto" reference to non-cryptographic assets.

Now that ECDSA has been introduced as another architectural component, and one of the components in the double-spend solution of DLT-based digital asset, we can continue on to the next distributed ledger architectural primitives—the consensus mechanism component of DLT.

Consensus in DLT

The idea of consensus was introduced in the 1970s by Leslie Lamport and Barbara Liskov. It is important to highlight the contributions of these two individuals to the model of consensus systems used in DLT today.

Leslie Lamport is an American computer scientist and mathematician and best known for his seminal work in distributed systems. Lamport was the winner of the 2013 Turing Award for imposing clear, well-defined coherence on the seemingly chaotic behavior of distributed computing systems, in which several autonomous computers communicate with each other by passing messages. He devised important algorithms and developed formal modeling and verification protocols that improve the quality of real distributed systems. These contributions have resulted in improved correctness, performance, and reliability of computer systems. Some of Lamport's most notable publications are the following:

- "Time, Clocks, and the Ordering of Events in a Distributed System" (1978)
- "How to Make a Multiprocessor Computer That Correctly Executes Multiprocess Programs" (1979)

- "The Byzantine Generals Problem" (1983)
- "Distributed Snapshots: Determining Global States of a Distributed System" (1985)
- "The Part-Time Parliament" (1998)

Barbara Liskov is an American computer scientist who has made contributions to programming languages and distributed computing. Her notable work includes the introduction of abstract data types and the accompanying principle of data abstraction, along with the Liskov substitution principle, which applies these ideas to object-oriented programming, subtyping, and inheritance. And she is one of the earliest women to have been granted a doctorate in computer science in the United States, and the second woman to receive the Turing award in 2008.

I frequently encounter contributors who post articles on web platforms or podcast on the topic of consensus in DLT—mostly their contributions are limited to Proof-of-Work (PoW) and Proof-of-Stake (PoS)—and they oversimplify consensus systems that they clearly do not understand, even in their simplicity, involving distributed ledger. And worse, acknowledgement is not given to those who truly developed the technology decades before the introduction of the Bitcoin network; however, I will acknowledge the contribution of Satoshi Nakamoto later. I will also correct the record in the next few paragraphs.

Consensus Protocols vs. Consensus Algorithms

Consensus in distributed systems became relevant in the 1970s due to the deployment of ARPANET developed by the Advanced Research Projects Agency, a branch of the US Department. of Defense, which became DARPA in 1983, the year I received my first undergrad degree and joined the US military—but this isn't about me, and more about APRANET, and the Internet.

Consensus structures employ algorithms and protocols—an "algorithm" is not a synonymous term for a "protocol;" however, many frequently, and indiscriminately, use them as synonymous terms. Following is instruction on "consensus protocols" and "consensus algorithms," generally deployed in distributed computing and specifically in distributed ledger networks.

Understanding these two aspects is key to understanding their distinctive role as a distributed ledger architectural component and to understand the intended goals of the consensus protocols, which should be included in a project's white paper, and the execution of the consensus protocols in the written code of the consensus algorithm. To do this, let's first recognize how consensus in a distributed network is defined. Consensus, in computer science, is the process of coming to a complete agreement across several parties. However, a fundamental problem in distributed computing and multi-agent systems is to achieve overall system reliability in the presence of faulty processes.

It is widely publicized and accepted that Lamport is the first to have discovered the Byzantine faults in 1978 as published in "The Implementation of Reliable Distributed Multiprocess System." Lamport, along with coauthors Robert Shostak and Marshall Pease, elaborated on the consensus problem in the 1982 publication of "The Byzantine Generals Problem," which is one of the required readings by graduate students who go through my courses on distributed ledger architectural engineering.

However, to simply get acquainted with the thesis of consensus does not provide a complete representation of the complexities of designing and implementing consensus mechanisms into the architecture of a distributed ledger network. Architecturally engineering a distributed ledger requires a consensus structure that, at a minimum, includes designing several consensus components such as the node network configuration, the node messaging procedure, and a verification and validation method of ledger inputs that are aligned around the consensus protocol.

Each of these will be addressed individually as each has unique considerations and adds complexity as more layers are included in the distributed ledger stack. It is important to ensure the consensus components are consistent with the overall objective of the architectural design and intended use case of the distributed ledger. So, it makes sense to commence with the consensus protocol as it sets the stage for development of the consensus algorithmic code.

To begin, it is necessary to grasp what a consensus protocol is for, so when we get to the consensus algorithm, the distinction between these two is clear. A consensus protocol is defined as a set of rules that govern how a system operates. These rules establish the basic functioning of the different parts, how they interact with each other, and what conditions are necessary for a robust implementation. The different parts of a protocol are not sensitive to order or chronology (i.e., it doesn't matter which part goes first). A protocol also doesn't tell the system how to produce a result. It doesn't have an objective and doesn't produce an output.

Perhaps this definition doesn't make sense, it is possibly due to prior learning bias (remember to think critically; ignore bias). Many have probably been convinced through various sources that "consensus protocols" and "consensus algorithms" are one in the same, but from a technology perspective, this is not correct, and this will become much clearer as we transition "deeper into" consensus protocols. The consensus protocol serves as the developer's abstract rules, or laws, for how the entire network will behave. These rules should be established before fingers hit the keys to begin coding anything, and an important takeaway, each project forms different consensus rules or protocols.

These rules are often found in the white paper of the project. And on that note, if a distributed ledger project does not have a well-developed white paper prior to deployment, that is a red flag! This is because it suggests that the development team has not completely thought through their architecture and the underlying consensus protocols (i.e., rules) for network participant interaction. My extensive research experience with projects that do not produce a white paper is that the developers are taking the architecture and consensus protocol of an existing open-source project and simply giving it a tweak to make is somewhat unique. However, that doesn't mean there shouldn't be a white paper explaining the change(s) to the ledger architecture and consensus rules. Again, any time that a project does not produce a white paper defining the architecture and consensus protocols, this should raise a red flag for anyone evaluating the project.

Let's look at a few examples of consensus protocol rules for sequential linear and nonlinear block architecture, directed acyclic graph (DAG) architecture, Radix architecture, and hybrid architectures such as BlockDAG—more on distributed ledger architectures later. (NOTE: the following examples do not provide specificity on the projects or platforms for where these rules are applied.)

- Stack memory usage rule limits the amount of memory that can be used on the stacks. If a transaction uses more memory than the rule allows, it is invalid.

- The "longest" chain rule is the one that the majority of nodes accept as the "true" chain in sequential linear block architectures. This is determined by the cumulative work of each chain.
- The node network rules define the type of nodes, what the nodes will store, how the nodes communicate (i.e., the messaging system), and cybersecurity standards.
- Logical clock rules track events witnessed by each node.
- Cryptographic commitment rules are implemented to hold nodes accountable for logical clock values and prevent manipulation.
- Specifies the consensus algorithm to be used in the coding process, such as a version of PoW (hashcash, script, ethash, and others), a version of PoS (dPoS, or lPoS, pPoS, nPoS, Casper, or some hybrid of PoS), Markov Chain Monte Carlo (MCMC), Byzantine Fault Tolerance variations (BFT,—aBFT, pBFT, and others), and Radix to list a few.
- Rules that define security features like the hashing functions, to be used for such processes as address generation, delivering the previous block hash, and creating the Merkle Root hash. A couple of examples of hashing functions are the SHA-256 (Secure Hash Algorithm 256-bit) and MD5 used in the Bitcoin blockchain architecture and SHA-3 and Kecck-256 in the Ethereum platform. The hashing functions are not uniform across all distributed ledger projects. (NOTE: There will be more detail on hash functions in a later section.)

This concludes the introduction of the consensus protocol, and I trust that it clarifies that protocols are the abstract concepts of consensus laid out in the consensus protocol as well as in a project's white paper—and a red flag if it isn't. Now we can move on to the consensus algorithm and then transition to distributed network architectures because of the connection between the two.

So, a consensus algorithm system is only one of many architectural components that are included in a distributed ledger. The consensus system and individual mechanism are composed of multiple algorithms. The consensus system cannot be described as simply as stating it is a PoW or PoS. And unfortunately, many simply explain a consensus mechanism like PoW or PoS as a "mathematical puzzle." However, a consensus system is a cryptographically complex ordered operation that interacts with several other architectural components, such as the node network, which, at its roots, serves the purpose of securing the network distributing copies of the hashed transaction ledger. The lack of education surrounding the complexity of cryptographic methods in algorithms designed to protect a distributed ledger network has led to an oversimplification of the technology that leads to misunderstandings in how the platform operates in practice and nuances that can reveal vulnerabilities and off-ledger methods that are relevant to professionals fulfilling their responsibilities. This has also resulted in misunderstanding the heuristic analytics of a distributed ledger project and its various suboperating systems within the network. This needs to be corrected so professionals in various industries can break down a distributed ledger platform and determine when to use forensic science or heuristic science analytic methods; determine whether a distributed ledger project is robust, practical, and worthwhile as an investment; ascertain whether investigative leads from distributed ledger analytics are sound; and the list goes on. So, let's dig into the various algorithms that comprise the consensus systems in a more profound way than how it is typically shared. But not so deep that it requires a graduate degree in cryptography or computer science.

For purposes of critical thought, I find the best way to begin the explanation of complex concepts is to define it to ensure everyone is aligned around a common lexicon, which tracks with the critical thinking methodology. In that vein, a consensus algorithm as a distributed computing architectural component is defined as the coded instructions that each node follows to achieve consensus (i.e., the process of coming to a complete agreement across several parties). An algorithm describes, or defines, the steps that will need to take place. Unlike a consensus protocol, which is a set of abstract rules to achieve consensus as defined earlier, an algorithm is a set of coded instructions that produce an output or a result. The code can be a simple script or a complicated sequencer, but it is important to note that the order of the instructions in a consensus algorithm is essential. A consensus algorithm should work in concert with the node network as outlined in the consensus protocol.

As with most consensus algorithmic structures, the desired outcome is to fulfill the objectives of the stated rules of the consensus protocol while being mindful of the purpose and type of consensus algorithm. This is essential to appreciating the complexities in achieving the results desired by the development team related to the distributed ledger's use case. In other words, a consensus algorithm mechanism is more than just stating that a distributed ledger utilizes PoW, PoS, PoA, or PoC; the consensus algorithm that in the consensus system should support the broader context of the architectural design of the entire project.

I trust it is clear why investigators, analysts, policymakers, compliance enforcement, and students studying these technologies need to be cognizant of these aspects of a distributed ledger that may seem to be hidden to the unknowing individual. Frequently these are often hidden from sight and not properly disclosed by developers who suggest their platform is open source. It is for this reason that services and individuals that purport to analyze distributed ledgers are not conducting comprehensive heuristic analytics because of analytics that don't take into account that distributed ledgers are unique even though there may be some perceived commonalities. And it also addresses why simply stating that a consensus mechanism (e.g., PoW, PoS, PoA, PoC, or any others in the long list) does not define the entire distributed ledger consensus system. Simply naming a consensus mechanism is like stating the ignition switch of a vehicle is what makes it move. In fact, it is only a single component in a complex system of putting a vehicle into a state of motion. Of course the ignition switch has a function, but the function is limited to activating many other mechanical systems that inspire the engine (electric or fossil fuel) to power other systems that enable a vehicle to move. And even if the ignition functions properly, any failures in other processes (e.g., transmission, differential, drive shaft, fuel pump/battery), it will prevent the vehicle from fulfilling its primary objective of moving people or cargo to another location.

Just as with my crude automotive example, a PoW or PoS mechanism is frequently described as the center or entirety of the distributed ledger consensus system when it is only one small piece of the entire consensus system that involves the nodes, the DSA, the verification process, the validation mechanism, and the list goes on. So, the consensus system is unconditionally a combination of many consensus algorithms and supporting software. So, if one component of the system that orders the transaction sequence is not functioning, the ECDSA will not be able to perform its function of signing a transaction. For example, if the hashing algorithms that create the key pair (there is often a sequence of hashes to create the key pair) do not work, then without this private key the Unspent Transaction Output (UTXO) cannot be used because there is no way to produce a valid ECDSA for that

UTXO. The UTXO spend method used in the Bitcoin payment network and other similar project architectures endeavors to mimic a fiat currency transaction and makes a transaction possible. The UTXO verification works in conjunction with the DSA within the consensus system. The result of a successful outcome of the DSA and UTXO verification results in a transaction being added to the mempool, which is then available to validation nodes that enforce the consensus validation mechanism. As noted earlier, this example is relevant to certain types of distributed ledger architectures, but all project architectures are different. And this is why professionals must grasp the importance of understanding the unique working of each platform. And to this point, I will contrast the DSA algorithm/UTXO method in the Bitcoin payment network code with the double-spend prevention method components on the Ethereum platform. Ethereum is not a fork of Bitcoin (i.e., not a hard fork chain split), so it is not constructed based on the Bitcoin base code as with several other distributed ledger networks like Litecoin, Dogecoin, Bitcoin Cash, and the list goes on with approximately 105 networks that trace back to the Bitcoin legacy network. Ethereum developers chose not to utilize a UTXO spend method because the Ethereum platform is designed to emphasize the Layer-2 portion of the DLT stack rather than the Layer-1, as in Bitcoin. In contrast, the Ethereum developers adopted a different ECDSA DSA algorithm and utilize an associated account-base spend verification method, which is modeled to act similar to transactions processed through a bank account. Recall earlier I communicated that Bitcoin transactions are designed to mimic a currency transaction. Notable is that most of today's distributed ledger projects have adopted an architecture similar to Ethereum because they either build on the Ethereum platform as a side chain (e.g., Polygon) or exist as standalone distributed ledger projects designed to be interoperable with the Ethereum platform.

It is not important to detail how UTXO and account-based verification models process transactions within this section on consensus systems although, spending the time to do the technical research to gain a deeper insight into the UTXO and account-based transaction accounting methods is extremely valuable for those involved in heuristic analytics involving ledger transactions. My objective in these couple of paragraphs is to provide an understanding that consensus algorithms are designed to coordinate and order activities within the complexity of multiple consensus structures to fulfill the stated objectives of the consensus protocol, whether it relates to double-spend prevention, secure transaction activity, transaction validation, or transaction verification processes. So, at this point, a natural progression is to move to the node network architecture, which enforces the consensus by executing the code of the consensus mechanism.

Distributed Network Architecture and Topology

Having a robust network architecture that enforces the consensus rules and securely maintains an accurate redundancy of transaction details is critical. Distributed network architecture is far more complex than what is frequently explained by individuals who pontificate on this topic. I frequently ask people at conferences and grad students in my courses about their knowledge of distributed ledger and node operations as a gauge of what they do and don't know. So, next we'll explore distributed network architectures, but I also want to pause here to note that distributed ledgers are a subset of the category of distributed network computing. And at this point, before we move, it may be helpful to provide a short list of distributed network examples that exists outside the subset of DLT networks:

- Video-rendering systems like Netflix
- Airline and hotel reservation like Expedia
- File-sharing like BitTorrent
- MMO (Massively Multiplayer Online) gaming like World of Warcraft
- E-learning applications like Coursera
- Distributed supply chains like Amazon

Distributed systems are made up of a network of components (i.e., hardware, machines, or software) and connectors (i.e., cables, IP address, or a circuit board). In a distributed system, components are the units that perform specific tasks, while connectors are the communication modules that coordinate components. Components and connectors deserve a more insightful clarification at the outset and are defined as follows:

Components: These are modular units that can be reused or replaced. They can be individual nodes or other important components. Components comprise the node network in distributed ledger architecture, which will be covered in a later section.

Connectors: These are communication links that facilitate coordination and cooperation between components, which constitutes the messaging algorithm and will be addressed in a later section.

Distributed systems are designed to scale and manage new machines and services. They can have a variety of purposes, such as solving a large computational problem or coordinating the use of shared resources. And the architecture of distributed systems is a complicated network of nodes. In a distributed system, components and connectors arrange themselves in a way that eases communication. Components are modules with well-defined interfaces that can be replaced or reused. Similarly, connectors are communication links between modules that mediate coordination or cooperation among components.

A distributed system is broadly divided into two architecture topologies: (1) software architecture with typologies that include layered architecture, object-based architecture, data-centered architecture, and event-based architecture; and (2) system architecture with typologies that that include client-server architecture and peer-to-peer (P2P) architecture. Because the focus will be on P2P architectures, it is important to articulate that the term P2P in the context of distributed system architectures refers to computers (electronic devices) that participate in the network as peers to each other. P2P in distributed ledger networks are often misconstrued as referencing people connected in a network. As we move further into the depths of distributed ledger technology, the focus will be on distributed system architecture specific to P2P architecture and we will dive into the node network topologies and typologies beginning with node network topology and then concentrically dig into node typology.

The network topology is the physical or logical layout of how network nodes interconnect. Common topologies include star, mesh, and hybrid in order of complexity. Star node topology requires a central device, such as a switch or router, and connects all nodes. Although simple to construct, and easy to manage and troubleshoot, it has limited scalability. And of course, because of a central server or router, therein lies a single point of failure.

In mesh topology, nodes connect directly to each other, creating a web-like structure resulting in data redundancy as well as a fault tolerant connection. However, mesh topologies are convoluted and complicated to manage.

Lastly, the hybrid topology is a combination of different topologies, which provides flexibility and the ability to customize for specific needs. Nevertheless, architecting and engineering a distributed network includes many design complexities as well as challenges in managing vision versus practical functionality.

A P2P network has the working concept of having no central control of the distributed system but is governed through a system of algorithms and software. A node can either act as a client or server at any given time once it joins the network. A node that requests something is called a client, and one that provides something is called a server. In general, each node is called a peer.

If a new node wishes to provide services, it can do so in two ways: (1) register with a centralized lookup server, which will then direct the node to the service provider, or (2) the node will broadcast its service request to every other node in the network, and whichever node responds will provide the requested service.

P2P networks of today can be classified as Structured P2P (the nodes follow a predefined distributed data structure), Unstructured P2P (the nodes randomly select their neighbors), and in Hybrid P2P some nodes have unique functions appointed to them in an orderly manner.

Now that we have define the basic structures within the distributed network architectures, we need to move on to nodes to understand their role in the distributed computing network.

I will note that I'm not taking readers through the coding of a distributed ledger as would be the case if enrolled in one of my graduate courses where we would continue to discuss node deployment, scaling strategies, and load balancing; however, I will not cover these topics as these are outside the scope for this book. But I am introducing them as an additional component consideration to give readers an appreciation for all aspects in developing a distributed network to be fully conscious of the fact that deployment challenges require significant attention in design contemplations in order to have a robust node network system, which supports the overall consensus system. The next section focuses on the P2P topology architecture, moving on from a global view of distributed networks, and begins drilling into specific distributed ledgers.

The node network, which comprises the backbone of a distributed network, is a micro-ecosystem within the distributed computing architecture that is composed of nodes: the endpoints, communication, or redistribution points over a network that can receive, create, store, and send data along distributed routes. It is important to point out that nodes are arranged into a network architecture, which is well beyond having a basic mindfulness of node typology. Understanding how node elements are arranged is critical to exploring and defining tiered network architecture leading professionals to a better understanding of distributed network architecture. (Note: node messaging algorithms will be covered in a later section.)

There are several types of distributed network architectures, including client-server architecture, peer-to-peer (P2P) architecture, hybrid architecture, service-oriented architecture (SOA), microservices architecture, multi-tier architecture, and data-centered architecture.

Now that consensus algorithms and distributed node networks have been explained, let's move to the nodes underpinning the distributed ledger consensus system. As defined in a prior section, nodes are the endpoints, communication, or redistribution points over a network that can receive, store, create, and send data along distributed routes.

The nodes are perhaps the most elemental component in the distributed ledger, and yet, they are also the key structure in securing the entire network. Going back to my example of a key starting a vehicle, none of the algorithms will function without the initial processing contributions of the nodes.

The misconception about nodes is that some believe nodes are computers that a human interfaces with in order for the node to be able to perform its function in a network. This is the abstract idea that many of the individuals had when I was educating federal agents in the US federal government during the 2010s. Nodes, as the definition provided earlier explains, are electronic devices that run specialized programs and have no user interface, unless a personal computer is connected to a distributed ledger as a node. However, a personal computer running as a node is only using the CPU or GPU components of the computer and does not necessarily allow a human to interface with the network. In fact, household devices like a dishwasher or refrigerator can be hijacked by bad actors and used as a node by some distributed ledger architectures to pool computing power for transaction validation. However, in more onerous node network systems, specialized hardware and software are required, thereby shutting out those that may not be as sophisticated or possess the finances to participate.

As an example, the Bitcoin payment node network, starting in 2012, demands the use of an Application-Specific Integrated Circuit (ASIC) device for block transaction validation, and these currently range in price from a few hundred to tens of thousands of US dollars. ASIC devices are customized to perform complex calculations and are significantly more powerful and expensive than a graphics processing unit (GPU) chip installed in most personal computers today. However, in 2009 when the Bitcoin blockchain network was deployed, one did not need any specialized electronic hardware—a simple personal computer was sufficient to run validation computations. And with the eventual progression into pooling, the use of ASIC devices turned validation of bitcoin transactions into corporate industry operation, which I will elaborate on in a later section. As a side note, there is currently a 2025 proposal for abandoning ASIC hardware in favor of more efficient technology for Bitcoin validation nodes executing PoW. This shift is driven by the need for greater energy efficiency, especially in respect to the upcoming 2028 Bitcoin subsidy halving that will reduce the validation subsidy from 6.25 BTC to 3.125 BTC. The proposal also addresses the necessity for more powerful, energy-efficient technologies like 3nm ASIC chips and AI integration. Staying with the topic of nodes, let's move to a discussion on node typology.

Nodes and Clients in Distributed Networks

So, what is a node? As defined in an earlier section, a node is a communication endpoint or redistribution point and an electronic device that can create, receive, or transmit information over a communication channel. I also need to articulate that "a node" is sometimes referred to as "a client." The primary difference between a node and a client is their role and functionality. A client is a computer program or software that requests access to a server's service. For example, a web browser is a client that requests information from servers across the internet. A node, however, is a computer that runs client software, is connected to a network, and can send, receive, and store data, and that maintains the network by enforcing network rules. Without these integral components that facilitate P2P distributed ledger networks, it would not be possible to secure the network.

Why is this distinction important? I'll use the Ethereum platform as an example because Ethereum has probably the most distinctive use of clients and nodes. In the Ethereum network, clients are the software applications that nodes use to interact with other Ethereum clients, while nodes are the network participants that maintain and secure the distributed ledger network. However, at the risk of confusing this issue, nodes can be a client, but they operate separately to access a network. You can think of a node as an operating system (OS), like Windows or iOS, and the client as the computer. This is why, all too often, many web articles and "blockchain experts" provide learners and novices with incomplete information, that leads to an incomplete understanding of clients and nodes. However, this information is often critical in a transaction analysis or a criminal investigation when attempting to determine where data information might be accessible, and where it is not, when gathering evidence. I trust this exposition clearly makes the point that nodes and clients are not synonymous, but let's now shift to node typologies.

Nodes do not always perform the same role, and this is made apparent in the definition provided earlier. But I will admit that the definition does not reveal anything about node typologies. To articulate on node and client typologies, I will stay with the Ethereum platform because of the level of detail their documentation provides on this topic. Ethereum.org conveys that the Ethereum client architecture utilizes two clients: an execution client and a consensus client. And the two clients connect to their respective P2P networks because separate P2P networks are needed as the execution clients message transactions over their P2P network while the consensus clients message blocks over their P2P network. And there are three different types of nodes that consume data differently identified as light, full, and archive nodes. The Ethereum node typologies can be summarized as follows:

- Full nodes do a block-by-block validation, including a download and verification of the block transaction and state values (states will be discuss in a later section).
- Archive nodes are full nodes that verify every block from genesis and never delete any downloaded data.

- Light nodes only download block headers, which contains summary information about the contents of the blocks. A light node can request information from a full node to independently verify the data received in the block header.

I trust delving into the intricacies of nodes and clients reveals how important they are to a distributed ledger network. And as Ethereum continues to evolve, understanding the nuances of nodes and clients becomes increasingly crucial; what I have described related to Ethereum nodes and clients may change over time, especially based on some of the Ethereum hard forks that are currently proposed.

However, there are hundreds of distributed ledger network architectures that have introduced many node typologies in addition to the ones introduced on Ethereum. Other node types include validation nodes (aka miners), pruned full nodes, authority nodes, master nodes, staking nodes, lightning nodes, and super nodes. The list goes on, but I cannot possibly detail every node type because the list continues to grow over time.

I believe substantial information has been provided for investigators, distributed ledger analysts, policymakers, investors, and others to understand that there is much to be aware of when delving into distributed ledger network rather than creating a stereotype based on only having experience with a single distributed ledger network like Bitcoin or Ethereum.

As I wrote in a previous section, nodes serve as the pillars of a distributed ledger network to provide for network's fault tolerance and security. And although nodes vary in purpose, their commonality is that they all include a messaging functionality in order to participate in the distributed network, i.e., nodes contain a messaging algorithm. And this introduces the next algorithm that must be discussed as a primitive of distributed computing.

Messaging Protocols in Distributed Networking

A node messaging algorithm is what makes communication possible in distributed computing networks and is critical for the network to achieve consensus. It involves transferring and entering messages between nodes to achieve various goals such as coordination, synchronization, and data sharing. And as presented in the "Byzantine Generals

Problem" by Lamport et al., coordinating army battalions that are physically separated is a necessity for a general.[4] How to message the troops to ensure that messaging challenges are overcome is at the center of the messaging. Challenges arise, such as a messaging being transmitted incorrectly, the message may not arrive timely or at all, the message may be intercepted by the enemy, or the receiver of the message may choose to violate the instructions in the message.

In distributed computing, nodes are physically separated and frequently span geographical boundaries. This requires that nodes be provided the ability to communicate, which introduces the communicate protocol found in distributed networks. A communication protocol is a set of rules with the crucial function of shaping how nodes exchange messages. Synchronous and asynchronous communication protocols are two ways to communicate between components in a distributed system. The main difference between the two is that synchronous execution requires parties or components to work simultaneously in real time, while asynchronous communications don't need anyone to wait around for a reply.

Nodes typically communicate through asynchronous messaging algorithms, invoking remote procedures, sharing memory, or using sockets. Messaging algorithms are designed to allow multiple nodes that are geographically distributed to exchange data and coordinate actions, enabling effective collaboration toward consensus with a strategy of fault tolerance (i.e., no single point of failure).

Despite the fault tolerance of a node architecture, there are instances of nodes not performing as expected, such as crash (node stops functioning), omission (node fails to perform the expected action or fails to send/receive data), Byzantine failure (malicious actions by node operators), and network latency (delay in bits of data to travel through the network), resulting in messages that do not reach their intended destination or in message corruption.

Messaging algorithms, combined with other consensus algorithms, must compensate for these challenges. So, messaging algorithms need to be architected in such a way that developers can meet the various standards of performance, reliability, scalability, and resilience necessary for the distribute network use case. Because one process can have a gap or disparity with

---

[4] Lamport, L., Shostak, R., & Pease, M. (1982). The Byzantine generals problem. *ACM Transactions on Programming Languages and Systems, 4*(3), 382–401.

another in different distributed systems, it is important to design components to the specific requirements and steps suitable for different scenarios.

What is notable is that node communication protocols have been in use in traditional distributed computing network architectures for decades. So, the use of a node communication protocol in distributed ledger networks is not nascent. The gossip protocol was introduced in 1987 by Alan Demers, a researcher at Xerox's Palo Alto Research Center. Demers et al. published a paper titled "Epidemic Algorithms for Replicated Database Maintenance" in the proceedings of the sixth annual ACM Symposium on Principles of Distributed Computing.

The typologies of node communication protocols are Anti-Entropy, Rumor-Mongering (aka, Dissemination), Aggregation, and Gossip. Node messages are spread using a Push Model, Pull Model, or Push-Pull Model. It is notable that messaging algorithms (i.e., a specific mechanism) in distributed ledgers is based in the oldest and most canonical gossip protocol (i.e., a general communication mechanism). A gossip mechanism can provide fault tolerance and scalability by exploiting the redundancy, parallelism, and randomness of the gossip communication. However, there are trade-offs and limitations that should be considered, such as the cost of gossip messages, the convergence time, the impact of network topology, and node heterogeneity.

The following are examples of gossip algorithms, in no particular order, utilized in several distributed ledger network structures. The Gossipsub algorithm, optimized by a subalgorithm called Plumtree (Push Lazy-Push Multicast Tree), used by Ethereum developers. On the other hand, the Bitcoin network architecture was designed around the push-based gossip algorithm similar to Gnutella used by Napster. And Hedera, a DAG distributed ledger architecture, uses the Gossip About Gossip algorithm. Each of these examples emphasizes the importance of designing a messaging algorithm that is specific to a distributed ledger architecture and use case of the distributed network.

I trust it becomes abundantly clear why an investigator, analyst, investor, compliance, and others who need to engage with a distributed network should consider and comprehend how the node communication protocol affects the entire consensus system of a distributed network. It is essential to better understand aspects of how the entire system functions and points of where evidence can be extracted and analyze a convergent digital asset transaction involving on-mainnet and the potential for off-mainnet channels.

The last aspect I want professionals to understand surrounding the architecture of a distributed network is how developers determine what algorithms from the protocols to construct the entire consensus system.

The origin of distributed computing originated in the 1970s with Lamport, and development of consensus algorithms for distributed networks have been an active area of research for several decades. And with the introduction of DLT in the 1990s, the experimentation with new consensus systems began. These new consensus systems require the introduction of economic game theory as a way to anticipate human greed-driven behavior when designing distributed ledger network algorithms to ensure security of the network to thwart the activities coming from bad actors in the network, consistency in enforcement of rules by the network, and to incentivize participants to play by the rules of the network.

I teach game theory in economics courses, and I also teach game theory in the context of distributed ledger architectural engineering courses in the context of designing consensus algorithms. Although there is an awareness of game theory, I believe it is important to provide definitions to establish a common understanding.

The *Stanford Encyclopedia of Philosophy* published the definition of "game theory" in 1997:

> Game theory is the study of the ways in which *interacting choices* of *economic agents* produce *outcomes* with respect to the *preferences* (or *utilities*) of those agents, where the outcomes in question might have been intended by none of the agents.[5]

Britannica defines game theory as, "a branch of applied mathematics that provides tools for analyzing situations in which parties, called players, make decisions that are interdependent. This interdependence causes each player to consider the other player's possible decisions, or strategies, in formulating strategy. A solution to a game describes the optimal decisions of the players, who may have similar, opposed, or mixed interests, and the outcomes that may result from these decisions."

---

[5] Zlata, E. N., & Nodelman, U. (Eds.). (n.d.) *Stanford Encyclopedia of Philosophy.* https:// plato.stanford.edu/.

While I gravitate toward Britannica's definition of a mathematical analytics tool from the viewpoint of a financial economist, Stanford's philosophical definition encompasses the aspect that unintended outcomes may arise. This is especially true when an individual or group only considers a limited scope of variables, which is often the result of the limited knowledge and experience of the individual or group contemplating the variables to include in game theory analysis.

First, it is important to make the point that game theory includes various types for analyzing various game scenarios, of which there are five (listed in no particular order):

1. Cooperative and non-cooperative
2. Normal form and extensive form
3. Simultaneous move and sequential move
4. Constant sum, zero-sum, and non-zero-sum
5. Symmetric and asymmetric

When developing consensus system rules for the deployment, a set of consensus algorithms and software needs to be developed that align with each other—e.g., the secure hashing algorithm, digital signature algorithm, transaction double-spend prevention software, node network design, the type of nodes and clients necessary for the network, and an efficient node messaging algorithms, and other components have to be developed in such a way that when they are integrated; they all work together. And the deployment of a complete consensus system requires game theory analytics to analyze how people make decisions based on the use case motives for playing, or participating in the distributed network. Game theory analytics also take into account the activities/behaviors of the various people, called players in game theory, to incentivize the behavior desired by developers for participation on distributed ledger. Game theory also studies how players interact with each other and form strategies on how to play the game based on the actions, good or bad, from other players' actions, which can lead to collusion tactics.

I understand that the connotation of game theory will not be clear to the nonexpert, but as I noted with the previous subject of critical thinking, I'm not going to make anyone proficient in every aspect of game theory analytics as I do in classroom studies. However, my attempt is to provide a minimal introduction of game theory to civil and criminal investigators, attorneys and judges, compliance analysts, regulators/policy-makers, and others who engage in distributed ledger.

I trust this overview provides a new appreciation for game theory in the context and relevance of this topic to distributed ledger architecture engineering design. I also believe it is relevant to understand the premise of game theory involving the participation motivates by bad actors to exploit projects deployed on some ledgers over others—it's because developers deploy what they believe to be a great idea, but frequently lack a thorough development of a game theory framework for preventing bad actors from exploiting a project. Guardrails can be coded into the project in anticipation that bad actors will be present. For example, the development of the Bitcoin distributed payment ledger was developed with several safeguards, such as preventing double-spends, which had been an outstanding issue for many years involving digital currencies. However, it did not provide guardrails from converting it from a payment network into an alternative investment system.

To summarize this chapter on distributed ledger architecture and some of the history, it is my hope that a greater appreciation exists for the many topologies and typologies of distributed network technology, and within the topology are dozens of variations. Attempting to generalize validation algorithms is a major miscalculation in the same way that distributed ledger architecture is frequently generalized by many as "The Blockchain," when in fact, there are more than 850 different distributed ledger architectures, each with its own unique idiosyncrasies that are often misunderstood or lost when conducting distributed ledger analytics, investigative research, policy development, and setting compliance parameters. Each distributed ledger requires to be understood for its individually unique nuances relevant to determine exactly how the entire system functions—i.e., how it executes a transaction, verifies a transaction, validates transaction, how the node network architecture is arranged, type of node metadata, and the manner in which nodes communicate, to provide just a few examples.

Being aware of the distributed ledger architecture allows an analyst or investigator to scrutinize distributed ledger projects for aspects such as algorithmic schemes that will support certain heretical hypotheses preceding or during an investigation, forming a compliance plan, or a determination of compliance. Can a lack of understanding or not being well versed in distributed ledger algorithmic methods be a problem? It might be, which indicates that an expert in distributed ledger architecture and heuristic methods may need to be consulted to evaluate next steps.

A specific example of my work involves participation in a US federal department cybercrime headquarters unit where I supported the development of a heuristic analytics tools. My research related to the ring signature algorithm metadata, which is part of the Monero ledger architecture. In addition, I have decades of academic knowledge in distributed network architectural engineering and 20 years of practical investigative experience working with the US federal government supporting civil and criminal distributed ledger-based asset investigations. For the past three years, I have worked as a government contractor analyzing distributed ledgers within the banking sector and designing secure storage for distributed ledger digital assets associated with bank failures my practical experience and academic knowledge in distributed ledger architectural engineering. And let's not forget about the recovery and integrity of transaction and node metadata related to ongoing or future investigations that is indispensable as evidence. My objective in noting this is to raise awareness, not as a guide on digital data collection methods, so apologies to any who might be disappointed. However, I need to emphasize that collection methods of digital evidence should be followed to ensure that metadata will be collected in a way that will not prevent it from being admissible in court in the event of a civil or criminal procedure. And, in addition, an unbiased and immutably recorded chain of custody should be maintained, as well as having a well-documented collection method. This same knowledge is relevant to investigations, policy, academia, setting compliance parameters, and developing regulatory guidance.

So, with the introduction of the architectural engineering side of distributed networks, we are ready to move to the topic of distributed ledger access designs.

Chapter 2

Distributed Ledger Transparency: Types of Network Design

Distributed ledger network design refers to the process of planning and mapping a network architecture where computing power and ledger data are spread across multiple independent nodes, allowing for parallel processing and providing a fault tolerant environment. I believe a point of clarification is necessary on the meaning of "independent" nodes. It does not have an implication of "independent" ownership as some my infer. In computer networking, it simply refers to a device on a network that can function and operate on its own without significant reliance on other nodes to perform primary tasks. I encounter many definitions that attempt to capture and convey an understanding of DLT from the perspective of a specific distributed ledger network system platform. But those descriptive notions should be reserved for white papers on the respective operational design and not to define a technology. For example, I read many definitions for DLT that are written from the homocentric context of the Bitcoin payment network architecture. The architectural design and the technology utilized in the Bitcoin network ledger can only define the Bitcoin system technologies, which may be similar to architectural components to other distributed ledger design structures, but it is never identical. The flaw is recognizable: defining DLT based on the structures in the Bitcoin distributed ledger results in an incorrect explanation of the numerous infrastructure designs introduced by other developers. An example is using a definition of DLT architectural technology components based on the Bitcoin payment system and then attempting to understand the Ethereum enterprise platform through the lens of the Bitcoin centric DLT definition: It doesn't work. Framing it in a different way, if everyone defined all architectural structures of physical buildings in the context of the Empire State Building: It doesn't work. In physical structures we define architecture across a number of typologies such as residential vs. commercial architecture. So, residential can't be defined in the context of commercial architecture. I trust the issue here is obvious.

I read and watch so many commentaries on distributed ledger design characteristics that describe them incorrectly and provide descriptions that often present conflicts of consequence involving inconsistent use of terms in distributed ledger design. As a researcher and developer, this matter is of little consequence to me. However, as a passionate educator teaching not only graduate students, but also professionals in law, investigation, cybersecurity, and government about distributed ledger architectural, digital asset risk attributes, and how they are converged to work together, it is of primary concern to stem the propagation of confusion through the misuse of terms associated with distributed ledger design. Graduate students going through programs I teach on distributed ledger architectural engineering and design in a formal academic setting find it rationally illuminating to have distributed ledger architecture and design explained in terms of the technology and not from the web-facing colloquial nuanced use of technology terms. Although I have been challenged many times by individuals pushing the agenda that using street terms is easier for people to understand concepts, I find that it is vital to establish the ground rules for how these terms are used in the context of how the technology has been defined for decades. Again, DLT structures are not nascent, so we should default to the existing definitions and avoid catchy hype phrases or terms. Otherwise, professionals will never be able to truly grasp how distributed ledger networks work in the real-world context of an operational DLT system and be able to think critically about how to conduct a proper analysis. With that, I need to take on the drivel definitions of several terms and provide correct descriptions to ensure clarity for professionals as I do with grad students. So, the following design terms are explained to enhance the understanding of the transparency of different distributed ledger architectural arrangements.

Permissioned vs. Permissionless Design

Before confronting the topic of distributed ledger architectures in a later chapter, I need to provide a "return to sanity" moment; otherwise, other topics involving these terms in later sections will be taken out of context. The frequency of the synonymous use of the terms "permissionless" and "public" in respect to distributed ledger networks is TNTC: Too Numerous To Count. And this leads to the comparison of permissioned ledger access as opposed to permissionless. Permissionless is quite straightforward; however, permissioned ledger, for some reason, tends to create a lot of difficulty for some because they have been led to believe that a distributed ledger can't be "blockchain" unless it is permissionless. Now, just because the Bitcoin network has been architecturally designed as a permissionless ledger network, the Bitcoin whitepaper does not use or define blockchain as a technology. So, defining a permissioned distributed ledger network is as simple as providing the definitions for permission and permissionless. Following are Webster definitions of each:

> Permissionless: Without permission, or no permission required.
> Permission: The act of giving formal consent.

These definitions, I'm positive, are very well understood as defined here. And in the name's sake of transparency, there are clear barriers to transparency in permissioned systems, but that doesn't preclude an investment analyst, investigator, or regulator from obtaining information related to the respective states. A permissionless design is simply a distributed network that anyone with internet access and the mandatory network software and hardware can join; hence, it is immediately accessible to whatever transparency is provided. But transparency can be limited, even in a permissionless network—more on that in the next section. And as a side note, even a permissionless ledger design frequently has requirements for access, such as a specific computer folder (aka wallet folder), a compatible electronic device with specialized software installed—often at no cost to download—that opens a channel and provides the electronic device with the communication capability with the respective distributed ledger, and any other criteria specified. It's good to research these things in advance of jumping on a computer with the impression that it is like going to a webpage. But the point here is that all these requirements are considered barriers to entering a distributed ledger network but are not considered permissions as in the case of obtaining formal consent to gain access to permissioned ledgers. But these barriers to entry present a level of consent or agreement if one is willing to go through all the steps to connect with the network. And going through these steps introduces a digital footprint for digital forensic investigations, which I and others have conducted to eventually identify individuals of interest and bad actors/cybercriminals. So, while there is a level of privacy, as there is in banking, there is no anonymity.

In closing out this portion on permissionless and permissioned distributed ledger networks, a ledger's permission design does not depend on the network being decentralized, public, open-source, having some degree of transparency or level of privacy/pseudonymity, or being defined by a certain type of governance configuration. So, it may be fascinating for many to learn that some of the most prominent permissionless distributed ledger networks have a highly centralized control. This exercise of quiet control often comes through the distributed ledger's foundation or developer team. I will return to this in later sections because these characteristics are recurrently and inaccurately used as preconditions in defining permissionless ledger networks, and they have no technological or scientific basis in defining a permissionless ledger network and require further explanation. Many permissionless distributed ledger networks are erroneously characterized as being decentralized, open-source, public, etc. In fact, some permissionless distributed ledgers will have corrective methods for removing bad actors. That may well bring to light other aspects of permissionless distributed ledger networks that raise questions about the permissionless design paradigm. But in the end, it is simple to determine whether there is an absence of formal permission necessary to make a distributed ledger a permissionless ledger network.

As for permissioned distributed ledger networks, moving to the flip side of permissionless distributed ledgers is the meaning of permissioned. Please take note that the permissioned distributed ledger design can have a single level of permission that provides full access to the entirety of the operational functions of the network. However, that is not the standard nor the norm. Permissioned ledger network participants can have specific roles which limits access permissions – this provides significantly better security than permissionless distributed networks. There are validator roles, user-only roles, and any number of other roles that may exist within the architectural framework of the permissioned distributed ledger. So, if the permission is for a validator role, that is a permission granted by the administrator of the distributed network, which is a different permission than the validator role.

I have viewed various charts on the web comparing "permissioned" with "permissionless" that refer to permissionless distributed ledger networks as an "open" network and contrasting it with a permissioned ledger network as a "closed" network. It might be of interest for professionals to learn that an open network in computer science is defined as being constructed on open standards, nonproprietary devices, with interoperable software. It becomes very clear the term open network does not describe any permissionless distributed ledger network currently in existence.

I have been involved with many permissionless and permissioned ledger networks in law enforcement engagements. And now in my civilian status, I continue to provide technical support as a contractor to federal entities that regulate the financial and banking sectors. The government still requires my expertise from time to time, and I have had the opportunity to evaluate the technology and architecture of distributed ledgers and associated assets being utilized within the banking and financial sector on behalf of federal entities.

These engagements with federal entities led to the opportunity directing an analysis of the architecture of a permissioned distributed ledger network deployed by a bank that fell into failure. This led to reverse-engineering the architecture and complete deconstruction of the proprietary permissioned ledger network and salvage all the transaction data from the distributed ledger. Because bank permissioned ledgers are created with various use cases in mind, it required the development of unique methods for each use case to secure the cryptographic keys of the assets that were held in custody by the bank. I share this to articulate that these networks are not closed, but they do require permission to be on the platform. These permissioned distributed ledgers, proprietary or foundation projects, are typically not closed in the context of the definition provided earlier for computer distributed networks. Referring to permissioned systems as "closed" implies, in the colloquial context, that a permissioned distributed ledger network cannot interact with any outside network, which is not the case. Thus, a permissioned distributed ledger network has interactions with various outside networks, but to gain access a permission is required. Permissioned distributed ledgers frequently have third-party actors such as digital asset exchange services, which are frequently conducted through application programming interfaces (API), but they can also be third parties that support the infrastructure of the permissioned ledger network directly. For example, third parties are engaged by developers of permissioned ledgers for cryptographic key management, wallet services, etc. The third parties become ancillary services that are permissioned to interact with the distributed ledger for performance and service enhancement. All of this to note that the design of a permissioned ledger network frequently has a multi-level permission authentication that ranges from user access permissions to granting nodes permission to conduct operational support services to the ledger network. The point is to clarify that "closed" networks are not synonymous with "permissioned" networks.

To close this section, a permissionless vs. a permissioned distributed ledger network is better defined with a simple compare-and-contrast based on the measures involved in accessing a distributed ledger network. Attempting to elude the simple paradigm of the contextual definition of a word by adding words out of context (i.e., words that have technological definitions as well as informal definitions) often results in dissemination of misinformation and inaccuracies.

Private vs. Public Network Design

"Private" and "public" are two more terms that are compatible with the above terms of "permissioned" and "permissionless" but are frequently misused in labeling distributed ledgers. Professionals from many industries with little to no technical education are speaking at conferences and webinars on technology topics and their messages contain the hype or colloquial terms used in articles across the web that become the obvious source of their expertise. Based on my observations and interactions with many professionals, I postulate that the majority of those speaking on technology topics do not have the level of technology background or education to understand the implication of the terms they use in their efforts to inform.

As a personal example, I have been in the teaching role as adjunct faculty at a law school, and I still lecture in law classes when I receive requests from friends that are attorneys on faculty at different law schools. While I have an education in law, I am not an attorney, and I do not attempt to teach law to attorneys. When I have the opportunity, what I teach attorneys is about intricacies of a technology and how the law might apply given unique aspects of that technology that are not well understood.

An example of what I have presented to attorneys in is sharing about the technology aspects of distributed ledger digital asset risk using a taxonomical model that I created in one of my postdoctoral studies. Different digital asset taxonomies have different risk characteristics, and what they astutely assimilate into their knowledge toolbox is that the term "crypto" does not accurately deliver a risk-based analytic model for advising clients and the legal implications involving the use of broad categorical inaccurate terms like "crypto." And what I have observed working with attorneys in the federal government is that it is very dangerous to the future of technology when attorneys teach others about technology.

Of the many examples that I have to draw upon, one in particular is a professional who attempted to educate readers about the terms "private" and "public" to explain what was described as different types of DLT but confused the explanation by differentiating these two terms from the term "permissioned" (which I explain in the previous section). I am not sharing names, but this is an actual example that exists on several websites.

To set the context, the writer's profession is shown as a professional financial services product manager, and the editor who reviewed the article is described as a financial therapist and educator. It is also important to note that the article is published in a well-known web-based learning resource. The author explains that "public" distributed ledgers allow anyone access, whereas "private" distributed ledgers are only available to selected or authorized users, which is completely inconsistent within the context of distributed ledger technology design. The author goes on to explain that "permissioned" distributed ledgers simply means that there are different levels of user permissions or roles, which isn't totally incorrect. So, the author seems to be explaining that a private ledger requires user permissions and then uses the term "permission" to explain that levels of permission exist. This quickly becomes a confusing and circular argument between the terms "private" and "permissioned."

Now contrast this with the previous section, which defines these terms from the authoritative prejudice of computer networking technology. Permissioned access is simply a distributed network design feature that requires a permission to be obtained to gain access to the distributed ledger network; and those granted access may be permissioned as a user or may be permitted to perform specific roles as part of network processes, such as operating a node for validating transactions. And the element of "private" describes that the "on-ledger data" has limited access, such as read-only privacy (no read-write access), limited read-write privacy, or it could be write-only with no read option to protect the privacy of transaction data. The private aspects (aka privacy) of user interaction with the distributed ledger depend on the distributed ledgers design, which is often required by the distributed ledger's use case.

I want to also note that the artificial intelligence (AI) chat bots used in search engines get the "private" and "public" terms in distributed ledger architectures wrong as well. These large language model (LLM) generative pretrained transformers (GPT) are not intelligent; they only extract and assimilate webpage content. But to transition back to the terms private and public, in the context of distributed ledger architecture, the meanings of private and public in distributed ledger are very different than in finance and IT access permissions. Private and public in the distributed ledger framework refers to distributed ledger data access.

If the distributed ledger has a public ledger design, anyone on the ledger can view all the transaction data that are on the ledger. For example, the Bitcoin payment ledger is permissionless, but it also has a public data ledger that provides all users with a full view of all transaction data. On the other hand, the Monero payment network, which is also permissionless, is designed with privacy enhancements giving it a private distributed ledger design that protects certain data that is only visible to the sender and receiver; they are not visible to other users on the permissionless distributed ledger network.

So, to conclude this section in what may seem to have been a long road for some very simple design attributes, the terms "private" and "public" connect access parameters to the viewing of data in the distributed ledger, not access to the ledger. And that is what differentiates these two design parameters from the additional design parameters of "permissioned" and "permissionless." And these are important aspects for professionals to grasp.

At this juncture in the conversation of public, private, permissionless, and permissioned, I have alluded to these distributed ledger design features being combined. Combinations such as permissionless public, permissionless private, permissioned public, and permissioned private exist in different distributed ledger designs. Again, the architectural design should always be tied to the distributed ledger's use case. Figure 2.1 shows a matrix that visually displays the various combinations.

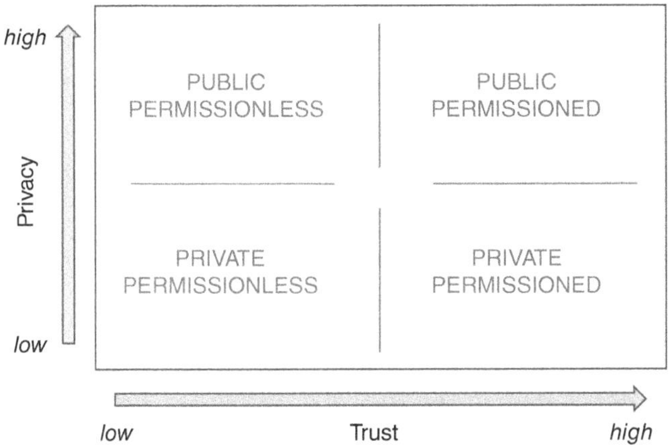

Figure 2.1   Privacy Trust Matrix.

Federated Network Design

I'll begin by noting that the federated network design is also known under the heading of consortium network design. A federated/consortium network design is a hybrid network design. Federated is referred to as a hybrid model of the permissioned and permissionless network design by those who often lack a prescribed learning on the characteristics of permissioned and permissionless network design. There are so many articles that call federated network design a different type of distributed ledger system, which it is not. This error is often the case with the permissioned, permissionless, private, and public design characteristics as well.

As it has been articulated in earlier chapters and will also be addressed in greater detail in chapters that follow, the distributed sequential linear blocked data ledger, colloquially referred to as blockchain, is but one taxonomic classification of distributed ledger technology. And distributed sequential linear blocked data ledger with different design characteristics incorporated into its architecture doesn't put it into a different taxonomic category. A distributed sequential linear blocked data ledger is a specific set of technologies that can have many different design characteristics such as the ones being discussed in this section.

To again use the physical construction architecture analogy, building a residential house with a lock on the front door to control access for security versus constructing the house with a revolving front door so that anyone has access to come and go as they please does not alter the fact that it is residential property—nor is it likely to be classified as a different class or type of residential property.

In an upcoming chapter, I will dive into the typologies of distributed network and data ledger architecture, but I am addressing the federated distributed network design in this section because this distributed network design type is most associated with the permissioned private design attribute.

The federated distributed network exists within the framework of the distributed network of sequential linear block architecture, but it is also incorporated into other taxonomic categories of distributed ledger architecture as well. But it is far from being a hybrid distributed ledger technology, as it is often described. The federated distributed ledger network design is its own unique design. So, what is federated/consortium distributed ledger design? A federated/consortium distributed ledger is typically formed by a homogenous or heterogenous group of like-minded institutions. So, as opposed to distributed ledger run by a foundation and/or a group of developers who write the code and maintain the infrastructure of the distributed ledger used by a network of many unnamed users, as with the Ethereum blockchain platform and Bitcoin blockchain, it is a group of entities that come together to form a distributed network with a common purpose. There have been several federated blockchain distributed ledger projects formed within the medical community, airline industry, supply chain partners, and government entities.

I trust it is easy to understand why I noted earlier that federated networks are frequently designed with permission levels—i.e., a federated permissioned distributed ledger; however, they can be permissionless as well. It will depend on the use case of the distributed ledger system and should always be the first thing to consider when designing a distributed ledger architecture.

And regarding the data, it can be designed with privacy in mind giving partial or no transparency involving the transaction date on the distributed ledger. But they can also be designed with complete transparency that allows all users in the network to view transactional data with read-write privileges, as in the case of multi-airline inventory distributed ledger network systems.

Federated distributed leger networks can afford a number of advantages, but I will specifically hone in on the architectural aspect.

Students are astounded when I demonstrate the flexibility of a federated distributed network. Federation peers, or members, can operate an independent distributed ledger network while at the same time being a peer in a federated/consortium distributed ledger network when it complements their entity operations. And in this framework, I want to draw

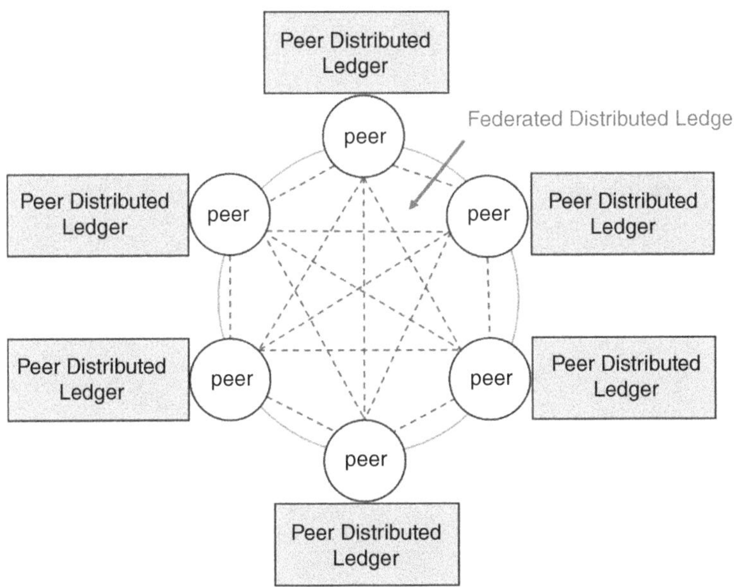

Figure 2.2   Federated Distributed Ledger.

attention to this architecture because it is not a theoretical project proposal; I have had the opportunity to work with an operational version of this architectural design. (Refer to Figure 2.2.)

In closing, I trust this chapter on design and transparency aspects of distributed ledger architecture has been educational and has helped clarify design characteristics that may not have been well understood previously.

Chapter 3

Distribute Network Secure Data Ledger Architectural Design Typologies

This chapter examines the definitions and architectural typologies of the currently prevalent common design models for distributed network data ledger architectures and I will concentrate on the more common architectural engineering design elements that have been brought together under the umbrella title of distributed ledger technologies (DLT). However, in the following chapter I will move through an examination of the alternative and less common architectural design structures along with their use case model.

It is important to note that this chapter is a prerequisite to understand the organization and classification of the various types of distributed network ledger structures and to an understanding of how to differentiate between them. Distributed network ledger systems, and alterative network ledger frameworks, utilize distributed computing, distributed networks, and secure ledger structures that often elude professionals in law, analytics, compliance, investment advisory, compliance, and regulatory/policy/legislative sectors. Because of the importance of having a firm grasp on being able to distinguish the differences between these various distributed network ledger systems, the following pages are dedicated to unpacking the distributed technologies and data ledger structures to ensure nothing is left to conjecture in what is the longest chapter in this book.

Distributed technologies and data ledger structures originated in the 1970s under the model of "distributed disk innovation" as an area of development within the early development of distributed computing systems. In this early development phase, the idea of disseminating data across multiple computers on a network to improve efficiency and reliability began to take shape with early projects like Andrew File System (AFS) and Sun Microsystems' Network File System (NFS) as some of the first widely implemented distributed network systems.

However, DLT, in concept, dates back to the Romans (31 BC–1453 AD) with various civilizations, such as the Rai Tribe on Yap Islande (origin unknown-early twentieth century), subsequently producing constructs for arriving at a consensus, long before the Bitcoin payment network. The phrase distributed ledger technology wasn't introduced until 2011. DLT was more regularly used as a synonymous term for blockchain by 2013, and the Google Chrome browser started to use DLT in 2018.

As with the contrived term of bitcoin with no verbatim roots in computer science, the same problem is true involving DLT. Discussions on DLT frequently introduce varying definitions that are consistently quite misleading from the perspective of the underlying technology. These numerous definitions for DLT are disseminated in publications, circulated by various media sources, and embraced by companies operating in the DLT digital asset sector. However, sometimes a definition for DLT is merely made-up to serve a promotional agenda that propagates the prevailing misunderstandings about the technologies of distributed networking as decentralized, distributed computing as mining, and data ledgers as databases. All the while, using additional common hype terms circulated by marketing departments or foundations to achieve what I believe to be the goal of adoption of whatever they are offering.

Many of the DLT definitions are devoid of any scientific basis or consideration for the differences among distributed networks, distributed computing, and data ledger frameworks used in the architectural engineering design of a distributed network data ledger. This use of idiomatic terms, like decentralized, open source, blockchain, anonymity, database, and many others to create a mix of concepts, provides a false perspective of what is a singular framework.

While attempts to define DLT is varied due to the fact it is a contrived term that has no roots in computer science leading to perceptions of its existence, it is a phrase that should simply be understood as an umbrella term that embraces the various distributed network data ledger architectures rooted in distributed computing and distributed networking to widely disseminate a singular version of a data ledger structure. Forget the nonsense about the notions of decentralization, blockchain, open source when examining DLT.

Professionals struggling to understand DLT need to first grasp that DLT is a convergence of several technologies. Underpinning DLT is the convergence of several technologies that must be appreciated before being able to explain and accurately understand that distributed ledger technology is not a thing in and of itself, it's a convergence of technologies. It's the various architectural components of distributed computing, distributed networking, data ledger structures, cryptography, and a number of other important components that give effectuation to DLT.

When I contemplate an issue, my preference is to remove the hype terms and view it through the lens of the scientific process which is generally defined in most textbooks as consisting of systematic observation, measurement, and experiment, alongside the formulation, testing, and modification of hypotheses. It is notable that "criticism is the backbone of the scientific process." So, as noted previously, DLT is the convergence of distributed computing and distributed networking technology, cryptography, data ledger structures, and this convergence would be more accurately be represented under a heading such as **"Distributed Network Secure Ledger Technologies** (DNSLT)," but that doesn't exactly roll off the tongue like DLT. To that end, I conducted some research and requested a GPT (General Pre-trained Transformer) AI bot to provide a summary of all variations of DLT as well as my new umbrella term to determine if there were perhaps any necessary changes in my process of developing a more suitable nomenclature. The response: "it's a system that allows multiple parties to share and update a digital record of transactions like Bitcoin blockchain." Very simple, but far from providing any clear and accurate insight into understanding the technologies of a distributed ledger. This little exercise provides context on how people arrive at equating DLT with the concentric knowledge around Bitcoin, blockchain, and similar typologies, and it fails to expose the technologies responsible that make the Bitcoin payment network possible.

In previous chapters, I presented historical information about distributed computing, distributed networking, cryptography, and data ledger technologies that have been in existence for decades, which debunks the AI bot's responses using web content, which to a novice appears as truthful information. To give credit, so I am not perceived as being anti-bitcoin, the most notable success of the Satoshi Nakamoto team is the design of the Bitcoin network as the first distributed ledger architecture that converged an asset transfer element, which is referenced as "bitcoin" in the white paper, and was an exercise that took years to bring to fruition.

So, with this very long introduction, I am working to establish a new thought paradigm about what should be known in the context of distributed-ledger technolog**ies,** (strikethrough, bolded and underlined for emphasis) as we move forward. In the next several sections I will address the three primary primitives that come together to form the distributed-ledger technologies that composes distributed computing technology.

Distributed Computing

Starting with the primitive of distributed computing, the accepted and simple computer science definition that provides the context of how to think about it is that distributed computing is the method of arranging multiple independent computers in a way that allows them to work together to achieve a common computational or data storage goal.

As usual, I am beginning with definitions. Distributed computing, which I covered from a technical and historical perspective in the first chapter, is a key primitive in DLT. It is critical in DLT for conducting the work of security by computing hashing algorithms, deploying digital signature algorithms to verify users when signing transactions involving cryptographic keys, and encrypting transaction data.

The distributed computing environment is why the node network of a distributed ledger structure is frequently designed with nodes that are multi-functional or divided into groupings of nodes that have specific functions. I defined the different types of nodes in the first chapter, but to make the point here, the Bitcoin node network is composed of full nodes that maintain complete copies of block ledger data, light nodes for participants that only store limited block ledger data but can rely on full nodes for complete copies of the ledger, and validation nodes that have the computational power to validate blocks for inclusion in the distributed data ledger.

Distributed computing, as a primitive of DLT, has several notable architectures that are worth mentioning. The three main distributed computing architectures are the peer-to-peer node model where each node is equal and can act as both a client and a server, the client-server model where a central server assigns tasks to clients, and the multi-tier model that uses resources from multiple client-server architectures.

So, having this distributed computing component serves an important function in distributed ledger networks of computing power and data storage. But that is just the distribution of computing power, and that takes us to the aspect of distributed networking in distributed ledger networks.

Distributed Networking

I covered distributed networking in more detail in the last chapter, but to provide a very brief recap, in computer science a distributed network is a coordination of computers that communicate with each other. So, in the case of the earlier example of the Bitcoin network, the light nodes need to communicate with full nodes, and this demonstrates the reason why a messaging mechanism must be introduced into the distributed ledger design, so the network nodes can communicate with each other.

I am often given white papers for review, but I also review nonscientific sources for definitions of distributed networks. I uncovered many instances that are too numerous to count on the number of times that the phrase "Distributed networks are also known as decentralized networks" included in defining a distributed network. In a couple of chapters, I am addressing the term "decentralized" and how it is misunderstood and mis-used in the context of distributed ledger networks. So, more to come on that, but it is completely inaccurate to express that a distributed network is decentralized because decentralization is morphologically rooted in removing centralization of decision-making and control. Distributed networks are only interested in being distributed and not in who owns or controls turning them off or on.

Data Ledger Structures in DLT

As I delve into the characteristics of data ledger structures, take note that these structures take several different design forms, and it is imperative that I establish at the beginning that there are a few different types of data ledger structures incorporated into distributed data ledger architectures such as the Bitcoin payment network, Ethereum enterprise platform, and various other projects that are in operation today. These data ledger structures have existed for decades, but many professionals are still not acquainted with them as they are typically disguised behind the naive term of blockchain—our retired term. This oversimplification of data ledger structure is most often used for achieving increased adoption. It is notable that there are various types of data ledger structures being integrated into the architectures of today's distributed ledger network projects in different ways than currently perceived by professionals.

Data structures have a long and storied history in computer science, with roots dating back to the early days of computing. In the early 1950s, researchers began exploring ways to store and organize data in computers, leading to the development of some of the earliest data structures. One of the first data structures to be developed was the array. They were a simple data structure that allowed programmers to store a fixed-size sequential collection of elements.

In the 1960s, researchers began exploring more sophisticated data structures, such as linked lists and trees. Linked lists were developed as a way to store data dynamically, allowing for the efficient insertion and deletion of elements. Trees, which are a type of data structure that consists of a set of nodes connected by edges, were developed to represent hierarchical relationships.

In the 1970s, researchers began exploring more advanced data structures, such as hash tables and graphs. Hash tables, which are used to store data in a way that allows for fast insertion, deletion, and search operations, were developed to solve complex problems in computer science. Graphs, which consist of a set of vertices connected by edges, were developed as a way to represent complex relationships between data points.

As computer science and technology have evolved, so too have data structures. In the 1980s and 1990s, researchers continued to develop and refine data structures, leading to the development of even more advanced data structures, such as heaps and balanced trees.

As an additional insight, it is interesting to note the AI search queries that I conducted for "data ledger structures" produced some rather inaccurate results. The AI results exclusively referenced the term "blockchain" and accounting ledgers despite the centuries long existence of other sophisticated data ledgers. There is an obvious lack of historical perspective in this area, which has led to a significant decline in understanding and has increased confusion about data ledgers in the distributed data ledger architecture. It is important to understand that digital assets exist in code separately from the transaction data captured in the data ledger, which is then distributed across the network.

In addressing the technologies and structures underpinning distributed ledger projects, it is critical to gain an insight into what a "data ledger" is and how it works in collaboration with other DLT architectural components. This emphasizes the fact that distributed network and distributed computing technologies are distinctive from data ledger structure and deserve to be conveyed independently. The *Professional Editors' Guide* notes that a hyphen is used to unite separate words into a compound form that functions as a single unit. The use of a hyphen would speak to making the distinction and unity of distributed network and computing alongside data ledger structures, i.e., "network-ledger," thus uniting the two as one all the while maintaining their distinctiveness. However, this is mostly a side note with the understanding that it will not have much influence. But it is worth the effort to provoke and give insight into the matter, especially since distributed ledger technology is a nascent and contrived phrase, or "distributed-ledger technology" if one is so inclined.

As previously discussed, many attempt to define or describe DLT, but they miss the contribution of the discrete importance of data ledger structures that includes block, blockless, and hybrid data ledger designs for the purpose of compiling transaction data into a ledger with an associated attempt at immutability to ensure that digital asset transaction data is preserved and unchanged.

I confess that many find understanding DLT in greater detail as a convergence of technologies difficult to ingest.

But regardless of whether a block or blockless data ledger structure is utilized in a distributed-ledger architecture, they both serve the same purpose: preserving a complete transaction data ledger of all historical transactions conducted on the distributed network mainnet.

It is my hope that by providing this information, it will enlighten and educate. So, let's dive in.

Data Ledger Structures: Block Ledgers

Starting with block ledger structures, it might be surprising for many to learn that "blockchain" is a made-up term. The term blockchain is not rooted in computer science; however, the technology underpinning the idea of chaining blocks of data has profound roots in computer science. The term blockchain is linked to the words "chain" and "block" that appear independently in the Bitcoin payment network white paper. The two words do not appear together as "blockchain" in academic or colloquial writings prior to 2008—the year the Bitcoin white paper was released. In subsequent years, I began to see the word "blockchain" appear with greater frequency in various web sources, much to my dismay It was during the years of 2009 and following that I was educating federal agents and legal counsel on the technology and web sources began to spew a multitude of terms that were the creation of developers flooding in from the web development community using new hype terms to promote adoption of something that many didn't understand with the promise of wealth. One of those was blockchain and Wikipedia notes (en.wikipedia.org/wiki/Blockchain) that the word blockchain was ultimately popularized by 2016; although, I suggest it was rooted in conversation well before 2016.

Regardless of its popularity, the term deserves to be retired for many reasons, if not solely for the inaccuracy in how it is applied as an artificial and superfluous term because data block structures originated in computer science in the early design of hard disk storage systems in the mid-1950s where data was divided into fixed-size chunks called "blocks" and these were utilized to efficiently access information on what existed as rotating disks. In the early 1970s, IBM formed a group that designed a block cypher to protect its customers' data. In 1973, the United States adopted it as a national standard under the Data Encryption Standard (DES). It remained in use until it was cracked in 1997. And prior to the work by IBM, Dr. Shannon introduced the idea of substitution-permutation networks (SPNs) in 1949, which are a type of block cipher. Block ciphers are a way of encrypting messages by breaking them into blocks and encrypting each block separately. I'll share a little more on block ciphers and block streams toward the end of this section.

Data ledgers have been in existence for many centuries as they trace back to well before the early research in computer science and didn't require a new term to describe its well established existence. In computer science, a data ledger is a record-keeping system that stores and verifies transactions over time. Ledgers can be digital or physical, and they can be used to track financial transactions, assets, or other data. Data ledgers are designed to ensure that data are immutable and verifiable, which means that every change to the data is recorded and cannot be altered.

There are currently two block ledger design approaches, both of which are rooted in computer science data ledger designs and have been used in distributed ledger architecture for over a decade which are linear sequential and nonlinear sequential block ledgers. It is worth noting that most block ledger implementations are of the linear sequencing block ledger classification. However, nonlinear sequenced block ledger has attained a significant presence as a superior L1 scaling architecture over sequential linear block ledger design. But it is notable that nonlinear block design is present in L2 solutions utilized to scale the L1 distributed ledger network to increase TPS and causes a significant amount of consternation for those providing analytic services as they have limited capability in this ledger type.

When the term blockchain is used to describe an entire distributed ledger network, it is grossly inaccurate because the term blockchain sequesters the entire system of structural component, thus overstating the competencies of the data ledger. In reviewing various web references describing blockchain, the content notes that a blockchain generates immutability, decentralization, distribution, database qualities, and executes payments. To elaborate on this, blockchain immutability is not certain and is a function of the node network, decentralization is a governance concept that cannot exist in code, distribution is another function of the node network, digital asset transactions are a functions of cryptographic algorithms entirely outside of the data ledger, and a ledger is not a database. So, over time the vast majority of sources that people use for information have fundamentally attributed the separate functions of the node-messaging complex, distributive computing capabilities, the cryptography of Digital Signature Algorithm, and the attributes of other architecture components to the data ledger component hidden behind the term blockchain.

I'll wrap this up with an illustration that I trust will solidify the point of this analysis. When I use the phrase "Bitcoin blockchain" to address the "Bitcoin cash system" (in white paper vernacular), blockchain (the ledger) dismisses the fact there are numerous more important and complex architectural components that get ignored. It is clearly another misused and contrived term in DLT that has exhausted its usefulness, and it is time to retire blockchain as a term used when referring to a distributed ledger platform (i.e., no more Bitcoin blockchain). This is similar to when the Fed announced in front of the Senate Banking Committee in November 2021 that they would be retiring the use of the term "transitory" after years of citing that inflation is transitory (i.e., temporary). Jerome Powell said, "The word transitory had become unclear" and that it was time to explain more clearly what the Fed meant by the term. That would be a fitting end for those in the DLT space to be bold like the Fed and retire blockchain because it is imprecise and it is time to explain more clearly what is meant.

Following is a simplistic visual of a basic sequential linear data ledger model, often visually recognized under our retired term of blockchain. Block data ledgers fundamentally exist to function as a transaction ledger in distributed network frameworks. A block data ledger structure in the form of a sequential linear block arrangement as shown in Figure 3.1.

But there are also sequential nonlinear block ledger arrangements that take the form of a data block-tree (or B-tree) data structure, see Figure 3.2.

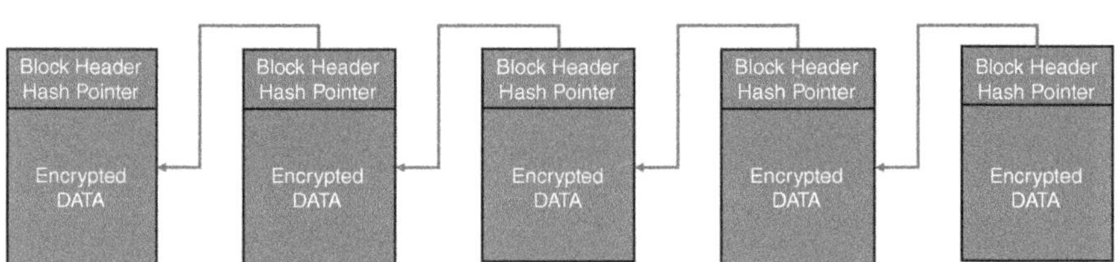

Figure 3.1 Block Data Ledger Structure.

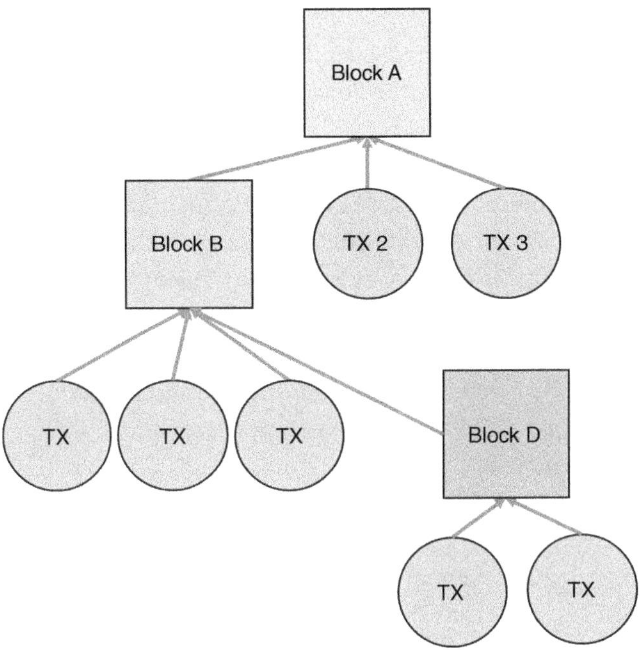

Figure 3.2 Blocktree Design.

As the diagram visually portrays, blocks are formed in a nonlinear, but still sequential, tree structure rather than linearly as in the sequential linear block data ledger structure. But mindful of the fact that block-tree sequential nonlinear data structures are no less a block data ledger structure than its counterpart, the sequential linear block structure.

A blocktree ledger has many advantages over a linear block data ledger structure and is used in several DLT L2 projects. Blocktree structures will come up again in the next chapter when noting the use of b-trees in L2 rollups. It is worth providing some insight into how the sequential nonlinear block data structure works in rollups as a precursor to what comes later. Rollups create data blocks of L1 transaction data processed off-ledger by the L2 rollup for purposes of scaling L1 for increased TPS. The nonlinear part of the data structure is advantageous because these data blocks are separating L1 transaction to be processed by the L2 rollup to later be reintegrated into the L1 data ledger as a hash of transactions. The L2 rollup only periodically forwards a data block from L2 to the L1 mainnet data ledger in a nonlinear fashion. This is exactly the reason that tracing services have difficulty visualizing transactions in L2 off-mainnet transactions because of the obfuscation introduced by blocktrees and off-ledger L2 rollup block hashing before reintroduction of the L2 rollup hash into the L1 mainnet block hash.

It is fitting to note that the first distributed data ledger is called the Haber-Stornetta time-stamp certificate ledger deployed in 1995, which I referenced previously. The foundational features of the Haber-Stornetta system for time-stamping includes hashing of data into blocks and securing the blocks with the Merkle tree, chaining blocks using hash pointers and using a distributed network system to share the ledger the entire network—all foundational components of a DLT architecture.

An interesting fact is that this first distributed ledger network was developed as a fraud detection mechanism for digital documents (no currency assets involved). How it works in practice is that a user generates a document and calculates the cryptographic hash. The user then sends the document to the time-stamping service that collects multiple document hashes and creates a Merkle tree. From the Merkle tree, the root hash for the block is calculated. Finally, the new block's root hash is linked to the previous block's hash, thus creating a sequential linear block data ledger. The Haber-Stornetta system is still in operation to this day.

It is fitting at this point to return to the beginning of this chapter and graphically represent the basic structure of a distributed ledger system. When I converge a distributed computing client and distributed node network and layer it with a data ledger structure I achieve a basic architectural structure for a distributed ledger network, which is represented in the simplistic visual aid shown in Figure 3.3.

There are of course many components not represented in this diagram, but the basic component of the distributed network of nodes that store and message the most current version of the ledger across the entire network is shown. The result is a data redundancy that prevents loss of data, and fault tolerance so there is no single point of failure in communication of nodes and clients.

It is worth noting that with the introduction of the Ethereum platform is 2015, it has made understanding DLT architecture more confusing for professionals because it isn't just an L1 network anymore like the Bitcoin payment system; however, developers have added significant complexity of Bitcoin transaction analytics by further developing the L2 infrastructure and adding code for runes and inscripts. The Ethereum platform has stretched the capabilities of the mainnet L1 distributed ledger architecture beyond realistic capabilities by expanding the use of the distributed

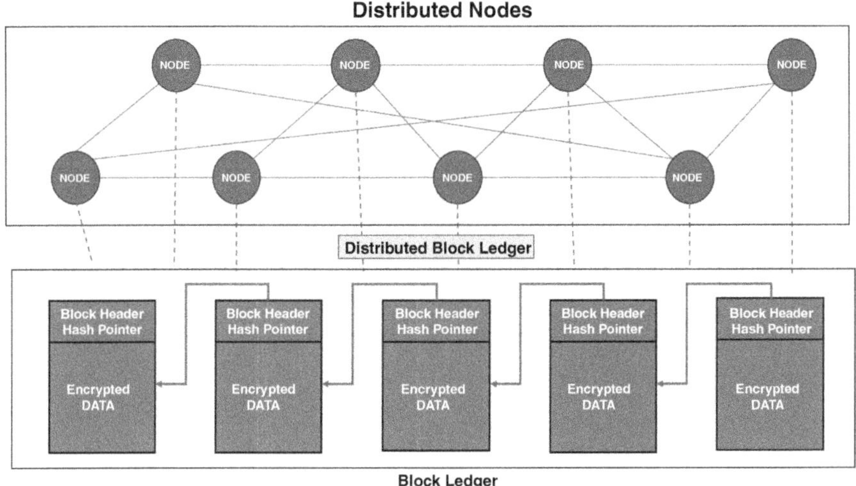

Figure 3.3 Distributed Ledger Network.

ledger of the mainnet to include the off-ledger transaction data of the L2 enterprise DLT stack where the majority of transactions from L1 are now processed on L2 (off-ledger) for L1 scaling purposes.

For years, Ethereum developers have been in the process of converging many adjacent ledger systems with the Ethereum mainnet to bring about platform enhancements in an attempt to expand performance such as improve interoperability of L2, increase scaling of L1 by moving transaction processing to L2 (off-mainnet), increase scaling of L2 through the introduction of rollups, and significantly increase the transactions per second (TPS) from an approx. average of 20 TPS to 100,000 TPS, the introduction of account abstraction (AA) wallets, expand privacy with zero-knowledge proofs (ZKP), and so much more. The Ethereum platform is an amalgamation of technologies that is attempting to engineer some very lofty goals that currently appear to be crashing in around the developer team and the Ethereum Foundation. As a distributed ledger architectural engineer, I forecasted that Ethereum would encounter major obstacles going back to 2019 and that it would start to look a bit like Frankenstein's monster.

In the real world of data block ledgers in DLT it is all about the code—like *The Matrix*. Figure 3.4 shows a sample of how a sequential linear block appears in its natural environment for professionals that have perhaps never seen blocks in code form.

```
[
  Block {
    data: { isGenesis: true },
    hash: '027f7198ae7fe53b98072241c6b8a8ed8c9bb4f05dd26f71335158fc44b92ad0',
    previousHash: '0',
    timeStamp: 2021-11-19T23:24:17.974Z,
    proofOfWork: 0
  },
  Block {
    data: { from: 'Viet', to: 'David', amount: 100 },
    hash: '00f0fdb96643d30262c04c6e9885a4b3014deac69e0f0f252530e50921165403',
    previousHash: '027f7198ae7fe53b98072241c6b8a8ed8c9bb4f05dd26f71335158fc44b92ad0',
    timeStamp: 2021-11-19T23:24:17.974Z,
    proofOfWork: 278
  },
  Block {
    data: { from: 'Adam', to: 'Beck', amount: 150 },
    hash: '00e8d7ea3e2afd40c8e902c1a7e3ed72a45481b4f9729b10fe037510d63a4cf0',
    previousHash: '00f0fdb96643d30262c04c6e9885a4b3014deac69e0f0f252530e50921165403',
    timeStamp: 2021-11-19T23:24:17.996Z,
    proofOfWork: 71
  }
]
===== Is Valid: true =====
```

Figure 3.4   A Block in Its Natural Environment.

Learning about distributed ledger architectural engineering methods for coding a distributed ledger as a project is what graduate students experience when they go through a graduate specialization program I developed and taught as the program professor for several years at an accredited university in Tempe, Arizona. Many of the students going through the specialization program were cybersecurity graduate majors, and I designed the program using kinesthetic learning with a coding lab environment so noncoders were able to participate. In addition, I use project-based techniques of testing rather than using traditional testing methods. These graduate students learned how to code a simple sequential linear data ledger framework and then incorporate it into a distributed network environment and then move on to ultimately have a rudimentary, fully deployed distributed ledger project. Because they went through the process of doing and seeing something that is not shared with the masses, they quickly learned and understood that block-based distributed ledger architecture requires the integration of different technologies and is so much more complex, and at the same time made more logical sense, than imagined. That is an experience that students appreciated.

In wrapping up block data structures in distributed ledger architecture, it is worth noting a distinction involving block ciphers and stream ciphers. These are not data block structures seen in distributed ledger architecture, but it is valuable to understand the basic function of block ciphers and stream ciphers as they are distinctly unique mechanisms. Starting with the block cipher, it is a cryptographic algorithm that encrypts data in a fixed block size using symmetric cryptography (i.e., a shared key). The encryption algorithm processes each block of data separately to transform plaintext into ciphertext. Block ciphers are appropriate for mathematically complex computation and permutations to ensure the encrypted data remains secure. But block ciphers involve discrete datasets and are not suitable to be linked into a data ledger format.

Stream ciphers are algorithms that encrypt data one bit or byte at a time rather than in fixed block sizes. This generates a keystream that is combined with the plaintext to construct the ciphertext. Use cases that utilize stream ciphers include scenarios where data need to be encrypted in a continuous flow, or stream, making it suitable for real–time applications and can be categorized into synchronous, asynchronous, and one–time pad (OTP). This concludes block ledger structures so let's move on to the next section on blockless data ledger structures.

Data Ledger Technology Structures: Blockless Ledger Architecture

The examination of DLT data ledgers does not end with block ledger networks. Two very different DLT architectures that surpass the capabilities of block ledger structures are the Directed Acyclic Graph (DAG) and Radix data structures. I will start with DAG as it is a little easier to grasp.

DAG data formations, as with block data storage, existed well before its integration into a distributed computing framework. Let me start by simply defining DAG through its acronym:

Directed: The data structure only moves in one direction.
Acyclic: The data structure cannot return to a previous state from the current state; it is "noncyclical."
Graph: When visualized, the data structure appears as an interconnected set of relationships between vertices.

The origin of DAG extends back into a period long before there was ever a thought about chaining blocks as a ledger and converging it with a distributed network and a digital asset. DAG can be traced to the early development of graph theory and the foundational concept first hinted at in Leonhard Euler's famous paper titled "Seven Bridges of Königsberg" from 1736. The "Seven Bridges of Königsberg" in Königsberg in Prussia (now Kaliningrad, Russia) is a notable problem in the history of mathematics that presented the challenge to devise a walk through the city that would cross each of those bridges once and only once (Figure 3.5). After simplifying the map of the city to a graph, Euler introduced his formula relating to the number of edges, vertices and faces.

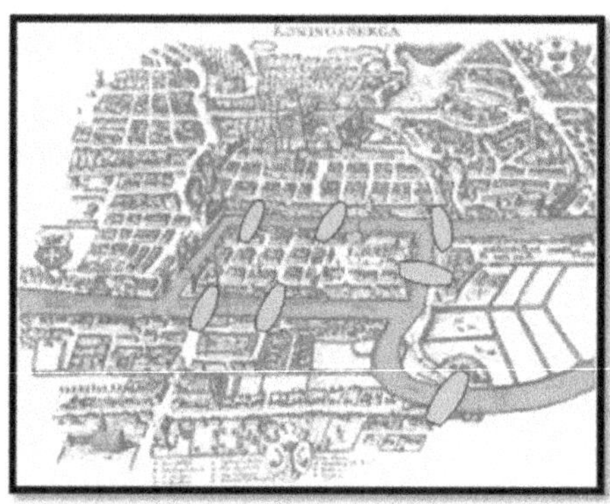

Figure 3.5   Seven Bridges of Königsberg.

DAGs represent a specific type of graph with directed edges and no cycles, which makes them beneficial for use in various scientific domains such as computer science. Today DAGs are used extensively in fields that include data engineering, machine learning (ML), and distributed systems, but they are not block data structures. DAG is used to represent complex workflows, data pipelines, and version control histories (also known as revision control, source control, and source code management) because of its ability to clearly show dependencies between tasks or events without creating circular loops.

A very early use case of DAG is in the creation of family trees. However, the definition of a tree did not appear in graph theory and did not include most family trees because in many family trees during that period, at some point distant relatives mated, forming a common ancestor on both the paternal and maternal sides of the family thus violating the rule of DAG by introducing a circular loop. However, a family tree can be considered a DAG if each node is a person, and each parent-offspring relationship is drawn as an arrow pointing toward the offspring, which is directed by the arrows and acyclic with no person being a parent of themselves.

This is significant because all directed acyclic graphs have a topological ordering (i.e., there is at least one way to put the vertices in an order such that all edges point in the same direction along that order; Figure 3.6). And a directed graph is a DAG if and only if it can be topologically ordered, by arranging the vertices as a linear ordering that is consistent with all edge directions.

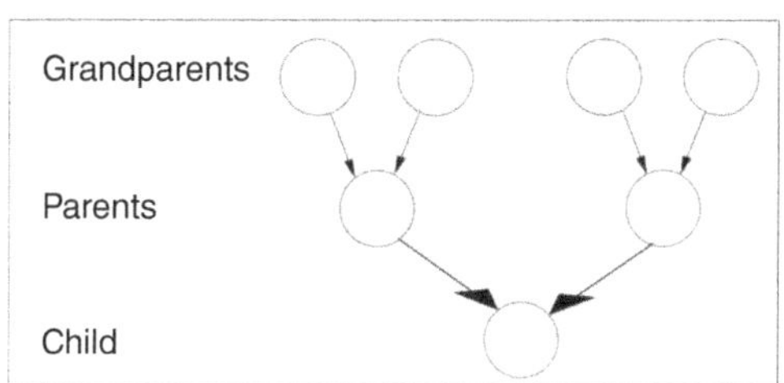

Figure 3.6 Directed Acyclic Graph.

All of this is relevant because, just as with block ledgers, it is not dependent on a distributed network for its existence. And with that noted, the first notable purported use of a DAG architecture in a distributed network environment was the Dagcoin project established by Nils Grossberg in 2017, which was proposed as a design that utilized a DAG structure; however, it turned out to be an approximately €8 million scam. The Dagcoin launch came on the back of the 2017 OneCoin launch, which is a scam operation that I discuss in the closing and is also connected to Nils Grossberg. Estonian police arrested Grossberg and several accomplices in 2022 in connection with OneCoin and Dagcoin. So, I will move to the first widely implemented DAG distributed ledger network, IOTA. Named after the smallest letter of the Greek alphabet and developed by David Sonstebo, Dominik Schiener, Sergey Ivancheglo, and Serguei Popov, IOTA's architecture was conceptualized in 2015, and it was deployed in 2017.

DAG ledger architecture is a more complex architecture than block ledger architecture, but it provides a considerably faster TPS, improved scalability, a significant cost reduction, and a diminished risk factor given enhanced transaction dependency. I will note that the TPS is significantly higher than block ledgers because DAG architecture has two important properties: (1) each transaction is a vertex (may also be referred to as a node) in the graph with the edges connecting nodes to each other, and

(2) each edge has a direction so the edges cannot form cycles, which ensure that transaction progress is in only one direction. An important DAG construct for professionals to grasp in all sectors researching a DAG architecture is to recognize the vertex classifications. Following is a list with a short description:

Root: A vertex with no incoming edges, often considered the starting point in a DAG

Leaf: A vertex with no outgoing edges, representing the end point of a particular path

Parent: A vertex that directly influences another vertex through an outgoing edge

Child: A vertex that is directly influenced by another vertex through an incoming edge

Professionals will find that various projects will utilize their proprietarily unique terminology in place of the standard mathematical terms associated with the DAG structure in an attempt to be unique, but many times it results in confusion for those who are novice or naive to the technology and the project. A few examples: IOTA uses the term "Tangle" for their DAG graph, a Leaf vertex is called a "Tip," and the IOTA foundation runs a special vertex (node) that is utilized to issue a zero-value transaction named a "milestone" that is inserted at given time intervals for consensus referencing. Let's contrast IOTA terminology with another DAG distributed-ledger project architecture, Byteball. Deployed in 2016 by founder Tony Churyumoff, Byteball uses terminology that orients with "blockchain" type terms. So, a professional reading a web article will note that Byteball will reference the DAG graph as a DAG-chain, which is accurately a "graph" and not a chain as articulated in the DAG acronym. There are other idiosyncrasies in terminology that I will not get into further because it can become confusing mixing terminology of DAG with invented terms, such as blockchain, that may conceptually sound correct, but cause puzzlement and mistakes when conducting heuristic analytic studies, developing investigative leads, or developing an investment risk assessment. The takeaway here is that using a platform's published terminology to determine the architectural design can be very misleading and can have a negative impact and erroneous outcomes during investigations, analysis, policy/regulation, and many other implications as already noted.

To summarize, DAG can be integrated into a distributed network-ledger architecture, but unlike block ledgers where blocks are compiled and added sequentially in a linear or nonlinear pattern, a DAG processes transactions concurrently across the graph using a nonlinear and non-block methodology; hence, DAG presents transactions as a graphical net of interconnected data points. And each connection between transaction vertices is a directed edge that prevents cycles from being formed, but then that new transaction vertex must reference previous validated transaction vertices for its own validation, utilizing a consensus mechanism to ensure all vertices agree on the validity of the ledger state. And like all distributed ledger environments, a gossip protocol is invoked to communicate new transaction data that are shared with the entire network. As a very simplistic aid, DAG can be visualized as something like Figure 3.7, but it looks nothing like this in its coded environment.

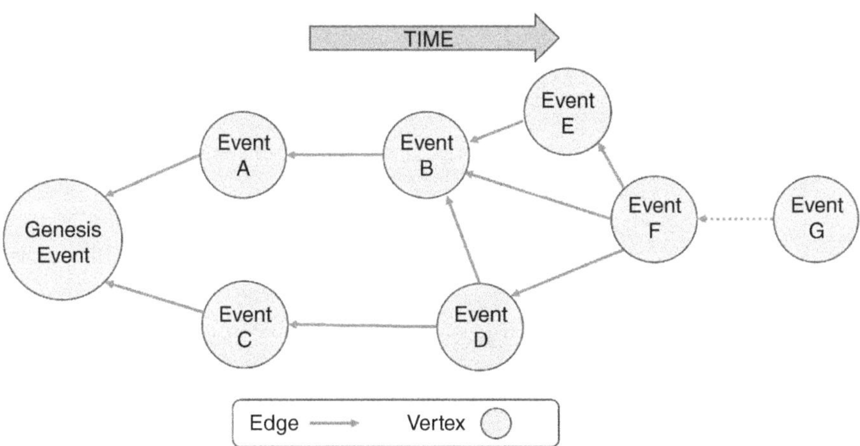

Figure 3.7 DAG.

But DAG is not the only blockless nonlinear DLT architectural design option. There is another data ledger structure, albeit not as commonly acknowledged as block and DAG data ledger models. However, it worth considering the Radix DLT platform which employs a "Radix Sort" data architecture. Radix was initially introduced as eMunie founded by Dan Hughes, but was later rebranded as Radix in 2013, which coincidentally takes on the same name as the underlying technology of the Radix platform.

"Radix" refers to the base of a number system, like the base 10 in decimal, while "radix sort" is a linear sorting algorithm that utilizes this concept by repeatedly sorting data based on individual digits (or "radix") within a number, starting from the least significant digit, to achieve a final sorted order; essentially, "radix" is the core concept that the radix sort algorithm leverages to sort data. For clarity, Figure 3.8 is an example of the radix sort process.

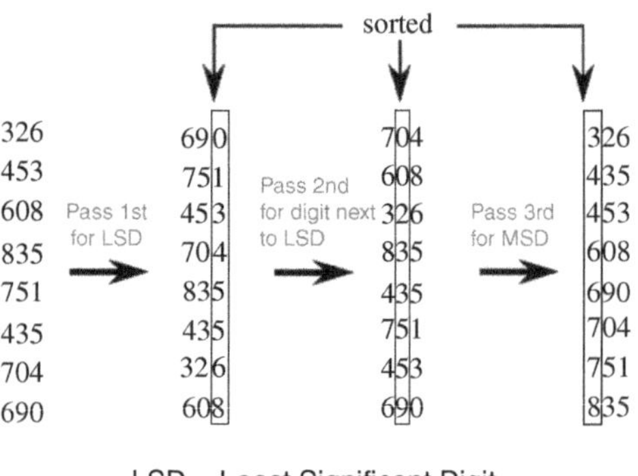

Figure 3.8   Radix Sort Process.

The concept of "radix" is deeply rooted in the early days of computing, with its most significant historical connection to the "Radix Sort" algorithm developed by Herman Hollerith, a German-American statistician, in 1887, while working on tabulating machines, where he used the idea of sorting data based on individual digits (radix) of a number to efficiently organize punched cards, and this later became a foundational part of IBM technology as his company evolved into the International Business Machines Corporation in 1911.

Today, radix sort is still used in various computer applications, particularly when dealing with large datasets of integers or binary strings because it can be significantly faster than other sorting algorithms in certain scenarios. Radix sort isn't used widely today because it's considered a specialized sorting algorithm, meaning it performs best only on specific data types (like short integers with consistent digit lengths) and can be more complex to implement when dealing with diverse data structures or large, variable-length keys, making it impractical for applications where flexibility is needed. However, in the use case within a distributed network ledger environment, it works quite well as the data structure is fixed length and consistent format.

It is notable that, in 2019, the Hughes Radix application published that it replayed the entire 10-year history of the Bitcoin ledger data in 30 minutes. To ensure everyone is tracking, the entire 10-year history of the Bitcoin transaction ledger was the period of 2009–2019. It was reported on the Radix blog (available at https://www.radixdlt.com/blog/replaying-bitcoin) and several other media sources that the entire 10-year Bitcoin transaction ledger was processed in 30 minutes. This is a testament to the increased efficiency of "Radix Sort" utilized by the Radix platform over the more convergent architecture of many different technologies and algorithms (e.g., DSA, PoW, node computing network, node gossip messaging protocol, block data structures, and the list goes on) that form the Bitcoin payment network. I recall writing an internal memo to superiors, while working for the federal government in 2019, providing a notification of the achievement of the Radix platform. It was a phenomenal accomplishment that to this day is largely unknown.

Additional details provided by Radix DLT indicate that the transactions per second peaked at 1 million, with full transaction and signature validation, on a network of approximately 1,000 nodes that are evenly distributed globally. This is significantly faster than any other permissioned or permissionless distributed-ledger project and faster than non-distributed-ledger payment platforms such as Alipay and WeChat Pay (the top two Chinese payment platforms) as well as PayPal based in the United States.

Radix DLT is the only project that I am aware of that employs the radix structure, which is neither a block design nor DAG blockless design, but like DAG, is catagorically a radix blockless data ledger structural design. In a Radix DLT white paper are a couple of diagrams that visualize the Radix DLT transaction management outside the bounds of a monolithic block data structure and implement logical clocks, which is a system based on Leslie Lamport's logical clock theory; refer to Figure 3.9.

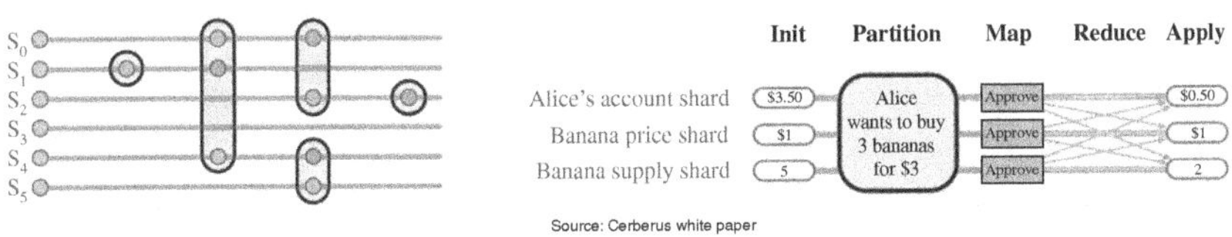

Figure 3.9 Radix DLT Transaction Management.

And with that, I conclude my overview of the most relevant current day blockless ledger systems. Next, I will highlight the hybrid ledger architecture.

Hybrid Ledger Architecture

A hybrid ledger design is one that combines at least two different, but compatible, ledger designs to employ the benefits of each of the respective ledger models. The most common hybrid formation that I have observed at the time of this writing is the blending of the DAG and block ledger models that I label a block-DAG ledger architectural design. Some of the benefits in this hybrid model combine the data security provided in the cryptography of block ledgers with the improved efficiency of significantly greater speed of adding data blocks by utilizing DAG's faster validation times, which has the tangent benefit of lower transaction costs. Overall, combining DAG and block ledger methods ultimately results in handling larger volumes of data, making it ideal for use cases requiring low latency (i.e., near-instantaneous or near real-time settlement [NRTS]) of transactions and high throughput (i.e., amount of data moved successfully from one place to another during a given period). For those not familiar with latency, throughput, and bandwidth in data flow, Figure 3.10 may help.

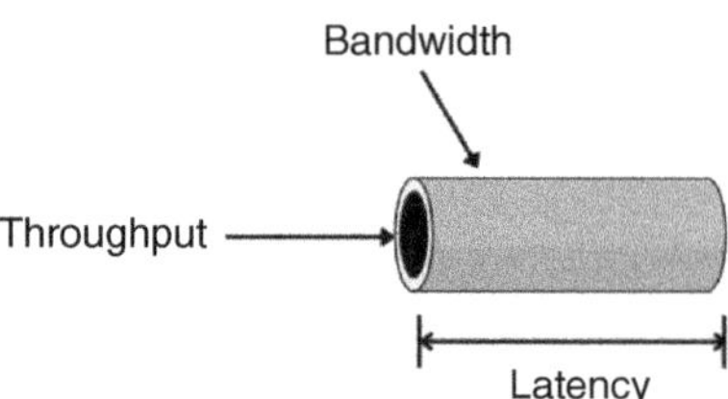

Figure 3.10   Latency, Throughput, and Bandwidth.

In the next several paragraphs I provide an overview of the architecture of two projects that I have followed for years from an academic perspective that applies to the block-DAG hybrid model. And I will note there is no bias applied to the order in which I address these projects.

It becomes quite complex and difficult to ascertain when a directed acyclic graph is converged with a distributed network environment predominantly because the design of distributed computing and network design also lacks standardization when adding the graphical aspect of DAG. So, the confusion escalates around separating the block ledger component and the DAG ledger component from the distributed network component in a hybrid architecture.

An example of the confusion that can arise is typified in an article written by the editorial staff of a well-known "crypto sector" media source that authored an article about Fantom—a hybrid ledger DAG distributed-ledger project. For readers to understand, the article wasn't written in some prehistoric period when DAG wasn't well understood; this article was written in 2023 and updated in 2024.

The body of the article focused on Fantom employing a DAG distributed network ledger environment, but the title said it was a beginner's guide to Fantom as a highly scalable blockchain. In a test of the critical thinking skills of graduate students, which I do frequently, in one of my intermediate classes on distributed network and ledger architectural engineering, I presented the article as one of their reading assignments for the next class . In that next class I asked students, "Does Fantom utilize a DAG ledger or a block ledger in their architectural design?" Students responded that, based purely on the reading of the article, the mixed DAG and block ledger terminologies could go either way and that the article could be hyping the use of DAG to make the Fantom project stand out from hundreds of other block ledger projects. This led to some discussion, as can be expected, as to whether the media source didn't have some financial interest in hyping the Fantom project. But that aside, an astute student who followed my teaching by always reading the project white paper, came to the conclusion that the Fantom white paper provides evidence that its ledger design is based in graph (DAG) and block.[1] This isn't just a matter of semantics as the visual representations from previous sections demonstrate clear support for the difference between "block" and "graph" ledger design respectively (see Figure 3.11).

But to continue with Fantom, it was founded by Dr. Ahn Byung Ik and deployed in 2019 but rebranded as Sonic Labs in 2024. This platform serves as an example of a hybrid architecture combining a linear block ledger with a nonlinear blockless DAG ledger to create a distributed

---

[1] Fantom 2018 white paper URL: https://fantom.foundation/_next/static/media/wp_fantom_v1.6.39329cdc5d0ee59684cbc6f228516383.pdf)

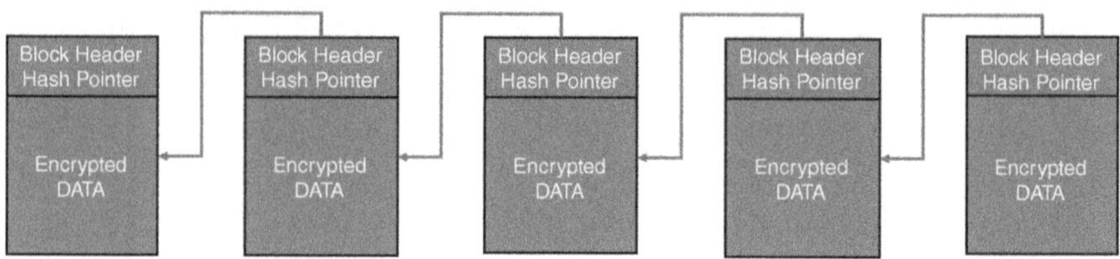

Figure 3.11 Block vs. DAG Data Structure.

network ledger architecture with faster confirmation times, improved latency, increased throughput, and decreased cost.

To accomplish this, Sonic Labs uses a sequential linear block data ledger framework that is Ethereum Virtual Machine (EVM) compatible for its L2 development environment. But the Sonic L1 mainnet required a robust node network to speed consensus approval to reach the desired throughput, and that is where the DAG node network provides a superior consensus network framework called Lachesis, an appropriate name as the DAG determines the destiny of a transaction. If that doesn't track from some readers, in Greek mythology, Lachesis (the Allotter) is the middle sister of Clotho (the Spinner) and Atropos (the Unturnable) who are the three goddesses who control human destiny and known as The Fates, or Moirai. The consensus system combines Proof-of-Stake (PoS) with Asynchronous Byzantine Fault Tolerance (ABFT), which is more compatible with the requirement of the Directed Acyclic Graph (DAG) nonlinear structure.

The DAG graph validation distributed ledger network performs the computational tasks of transaction (TX) verification prior to being included in an "event block" for validation. This is very much in contrast to linear block ledger projects design mechanics where verified transactions enter the mempool, or similar holding state, before validation nodes select grouping of transactions that will be sequentially tested computationally to determine if they will be a suitable fit. Ultimately, only one node will be able to add a block of transactions that meets the mathematically computed fit and then be communicated by the validating node to the entire network where the other nodes in the network will provide a confirmation on the validity of the newly validated transaction data block. Finally, the new block of transaction data will become part of the sequential linear arrangement of blocks linked by a hash point to the previous data block (demonstrated in Figure 3.12). This process is slow, time consuming, and resource intensive, thus expensive.

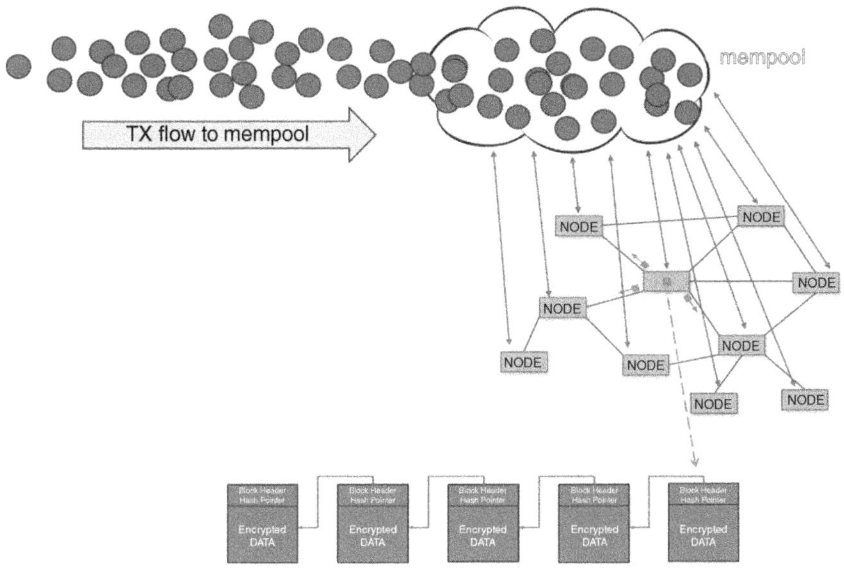

Figure 3.12 New Data Becoming Part of Mempool.

The design of the DAG node network provides an environment for the validation nodes to provide the capability to verify transactions and form blocks of verified transaction working with any block of data rather than needing to follow a sequential stream, which is quite different than the constraining architectural design of the Bitcoin payment network and the Ethereum platform. DAG ledger in the framework of a consensus system allows validation nodes to work independently to verify transactions and join them into blocks in a nonlinear methodology into what are known as "event blocks," which is a slight variation to the graphical representation of DAG that I presented earlier where the vertices denote transaction events.

The event blocks are then broadcast to the distributed node network infrastructure in a nonlinear manner to achieve consensus that does not rely on data blocks being ordered and validated sequentially, which I described when addressing sequential linear and sequential nonlinear block ledgers earlier in this chapter. And once most of the validators agree on the contents of the event blocks, it is added to the Sonic main block ledger as a root block event. The rudimentary graphic in Figure 3.13 may help provide visual learners with a better perspective of the architecture.

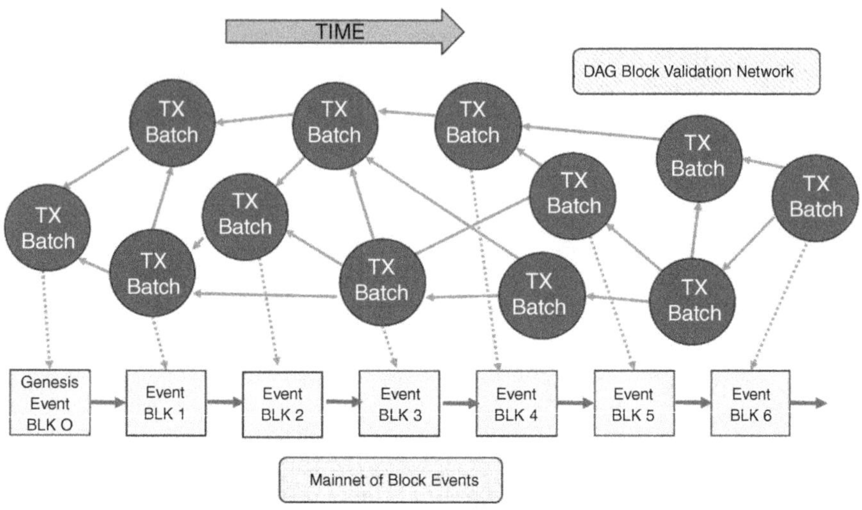

Figure 3.13 Architecture of a Distributed Network of BlockDAG Data Ledger.

To summarize the process:

1. Transaction Submission: A user initiates a transaction on the Sonic network.
2. Validator Node Processing: Validator nodes collect transactions into batches and create "event blocks."
3. Consensus Building: Most validator nodes must agree on the order of event blocks, reaching consensus on the transaction data.
4. Block Finalization: Once consensus is reached, the event block is finalized and added as a block.

Sonic Labs' hybrid Block-DAG architecture has provided some substantial improvements in increased throughput and reduced latency and transaction costs as provided in a January 2025 report (https://www.soniclabs.com/). Some of the statistics provided by Sonic Labs demonstrate a confirmed capacity of 10,000+ transactions per second, confirmation times of approximately 1 second, finality times averaging 720 milliseconds, all with an average transaction cost of less than $0.01. These improved metrics in a distributed network ledger architecture are a computer science version of heterosis. In the biological science of genetics, heterosis, or hybrid vigor, is a phenomenon where hybrid progeny have superior performance compared to their parental inbred lines. Following is one additional example of the hybrid distributed network ledger model to close out this section on hybrid architectural models.

This next example of a hybrid distributed network ledger model is found in the Hedera project. The Hedera Hashgraph project was launched in 2018 founded by Dr. Leemon Baird, the creator of Hashgraph, and Hedera cofounder Mance Harmon.

The reason I want to present this architecture is because it provides a stark contrast in block–DAG hybrid architectural design approach. The Hedera platform uses a linear hash-lattice framework within a DAG ledger consensus infrastructure. In other words, transaction data are stored as hashes as a substitute and arranged in a directed acyclic graph (DAG) lattice arrangement. So, the convergence of the various technologies utilized results in an overall lower cost of computing in contrast to alternative forms of sequential linear and nonlinear block architectures. But I will note there are block-lattice architectures as well, but again, Hedera is unique in its use of hash-lattice versus block-lattice.

The flow of transaction processing in this architecture follows this general sequence:

- Each transaction is assigned a unique time-stamp.
- The time-stamp is determined by calculating the median of the times each DAG node received the transaction.
- Transactions are processed and absorbed into the network's shared state based on the order determined by their consensus determined time-stamp.
- And once the transaction has achieved consensus, it is recorded in the hash-lattice ledger.

Figure 3.14 shows a hash-lattice, which may be helpful to fully understand the difference between the nonlinear and linear DAG architectures:

Notice the node ordering at the left side of the lattice graph that contextualizes the linear DAG design of the hash event vertices. This is representative of the Hedera platform DAG hash-lattice architectural design. In Hedera, topological sorting is the linear ordering of a DAG where every edge marks the end of one vertex and the beginning of another. In many ways, topological sorting is a type of schedule that ensures tasks are completed in a specific order.

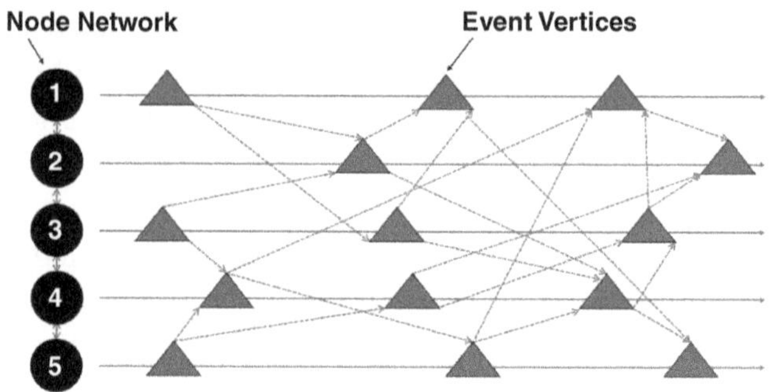

Figure 3.14   Hash-lattice.

Another aspect of DAG is transitive closure and is one of several architectural component features that separates directional acyclic graphs from a data block structure. When a transitive closure is constructed in a DAG, it may allow programs to reach nodes in fewer steps.

So, I trust readers have gained a realization though the content of this chapter that there is much more complexity and variability underpinning this technology set that is so far beyond what is inaccurately referenced as "blockchain"—a contrived term that doesn't represent the sophistication of this technology area. I also trust that I've provided significant evidence that there has been, and will continue to be, significant evolution in the development of next generation ledger convergence with distributed network technology to form new architectural design models. Who knows, maybe it will reach revolutionary leaps with quantum networks, but more on that in a later chapter.

I want to add a developer's note to the topic of evolutionary change that may provide retrospective insight for readers who struggle to maintain a continuing education mindset and have no clue about the advancements conveyed about the tech in this chapter. Many of the evolutionary developments come by way of solving the "theory of constraints" and the "shortest path wins" theory to develop solutions, formally or informally, including methods that have been theorized over the decades. The "shortest path wins" theory essentially states that, in a system where multiple paths can be taken to reach a destination, the path with the least cumulative cost of time, energy, distance, etc., will naturally be the one chosen. This is because it represents the most efficient way to travel between two points, assuming all other factors are equal. In graph theory, the shortest path wins theory is associated with Dijkstra's algorithm, developed by Dutch computer scientist Edsger Dijkstra in 1956. The theory was published in a 1959 paper titled "A Note on Two Problems in Connexion with Graphs." In addition to Dijkstra's algorithm, the shortest path wins theory has other key aspects such as greedy approach and graph representation.

The theory of constraints (ToC) was conceived by Dr. Eliyah Golratt, an Israeli business management guru, in his book titled *The Goal*, published in 1984. ToC is a methodology for identifying the important constraint in a system and upgrading the constraint until it is no longer the limiting factor. The ToC includes a methodology for identifying and eliminating constraints (The Five Focusing Steps), tools for analyzing and resolving problems (The Thinking Process), and a method for measuring performance and guiding management decisions (Throughput Accounting). There is so much more to share on ToC, but I will leave that for readers to research and apply.

With this information, it should be of no surprise why DAG (directed acyclic **graph**) has become so pronounced in some of the most efficient renderings of providing new ledger designs that amplify the efficiencies in distributed network ledger architectural designs.

The next chapter will dive into alternative distributed network designs that are innovative but often elude those rooted in the "blockchain" frame of thinking and are not adequately addressed in policies involving digital assets, tokenization real-world assets (RWA), compliance vetting, cybersecurity, and post-quantum computing (PQC) cryptography resistance, and the list goes on. l trust this next chapter will be insightful, enlightening, and educational.

Figure 3.15 Cars as Architectures.

I'll close with a diagram (Figure 3.15) of what I have been stating in lectures and speaking engagements for nearly two decades—block ledger architectures are like the Edsel cars of the past.

Once professionals in the various industry sectors that interact with digital assets come to this knowledge, it will open up an entire universe of digital asset transaction methods that were never considered by policy-makers, compliance officers, investigators/LE, regulators, and financial services. And I will provide an overview of some of these digital asset transaction methods in later chapters. But let me first move to the next chapter on alternative distributed ledger network architectures.

Chapter 4

Alternative Ledger Frameworks

In this chapter, I am providing an examination and analysis of alternative ledger structures. I have separated the alternative structures examined in this chapter from the prior chapter on DLT architecture to avoid any confusion between these two. The design structures in this chapter, as opposed to those in the last chapter, are recurrently described in web articles and other podiums as being on an equal topological level as other DLT architectures under the retired term of blockchain. While these alternative ledger frameworks use data ledger structures, they do not have the DLT stack that addressed in the last chapter, which makes them quite unique.

To provide a brief insight into what to expect in this examination of alternative frameworks, they are constructed with the idea of functioning in what is sometimes described by project developers as a Layer-0. However, the Layer-0 of these alternative systems is still the TCP/IP algorithms of an internet. Using an analogy, these alternative projects are more like GoDaddy, a web-hosting company that provides a prebuilt infrastructure with all of the modules for deploying a live website ASAP (as soon as possible). The only thing left for someone wanting to deploy a website is to create the design.

This is the objective of these alternative systems. They provide the equivalent of an L1 infrastructure that supports developers building what is equivalent to an L2 enterprise project by eliminating the burden on the developer of having to design and cultivate an entire DLT architecture. So, let's jump into examining the two primary models in the alternative ledger framework space.

Relay-Parachain Model

In addition to the typical DLT architectures described in the last chapter, it is important to also understand the general framework of alternative architectures as well. Relay platforms and its relationship to parachains is just one of a handful of alternative architectures. The architecture of a relay platform with its parachain projects is very different from standard L1 and L2 distributed ledger architectures such as the Bitcoin payment network or the Ethereum enterprise development platform. Although, I want to note that the relay-parachain model has something common with the Ethereum platform, they are designed as developer enterprise platforms. This section is to help those endeavoring to understand and differentiate the functionality and capabilities of these unique projects and how they are different from the common architectural designs that most think of in the context of a Solona, Ethereum, or Tron to name a few in the L2 enterprise space.

It is important to begin by pointing out that a relay base supports parachains in what I will describe in biological terminology as synergically collaborative parasitic structures. The object of a relay base is to provide L1-type mainnet infrastructure for developers to introduce L2-type options in a less complex environment. As a result, the relay-parachain structure uses a direct relational method rather than having many independent L1 platforms with L2 interoperability. Before moving into describing the fabrication and mutuality mechanics of the rely-parachain model, it is ideal to describe the individual structures of the relay base and the parachains.

To begin, the most well-known of the relay-parachain structures was introduced as Polkadot and Kusama in a white paper release in 2016. The founders include Gavin Wood, who is also a cofounder of Ethereum, Robert Habermeier, and Peter Czaban. I will not be able to adequately cover as much of the detail and intricacy in the design and mechanics in the development of the relay-parachain model as I want in this book; however, reading the project white papers and updated developer papers will provide a relatively reliable source of information for further reading. In the following examination of the model, I provide sufficient detail to afford a clear understanding of the essential workings of the relay-parachain environment and how it is unique in comparison to the legacy DLT architectures discussed to this point.

It is best to begin by categorizing and describing the relay base of the model because it acts as the central point of communication and provides the algorithms that allow for the interoperability between different parachain networks and coordinates interactions between the various heterogeneous connected networks called parachains, short for parallelizable chain. The relay base typically has minimal functionality, e.g., the relay chain does not support an L2 contract infrastructure; however, the main responsibility of the relay chain is to coordinate the interoperability of the system of parachains by securing and facilitating secure communication between them, i.e., the relay base is the heart of the relay-parachain model.

One of the ways that a relay base supports the interoperability of the entire network of parachains is through bridges, which are fundamental to interoperability of the network by acting as a secure communication channel. Other main components of the relay base are the validators, nominators, and collators. But it is notable that most of the computation across the network in its entirety is delegated to the parachains.

Now that a high-level overview of the relay base has been developed, I will move on to address the parachains. Some parachains may be specific to a particular application, while others may focus on specific features, such as contract deployment. And some parachains are occupied developing experimental projects that may not even be related to DLT. However, the conditional standard is that the project must be able to generate a proof that can be validated by the validators assigned to the parachain core—a core on a relay base is like the core in a computer processor chip.

Parachains defer on governance issues that manage upgrades and other sensitive actions. That is, they do not have their own proprietary token issuance or separate governance systems. This is consistent with what I wrote previously regarding the primary responsibilities of the relay base. Parachains receive benefits like shared security, forkless upgrade, a trustless communication format, and L1 mainnet governance. And the proprietors of the relay base benefit from the revenues generated by the parachain developers.

At this point, an overview of some intersections of the relay-parachain model are necessary. The communication channel is where parachains send messages to each other, which are routed through the relay base; the parachains cannot directly communicate with each other, thereby creating a firewall to ensure that all interactions are verified, validated, and secure. And relay-parachain bridges provide a channel for random transfer of data.

It is relevant to delve into relay-parachain bridging. As with L2 bridges between full-stack DLT projects, the only objective of a relay-parachain bridge is to connect with DLT networks such as Ethereum's L2. Bridging a parachain to an L2 contract involves development of a dedicated L2 bridge contract deployed on the parachain as well as the L2 distributed ledger mainnet ledger network. And this introduces all kinds of new complexities. From an investigative, heuristic analysis, regulatory oversight, or investment perspective, a professional needs to comprehend the extent of complexity required to converge these diverse architectures.

Some key points to be aware of are that a messaging algorithm is needed for the L2 network to communicate with the XCMP on the relay-parachain platform as well as a token lock, and wrapping contract being necessary to move a digital asset to and/or from the L2 contract for parachain bridge functionality (e.g., initiating transfers, verification and validation, off-ledger commits to the L1 mainnet and relay chain). Most importantly when analyzing the process devised to achieve interoperability between these extremely different structures is to recognize there are significant cybersecurity vulnerabilities that are introduced.

These processes are because the DLT full-stack L2 bridge differs significantly from a relay-parachain bridge in coding and connection complexities. The important takeaway is to recognize that when discussing bridging, a relay-parachain bridge is uniquely different in construct to an L2 bridge in a full-stack DLT architecture.

In the relay-parachain model, the main actors that make bridging possible are the validators, nominators, and collators.

To expand on these components, the relay's validator mechanism is responsible for verifying and validating all parachain transactions and maintaining state updates from each parachain, which in the end provides a consistent and constrained security layer for all parachains.

Nominators select a group of validators to nominate and promote a collection of validators into the active validator role to validate data blocks for the relay data ledger. In this process of nominating validators, nominators commit token assets to make the nomination. In return, nominators receive some of the validators' rewards. However, nominators are also assessed penalties if their nominated validators misbehave (aka slashing), which results in the removal of a percentage of a nominator's token asset from its account. It looks a little like franchising.

And then there are collators. Collators are full nodes that connect to the relay base as well as the parachain. While all parachains have their own state, the relay base maintains what is often referred to as a "state-of-states" by recording and maintaining essential information on all parachain state transitions to safeguard and create consistency across the entire network. So, for any project to become a parachain with access to the relay base, the parachain must participate in a slot auction in order to secure a time slot to be able to connect and network with other parachains.

Figure 4.1 is a diagram that provides a low-level visualization of the relay chain–parachain component interaction that I trust provides some context to comprehending the complexity of this model:

One last structure that warrants attention when researching or examining a relay-parachain platform is the "on-demand parachain" (previously known as parathread) component. On-demand parachains have a similar design as a slotted parachain as well as leveraging the same benefits as parachains such as shared security, governance, and XCM (cross-consensus messaging)/XCMP (cross-consensus message passing) transfers. However, the difference between parachains and on-demand parachains lies in the operational economic characteristics in how they interact with the relay base. Instead of acquiring a parachain slot, on-demand parachains follow a "pay-as-you-go" model, which charges fees per executed data block.

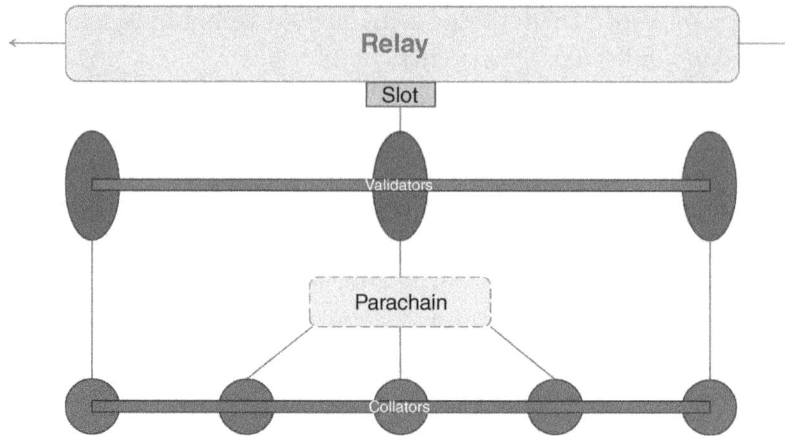

Figure 4.1   Relay-Parachain Visualization Graphic.

In covering the relay-parachain model, there are so many intricacies and complexities in this model's architecture that I do not have the space required to provide greater detail in this book, but I trust this overview has provided some insights. If additional insight into this structure is required, I recommend reading the white papers of Polkadot, other relay-parachain platforms, and parachain projects as well as documentation from developer teams on current upgrades to the infrastructure. These are fairly reliable sources of information but often convey the technical aspects in terms that are frequently used in web sources rather than someone writing about technology in the context of the verbiage of the technology being used.

Hub-zone Model and App-chains

Moving to the hub-zone model architecture, it is a relational structure that is important to examine to ensure professionals in various sectors make the distinction in how it differs from other structures. The hub-zone model is frequently conflated with the relay-parachain model. In the hundreds of sources (print and video) that I have viewed over the years, the hub-zone model is often characterized as a relay-parachain model, which isn't technically or functionally correct, but is somewhat understandable because there are some similarities from a macro-level design concept. However, from a micro-level technical structure perspective, their architectural components are very different. As I take you into the structure of the hub-zone model, it will become clear that the enterprise environment of the hub structure has spawned an entirely new environment of app-chains.

The Cosmos network is one of the most prominent in the hub development space. So, as I share the architectural structure of hub environments, this is a platform that I am using as a representative example in this section. The hub-zone architecture was introduced in the Cosmos white paper published in 2016. The architecture was founded by Jae Kwon, also the developer of Tendermint, and Ethan Buchanan who introduced the idea of an interchain as a web that can share assets and information. The Cosmos hub was deployed in 2019.

I will go into the various aspects of the hub-zone model architecture providing an overview to give a basic understanding. However, it may leave questions and a need for additional resources. Other resources, as I shared in the section on relay-parachains, are project white papers and developer documentation, which can sometimes be found in GitHub, as I will not get into many of the developer-level specifications. So, the simple explanation: a hub-zone architecture bestows the hub as the central point of the system. The hub provides structure for independent zone application projects. The objective of the hub-zone architectural design is to create a conducive environment for developers to create chain-apps. (More on chain-apps later in this section.)

So, the two basic structures that exist in the hub-zone structure are the hubs and zones. The hub is built for the purpose of connecting zones and is responsible for tracking the state of the connected zones as well as managing the inter-chain communication. The zones are heterogeneous distributed projects with each having developed a unique design base on use case objectives, features, and rules. This means that architectural components across zones can differ in the number of layers in the stack, the type of transaction verification and validation, as well as having the capability to develop a proprietary digital asset economy—or not.

Figure 4.2 should hopefully provide a visual perspective of the hub-zone structure.

In addition to the zones are the "peg zones." A peg zone is a hub zone that connects the hub-zone environment to a nonzone L2 full-stack DLT environment like Ethereum's L2. The peg zone acts as a two-way

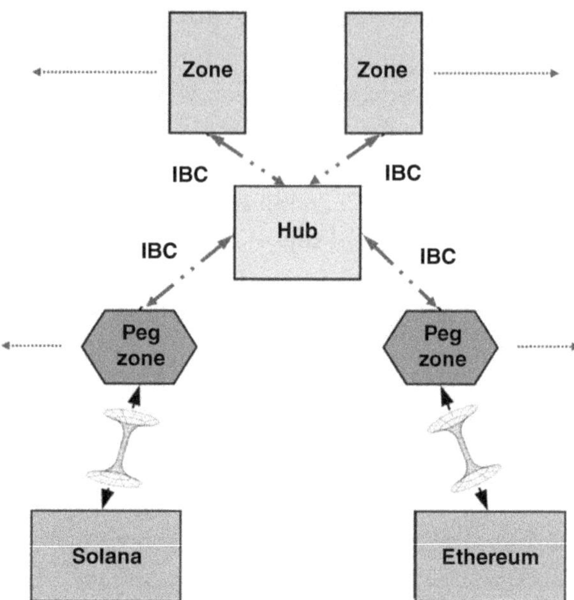

Figure 4.2 Hub-Zone Visualization Graphic.

peg to create interoperability to non-hub full-stack DLT architectures. However, this is a very complex process as the hub architecture is not directly compatible with independent non-hub-zone distributed ledger projects. But this obstacle was overcome, which has enabled hub-zone projects to receive and send data/assets with non-hub-zone projects.

To highlight the complexities involved, the following is an example of the process flow involving the components of the peg zone on a hub-zone model and Ethereum. The peg zone starts with creating an L2 contract on the blockchain that the peg zone will connect to. A witness component attests to the events in Ethereum, which is an Ethereum node to attest to state changes. The peg zone then acts as the translator blockchain to allow users to perform and query transactions on Ethereum. The signer then signs messages using the Ethereum digital signature algorithm (secp256k1) to sign and execute a transaction between the peg zone and the L2 contract on Ethereum. Finally, there is a relayer component to relay a batch list of transactions that were signed by the signer component that posts them to the Ethereum L2 contract, which will send a state commit to the L1 Ethereum mainnet—L2 contract state commits will be addressed in a later chapter.

A note about network security in the hub-zone model. Unlike the relay chain–parachain model where there is a shared security responsibility, the zone project in the hub-zone architecture carries the primary responsibility for its own security using zone validators. That leaves the hub responsible for development of its own validator system to ensure the integrity of the inter-chain communication.

Keep in mind as these structures are encountered, the developers use the buzz words that people on the street are familiar with. Also, it can be challenging conducting research on these projects because developers do not fully disclose the technology in the architecture of what they build. As a side note, it is a scenario like this that led to truth in lending and food content laws, so a consumer knows exactly what is being sold.

THORChain, a Cosmos zone project, has gained attention in the context of digital asset laundering operations, particularly by groups like Lazarus, for a few key reasons:

- It operates as a permissionless app.
- It allows for swaps of L1 coins without requiring an L2 token wrap.
- Its Continuous Liquidity Pool (CLP) offers substantial liquidity for an extensive number of DLT network.
- Its key feature is the absence of custodian in the swap process.

This concludes the overview on alternative structures to DLT full-stack architectures.

Chapter 5

The Distributed Ledger Stack

When looking at distributed ledger architectures, it can be confusing. I was listening to a CEO on a business news program who runs a lobbying group focused on influencing digital asset legislation in the US Congress. In the remarks made by the CEO, it was interesting to hear statement snippets like "the blockchain is" and "bitcoin is a representation of all crypto." The anchor of the business show applauded the CEO as being the smartest person out there in this technology. Unfortunately, the CEO had no depth of knowledge about DLT or digital asset risk classification. When asked about risk classes in the broader area of digital assets, the conversation went back to bitcoin as a long-term store of wealth and essentially ignored day-to-day volatility. However, there was never a conversation about the Bitcoin white paper title: "Bitcoin: A Peer-to-Peer Electronic Cash System."

This is unfortunately another case of a Bitcoin enthusiast leading the conversation with media providing essentially no technological understanding or training, which indicates that legislation in Congress is directed toward the interest of stakeholders in bitcoin rather than the technology that is moving past the present age of bitcoin as an alternative investment.

The statements by the CEO compress a massive number of distributed ledger projects and digital assets into a topic encompassed within the contrived term of "blockchain." More than 2.5 million circulating distributed ledger digital assets are simply described as being in the same class as "bitcoin." This is such a poor representation of the two areas of technology: digital asset risk analysis and distributed ledger technologies.

In Chapter 3, I articulated that there is extensive architectural diversity in the distributed ledger space that includes DLT projects using data ledger structures based in data block, blockDAG, DAG, and Radix that are messaged across expansive distributed networks supported by a distributed computing network running complex consensus mechanisms to maintain the security of the network. In this chapter I will discuss the DLT stack in a way that few outside of the classroom have seen and explain why technologies like the internet and DLT have a technology stack.

Since retiring from the federal government a couple of years ago leading the digital asset support and education component with a federal cybercrimes headquarters unit, I have been engaged in government contracts continuing to work with federal entities that regulate the private financial sector that engage with digital assets. They frequently focus on the digital asset and neglect the importance of the DLT stack. That is, until they need me to deconstruct it to render it inoperative.

I have had the opportunity to reverse engineer and deconstruct distributed ledgers that are terminated because of government action and, in the process, secure the cryptographic keys of the various respective digital assets and transaction information and metadata in the data ledger. This is a complicated and time-consuming process; however, the reason I share this is because entities that regulate the use of this technology, which occurs mostly in the financial services industry, are unaware of the architectural components of a distributed ledger infrastructure when developing regulatory parameters and boundaries. The focus is most frequently on the digital asset rather than considering what is permissible to prevent the addition of certain architectural components, such as an L2 oracle contract that not only feeds information to the L2 contract but introduces vulnerabilities into the distributed network ledger that as it is connected to the entire infrastructure of the financial institution. There are often other components like APIs and third-party developers who upgrade components of the DLT system that are not disclosed to regulators and introduce attack vectors as well. On the other side of architecture, I have also encountered institutions that called their system a blockchain when, in reality, it lacks many of the major architectural components such as a distributed node network, a secure messaging algorithm, and an actual distributed data ledger infrastructure. It ends up being more of a PayPal or Zelle systems than a DLT. As previously noted, the functions of a distributed system can literally be simulated on a single cloud server infrastructure. This is neither distribution nor decentralization, and calling it blockchain doesn't make it so. However, calling it blockchain doesn't convey a correct perception either.

This is why professionals need to grasp a hint of the science of distributed ledger architectural engineering to understand enough to know when to include a trained expert in the conversation involving distributed ledger architectural engineers to provide a detailed analysis.

I'll start the section on distributed ledger stack by adding a reminder that a distributed architecture is a distributed network system that distributes the computing application's workload across multiple clients and messages a data ledger across a network of nodes. And the distributed ledger architecture will consist of any number of various typologies. Currently, there are thousands of different distributed ledger networks that have been built. That is to say, it is not all about the Bitcoin payment system and the Ethereum enterprise platform regardless of the system's asset market capitalization. The point to be made is that distributed ledger technology architectures and their respective digital asset(s) are all very different in design, function, code, and transaction capability, and that aspect has to be acknowledged and respected in all instances by professions in all sectors that engage with DLT systems.

And with that backdrop, where does this diversity come from? The architectural stack system is what provides the capability for developers to provide so much diversity. Traditional distributed network computing systems have a basic, four-layer top-down stack structure, although some technology stacks are more extensive, giving them greater functionality and capability:

- Application layer—encodes/decodes the message in a form that is understood by the sender and the recipient.
- Transport layer (creates)
- Network layer (involves senders and receivers)
- Link layer (enables packet transfer between network nodes and across different networks)

But the focus in this section will be on the DLT stack, a group of technologies that fall into the typology of communication networking, compute networking, and data ledger structures. As I noted earlier, layering allows standards to be developed and to also be adaptable to new structures over time. Figure 5.1 should help visualize the distributed ledger stack:

Following is a summary of the different layers in the DLT stack. I believe a bottom-to-top order of review will provide more clarity in understanding the stack, despite stack order generally being portrayed from top-to-bottom, like looking at a cake with the cake foundation (L0) and the frosting on top (L3).

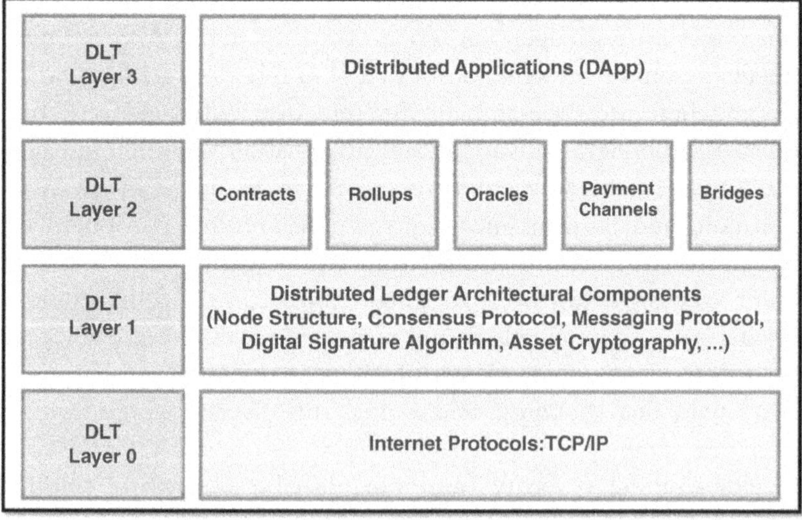

Figure 5.1 Token Topology.

Layer-0 (L0)—TCP/IP Layer

The distributed networking and distributed-ledger technologies have a stack, the L0 of the distributed ledger stack has the Transmission Control Protocol/Internet Protocol (TCP/IP) technology. TCP/IP is a framework for organizing the end-to-end data communications used by what was termed the Internet when deployed. The Internet is called the Internet because it is a global network of interconnected computer networks, literally "inter-networking". The term combines the prefix "inter-" (meaning between or among) and "net" (short for network). Essentially, it's a network of networks, where many individual networks are linked together to form a larger, global network.

The foundational protocols in the TCP/IP suite are the Transmission Control Protocol (TCP), the User Datagram Protocol (UDP), and the Internet Protocol (IP). Early versions of this networking model were known as the Department of Defense (DoD) model because the research and development were funded during the 1970s by the Defense Department's ARPA (now known as DARPA) and were deployed in 1990 to replace the limited scope of ARPANET.

It is important to make the distinction between the Internet and the World Wide Web—aka WWW, the Web, 3W, and several other terms that commingle the Web with the Internet. The internet and the Web are not the same technology, but they are often conflated as being the same. However, this distinction needs to be made clear for professionals wanting to understand the distributed ledger stack. Especially when I address the Web as an essential component of the L3 portion of the distributed ledger stack.

It is this TCP/IP distributed L0 that makes it possible for nodes in a distributed ledger network to connect. Although I will not expand on the TCP/IP layer, it is important to know what these layers are to comprehend the distinction between the distributed ledger layers in its stack, and the layers in the stack of the TCP/IP technology. The layers at a very high level are as follows:

- L4-Application layer: This layer deals with communication between the sender and the receiver, and several protocols exist in this layer. This is where the World Wide Web resides.
- L3-Transport layer: This layer is concerned with data traveling from one device to another. The data being transmitted is split into groups

called packets and is broken up into packets of a specific size. There are data receipt acknowledgments and transmittal of missing data packets to ensure that packets arrive in order and without being corrupted.

- L2-Network layer: This layer defines protocols that head the logical data transmission over a network, which looks at the headers of each data packet and reads the IP address (the packet's destination), and then delivers the packet to the device with that address.
- L1-Data link layer: This layer defines a packet's network protocol type, which includes Point-to-Point Protocol (PPP) and Ethernet protocols.
- L0-Physical layer: This layer is a group of applications that network communications and generate data that are transmitted and request connections for those transmissions. It also defines the transmission medium and method of communication between two connected electronic devices.

Layer-1 (L1)—Mainnet (Main Network) Layer

The distributed-ledger Layer-1 (L1) mainnet refers to the foundational and primary operational support layer of the network distributed ledger architectural stack. This is the layer that comprises the bulk of the DLT architectural components such as the messaging algorithms, node and client networks, the DSA, the digital asset code (if it is a coin asset—tokens assets are minted in the next layer), and the data ledger whether the structure be a typology of block, DAG, Radix, or a hybrid like BlockDAG.

The mainnet is where coins are transacted and minted. (NOTE: digital asset taxonomy, typology, and topology were discussed in a prior chapter.) However, some L1 mainnets have no asset associated with them as the mainnet serves pure and simply as a distributed ledger network system to achieve the purpose as a distributed supply chain management ledger, inventory management ledger, or any number of other use cases that distributed ledger was designed to perform. It wasn't until 2009 that financially related digital assets were converged with cryptographic transaction protections involving a distributed ledger system.

In this convergence of digital financial assets and distributed network ledgers, L1 is the layer that secures the L1 digital asset transactions through a digital signing of transactions managed by a cryptographic digital signature algorithm (DSA). Supplementary to the DSA is a common everyday computer folder, referenced as a wallet, that is kept on most any electronic device (e.g., table, laptop, desktop, remote server, smartphone, or any number of other methods) that contains software to manage the asymmetric cryptographic key generation processes. This process involves using repeating one-way hash functions and ECDSA to produce a private key, then the private key goes through a one-way hash to generate the public key, which is hashed again to produce an alphanumeric string that is called an address. It is intuitively called an address because, as is the case with property addresses, it associates a digital asset owner with the location of the asset on the distributed data ledger that recorded the acquisition of the asset. This is possible because the DSA, when signing the transaction, used the public key and the address to sign the transaction. And the public key/address combination has a hash link to the computer folder where the private key resides (and other software). All of this happens on L1, but note that this is not a function of the data ledger (i.e., block ledger, DAG ledger, etc.). Note that while the data ledger maintains a record of transactions and has its home on L1, the DSA, ECDSA, transaction verification, transaction mempool, consensus system for validation, messaging of the ledger, and many other transaction functions that happen in L1 are conducted, completely outside, of the data ledger.

As I segue into L2, L1 with a full-stack DLT architecture, the mainnet needs to be designed with a Layer-2 (L2) enterprise development objective in mind. This is because the mainnet technology components will have to support L2 contract development projects. Several of the L2 demands on L1 by L2 come in the form of providing a repository for certain L2 state variables that require permanent storage and the L1 data ledger stores these state values.

To provide some understanding around how complex and burdensome L2 state variables can be for L1 components to ingest, it is not just the data ledger component that is impacted. State values are variables declared in an L2 contract that are not within any function statement of the contract itself. In other words, state variables are declared outside of the code of the L2 contract functions embedded in the contract, and the state value is stored permanently on the L1 mainnet. Some of the states variables declared when reading an L2 contract and stored on the L1 mainnet are "totalSupply," "balanceOf," "creatorAddress," "tokenPrice," "isPreSale," "lockTime," "withdrawnAmount," "tokenExchangeRate," "allowed," "isPaused," "nonce," "startTime," "endTime," "whitelist," "balances," "ownerAddress," "tokenStandard," "decimals," "minimumContribution," "maxContribution." These examples of some state variable codes typically reflect the data being stored for future use by a L2 contract, like the total token supply, individual user balances, contract owner address, or parameters related to a specific functionality like a token sale or lock period.

I trust it is obvious how L2 adds an additional burden for the entire L1 mainnet—it's not just about the chaining of blocks to form a data ledger. But because many focus on the data ledger portion of L1 as the most important component, they attempt to treat the data "ledger" as a "database." And it isn't uncommon to read or hear speakers refer to the L1 data ledger as a database. It is for this reason that I need to educate on the distinctive difference between a data ledger and a database. To add emphasis, a data ledger (DL) is not a database (DB), although this is how many describe a DLT distributed data ledger. I will quickly note that a database in computer science is defined as "an organized collection of information that can be searched, sorted, and updated, which is stored electronically in a computer software system called a database management system (DBMS) with data organized in rows and columns for easy processing and retrieval. The DBMS allows users to create, modify, and query a database, as well as manage the security and access controls for that database."

On the other hand, a distributed ledger is defined as "records of transactions that are stored across a network with the copies of these records used to automatically compare and validate new transactions to ensure they are accurate and have not been altered." Data from a distributed ledger L1 can be collected and put in a database for analytic purposes, but attempting to use a distributed ledger as a database never makes sense and has real-world implications that result in designing inefficient DLT architectures. While I applauded the Ethereum objective of developing an enterprise DLT architecture when I read the Ethereum white paper written by Gavin Wood, I was quite critical after reading the second Ethereum white paper from Vitalik Buterin. My internal papers written while working in the federal government, I was consistently critical of the architecture and the design component that would lead to problems from a government regulatory and enforcement perspective, but it has also resulted in Ethereum having to endure numerous and complex hard fork upgrades. One of the major design flaws, which I convey to grad students going through classes on DL architectural engineering, is that the L1 design was modeled after the Bitcoin payment network in order for the Ethereum platform to introduce an L1 coin asset, ether, to fuel L2 contracts. As a result, Ethereum has had to introduce so many scaling solutions to increase TPS and reduce transaction latency. However, several subsequent DLT project architectures abandon the L1 asset in favor of minting an L2 asset for L2 contract execution.

Another aspect of the L1 is the capacity to fork—i.e., a developer-introduced change in the code of a DL's L1 components— will result in a soft fork or a hard fork, depending on the conditions that developers decide to deploy the code. Forks are frequently misunderstood and deserve more attention than I will provide here. Forks today are not discussed nearly as much as in the 2010s but are still prevalent today.

A straightforward and brief explanation of forks is that soft forks are typically a very rudimentary change in the code of the L1 mainnet that adds a feature or corrects a bug, or bugs, that have been identified. A soft fork that adds a feature is usually a voluntary adoption that users can adopt or not. Some soft forks are implemented to fix a bug or vulnerability that has been discovered and are simply integrated, often going unnoticed. It is relevant to note that soft forks occur in all DLT L1 mainnet architectures regardless of the data ledger structure of block, BlockDAG, DAG, and Radix.

On the flip side of the soft fork is the hard fork. An L1 mainnet hard fork is a significant change to the code that users must adopt. Hard forks are frequently communicated as a contention among users, but usually developers introduce upgrade changes to the code that is communicated as a split in the L1 mainnet with the data ledger being one of the L1 components. This is often inaccurately referred to as a chain split hard fork. But whether the hard fork is a chain split or non-split, the legacy system ends and the new mainnet code is implemented as in the case of the recent 2025 Ethereum hard forks of Pectra and Fusaka.

The chain split terminology essentially originated from the extensive focus on the data ledger component of the mainnet rather than giving attention from the perspective of the entire L1 mainnet. This focus on the data ledger by casual observers is also the cause for the obfuscation of the mainnet under the slang term of blockchain (chaining of blocks in the data ledger). L1 mainnet code upgrade hard forks are quite common. And when it comes to hard forks, the most well-known are those that stem from the legacy Bitcoin payment network. But it is interesting to point out that many went through multiple hard fork chain splits before a project achieved success. An example of a multiple split from the Bitcoin network, which includes successful and unsuccessful projects, is Dogecoin, a split from Luckycoin, which was a split from Litecoin, that was a split from Bitcoin. This is just one example, but there were 105 projects that began as a hard fork mainnet split from Bitcoin with many that never survived. This was an example of entrepreneurial developers using a common L1 mainnet to alter the base code from the Bitcoin architectural design.

Many of the early L1 mainnets have comparable architectures, but entrepreneurial developers began to utilize new algorithms to alter the basic Bitcoin code to improve transactions/sec (TPS) times, improve user experience, and any number of other objectives that were raised during the early 2010s. And out of that came approximately 105 Bitcoin blockchain alternatives (e.g., Bitcoin Cash, Dogecoin, which were chain split hard forks from the Bitcoin legacy network). This doesn't mean that identical algorithms were used. In fact, the DSA, asymmetric cryptographic key construction, hashing algorithms, node network design, messaging algorithms, and other architectural components will differ in various ways; however, they are all based in the same basic architectural protocol. And to avert any confusion surrounding algorithms and protocols, recall from an earlier section that I formulated the functional purpose and difference concerning these two paradigms. What makes each network with similar architectures different is that these chain splits modified an algorithm of the legacy ledger to create a unique algorithm. For example, the Bitcoin mainnet uses a HashCash PoW consensus mechanism that was developed by Adam Back, while Litecoin uses a Scrypt PoW mechanism within its consensus system adapted from the work of Coolin Perseval's Tarsnap. These are examples of innovations refenced above that I frequently use to demonstrate that what is often colloquially referred to as just Proof-of-Work, are algorithmic changes to the Proof-or-Work protocol. There are so many of these minor tweaks in each project's architecture that professionals are not often afforded the opportunity to appreciate and how they can impact investigations, regulation, policy, and compliance decisions. This makes the point that DLT architecture has largely been on the back of evolutionary change rather than revolutionary.

But with this example of hard fork splits originating from Bitcoin, it is necessary to point out that there are thousands of DLT projects that began as independent projects (i.e., they are not hard fork splits from the Bitcoin legacy network). Many of those early day independent projects didn't survive just because they weren't Bitcoin, but some of those projects, before they collapsed, spawned projects that split from the legacy project and still exist today. These non-Bitcoin projects focused on architectural designs features that contained enhanced features such as privacy that Bitcoin lacked. For example, Monero deployed in 2014 as a hard fork split from Bytecoin.

But one of the more significant independently developed DLT projects began in 2014 that has an L1 sequential linear data ledger just like Bitcoin's, but utilized very different architectural components and algorithms from what Bitcoin has. The original founders of this project (Gavin Wood, Charles Hoskinson, Anthony Di Iorio, Joseph Lubin, and Vitalik Buterin) conceived the concept in 2013 with the objective of having a significantly enhanced L2 infrastructure from what the Bitcoin design had. The L2 was being designed as an entrepreneurial enterprise development space, not as a competitor of the Bitcoin payment network. The platform was named Ethereum with a L1 asset named "ether" that would be used as fuel for L2 contracts.

Various comments from the founders of Ethereum highlight that they chose the name "Ethereum" because it references the concept of "ether," which is a hypothetical invisible medium that permeates the universe in science fiction. This fictional concept aligned with their vision of Ethereum as an underlying, imperceptible platform that would allow applications to run on top of it and essentially create a network to be a foundational element that facilitates other functions using ether, the theoretical medium of electromagnetic wave transmission.

At the functional use case level, the Ethereum platform, and future competitors, had no desire to focus on the L1 coin alternative payment market. The new design model was to create an entrepreneur enterprise development mainnet to support the L2 architecture where independent entrepreneurs could create contracts to develop new assets named "tokens" which could be used in the L2 network of contracts to develop trading, lending, and other financial projects. This is a good segue for me to transition to the next section on Layer-2.

Layer-2 (L2)—Developer Layer

I want to bring a notable reflection to L2 at this point. It is not uncommon for the mechanisms and processes in the L2 development space to be articulated as "decentralized" and "transparent" by developers, enthusiasts, evangelists, and others who promote a development project. As I go through the following L2 enterprise development tools, it becomes obvious that they are not decentralized, they are not fully transparent, and many have only deployed basic cryptographic methods outside of the secure multi-layer cryptographic methods utilized in L1 processes.

I will address the terms of decentralized, democratized, distributed, and transparency in later chapters, but it is important for professionals reading this to grasp and grab hold of where the misuse of terms in this area of technology, as well as other technologies, is misleading users who do not have a working knowledge of these mechanisms.

L2 Contracts in General

Layer-2 contracts are a staple in the development of scaling and interoperability of Layer-1 platforms like Ethereum, Solana, and many other platforms. As a result of the interoperability, entirely new practices have been made available to users involving the 2.5+ million L2 token assets currently in circulation. However, before going down the path of L2 contracts, it is worth spending time providing an overview of what are termed "smart" contracts from a conceptual, historical, and technical perspective.

The idea of machines using a binary code system using 0 and 1 (base 2) as a representation of alphanumeric characters has been around for centuries. It was Gottfried Leibniz who formulated a theoretical model of modern machines in "De Arte Combinatoria" published in 1666 and developed the early binary system, which he published in 1703 in an article titled "Explication de l'Arithmétique Binaire."

It was in 1994 that Nick Szabo, a computer scientist and legal scholar, described the concept of a smart contract in a paper titled "Smart Contracts." In that paper on digitally enforceable legal contracts, Szabo explains that digital cash protocols introduced in the early 1990s, many developed by David Chaum in the 1980s, were what he considered rudimentary examples of what he termed a smart legal contract. This is because it included aspects of paper currency transaction characteristics such as confidentiality, divisibility, and forgery barriers. In addition, Szabo noted that traditional technologies in the 1990s, which still exist today, that he considered POS (point-of-service) terminals and EDI (electronic data interchange) as examples of crude smart contracts.

Szabo defined a smart contract as a computerized transaction that executes the terms of a contract, and he goes on to note that the contract design, in satisfying the conditions, would minimize exceptions (malicious and accidental) as well as minimize the need for trusted intermediaries. But he detailed that one important task of a smart contract is the communication of semantics of a transaction to the parties engaged in the transaction, i.e., revealing the action(s) of the software hidden from a party to the transaction, while hiding the details of the transaction from the public eye. To illustrate the use case, the paper contains an application of smart contracts to synthetic securities—i.e., a digital representation of an equity, debt, or derivative financial instrument.

Dr. Gavin Wood, an Ethereum founder who wrote the Ethereum yellow paper, correctly labels the Ethereum L2 contract development space as a "contract-creation" transaction. It was the Ethereum white paper written by Vitalik Buterin, that began ascribing Nick Szabo's concept of a "smart contract" to the Ethereum L2 contract-transaction developments. This is one of the first significant instances of "hype over technology integrity" that I witnessed in the early days.

Another aspect of L2 contracts that requires clarification is the frequently touted self-execution characteristic. This is a misleading feature, and I've yet to see a clear motive from the L2 developer community as to why the self-executing promotional message is so often communicated to professionals as an important feature of L2 contracts. In computer programming, as I went through programming courses throughout my academic career, there is self-invoking and self-executing code. In computer programming, self-executing refers to a piece of code that automatically begins running as soon as it is loaded without requiring an explicit execution command. L2 contract require the contract to be called as well as requiring a certain amount of ether in gwei (the L2 contract gas fee) before the contract will execute. Now, I will note that there are "functions" within the contract that are self-executing once the L2 contract is invoked (or called) after meeting the contract requirements of calling the contract and submitting the gas fees. And the self-executing functions embedded in the contract cannot be stopped once execution begins, which is why self-executing code presents a major security exploit risk. Self-executing code poses security risks because malicious script (malware) automatically runs on a user's system without their knowledge or allows attackers to exploit vulnerabilities in the L2 contract code that have not been identified by the developers. This is also why websites are often exploited; it is the self-executing HTML code. Many websites use JavaScript code embedded directly within HTML pages that will automatically execute when the page loads, allowing for dynamic interactions without user permission. I trust this is a significant revelation to professionals on the risks associated with self-executing code.

Current day Layer-2 contracts, are essentially a vending machine enterprise of if-then-else loop code that are being spun up at an alarming rate using platform templates and ANI (Augmented Narrow Intelligence) GPT AI bots. This all significantly reduces the level of sophistication of the legal "smart contract" concept presented by Szabo in his paper (https://www.fon.hum.uva.nl/rob/Courses/InformationInSpeech/CDROM/Literature/LOTwinterschool2006/szabo.best.vwh.net/smart.contracts.html). Although it has taken a decade for this realization, it is heartening to see many developers using the term "L2 contract" on their websites and in conversation rather than "smart contract."

And giving this some cause-and-effect analysis, referring to the current day version of an L2 contract as smart is rather demeaning to the sophistication that Nick Szabo conceptualized as a legal "smart contract," which weakens the developmental future of a true legal smart contract. This is because it taints the true vision with a false version of what a programmatically executed legal contract should be. I will also remark that the missing component to having a cultured version of the legal smart contract envisioned by Szabo is AGI (augmented general intelligence) AI, which developers are still working to bring to fruition.

An evolutionary change that occurred was in the Ethereum platform, deployed in 2015, that has the objective to develop the L2 for entrepreneurial enterprise development as I've noted a number of times. But part of the original consensus protocol design is in how ether, the Ethereum L1 asset, would be used as fuel (i.e., gas fees) for Ethereum L2 contracts. This is the reason that ether (an L1 coin asset) has an unlimited supply given its architected use case versus the limited supply of Bitcoin in the Bitcoin payment system with a focus on currency and monetary principles.

It is notable that the original design of ether (ETH) is to serve as an L2 contract fuel, but it has become an alternative investment. While the precise figures are difficult to pinpoint without real-time data, as of December 2024 there were seven consecutive weeks of net inflows into ether ETFs with a record $2.2 billion during the week of November 26, 2024. (NOTE: The SEC approved ether EFTs in July 2024. This positive trend is expected to continue into 2025).

But on a technology note, I have forecasted since 2012 in my roles as an academic and federal government lead in digital asset technology that allowing ether to trade in a method that resembles a security on CEXs, and now spot ETFs (exchange traded funds), will create a shortage of ether for contract execution. Following a simple supply/demand curve model for ether, as held by investors (individuals who hold assets—i.e., not available for contract execution) will take ether out of the supply chain. Now, given the increase in contract creation in the L2 and enhanced user web interface through the L3 tier of the DLT stack, the demand for ether will increase, making interaction with an Ethereum L2 contract very expensive. In a May 2025 statement, Vitalik Buterin addressed the issue of gas fees and potential shortages of ether for contract transactions as an issue; although, he did not address the root causes for the shortages. However, he highlighted Ethereum's long-term scaling goals and proposed solutions to make Ethereum more accessible and reducing gas (ether) fees.

As a financial economist and DLT architectural engineer, I point out that these solutions only compound the problem. In making something more accessible at a lower cost, it only increases demand. That demand creates demand for more ether, which results in the increased price of ether. Of course, increasing the ether supply will circumvent this problem, but at the same time investors holding ether will drive the price up due to the increased accessibility, increase in the number of users, with a correlated increase in transaction fee revenues. There are competing and contemporaneous interests at play that present some very interesting problems for the Ethereum Foundation and Ethereum developers. It is interesting to watch the proposed hard forks that are coming down the road and the challenges developers will have with integration.

And with that venture into some economics and DLT L2 architectural design issues, I can't emphasize enough the importance of being able to translate L2 contract code. It is essential if there is to be an understanding of how associated fees impact transactions, who receives the benefit of transaction fees, the flow of transactions and fees through the contract, and what functions are executed by what is essentially a more complex version of a vending machine type contract—put ether in and there is an output (but not always what is expected due to fraudulent bad actors).

There are several L2 platforms that exist as competitors of the Ethereum platform with different architectures, different algorithms, different code for the L2 contract, and the list goes on. Some of these competitor L2 platforms are Ethereum Virtual Machine (EVM) compatible to be able to interact with contracts on the Ethereum platform—but not all are EVM compatible.

It is interesting to look at the L2 contract code used by different L2 development platforms, which can be block architectures (e.g., blockchain) or blockless architectures (e.g., DAG, Tempo). For example, Solidity is the coding language for L2 contracts on Ethereum specifically for Ethereum L2 contracts, which was developed by Gavin Woods, Ethereum cofounder and creator of Polkadot/Kusama. Incorporated into Solidity are elements of coding languages C++, Python, and JavaScript to design a language that caters specifically to the needs of distributed applications (DApp), which is the principal piece of L3 and will be addressed later.

On the point of programming and coding languages, I am not going to conduct a review of the advantages and disadvantages of each as I do with students; however, I will make the point in the next several paragraphs that not all L2 contracts use the same coding language. In fact, many of the L2 contract platforms have created proprietary coding languages from existing web programming languages. But knowing the advantages and disadvantages related to security, loop vulnerabilities, speed of execution, etc., of the code used by an L2 contract can be significant in the life of an investment advisor, investigator, analyst, and others who work in this area.

As a side note on my use of the terms "coding" and "programming" languages, from a computer science perspective, a programming language often implies a broader concept encompassing the theoretical aspects of designing and structuring code, while coding language is used to emphasize the practical act of writing code in a specific language, focusing on syntax used in a specific environment.

As noted by Ethereum developers, by incorporating familiar syntax and features from these languages, Solidity aimed to make it easier for developers to transition from web development into blockchain development. However, I have worked with L2 contract security review analysis and teach grad student in this area; this code development approach has allowed many coders from other industries with more accessible and user-friendly programming experience. But many of these individuals come with little to no experience with a cybersecurity mindset, like those from web development, which has led to the creation of many L2 contract exploits over the past decade. I will note this mindset has changed a little, but few are taking the initiative to obtain the expertise to have security reviews of their contracts prior to deployment. However, as an ironic twist, many are investing in contract generated assets or using L2 contracts who never conduct their due diligence to research the developers and determine if a security review has been done on the contract.

Now let's look at some other L2 contract platforms. Another prominent L2 development platform is Solana. While Solana L2 currently supports C and C++ contract developers, the preferred option for Solana L2 contracts is Rust. Rust was developed by Graydon Hoare in 2006, who at one point worked for Mozilla. The story that is told about his development of Rust came from his experience of living in a 21st floor apartment. He got annoyed with having to constantly climb the stairs because the software that ran the elevator, likely written in C++ or C as common in elevator software, frequently crashed. It is said that Hoare named his new language "Rust" after a group of robust fungi. Rust is considered to focus on memory, safety, and performance.

To wrap up coding languages, I will conclude with a short list of some of the other common L2 contract coding languages: Clarity, Pact, Michelson, and Plutus. However, despite the number of options available, Solidity currently holds the position as the most common L2 contract language largely due to its connection to Ethereum.

L1-to-L2 Contracts

In this section on bridge contracts, it is important to understand that this term is not unique to distributed ledger structures, so I'll point out that a "bridge contract" also occurs in a legal context with no relationship to DLT stack. With that interesting tidbit of information, I'll move on.

As an increasing number of DLT projects were being constructed after the introduction of the Bitcoin blockchain in 2009—users began demanding efficient methods of interoperability between DLT networks. A decade ago, interoperability just was not possible without a third-party. To transfer, sell, buy, or exchange DLT digital assets of different platforms required trusting a third-party, which was the antithesis of the thesis construct of DLT in removing intermediaries. Many third-party intermediary exchanges were not trusted in the early days of DLT asset trading—and perhaps many third-parties in third-party intermediary exchanges shouldn't be trusted today either. But it was the easiest way that would allow for trading of digital assets from across the several hundred DLT projects that existed back in 2011. In contrast, the current number of digital assets is approaching 3 million led by the minting of new L2 token assets.

Many in the space today don't care about intermediary involvement, as exemplified by the number of third-parties that participate in every aspect of DLT today. From a behavioral economics thought, my findings demonstrate that intermediaries are woven into the fabric of traditional life, so why not in DLT, especially as the traditional finance industry has integrated DLT projects into their systems. However, it is notable that a bank adopting DLT infrastructure and calling it a decentralized bank, as through some wave of a magic wand a DLT structure makes their infrastructure decentralized. Decentralization of control doesn't occur because of DLT. My experience in deconstructing the DLT structures of failed banks has provided me with plenty of insight on the point.

But prior to today's L2 construct of DLT L2 digital assets, regional and local meet-up groups were some of the earliest forms of transferring, buying, selling, and converting different types of DLT digital assets. I found it particularly interesting when observing the early development of trading DLT digital assets, that existing virtual asset trading in VR gaming since the 1980s constituted some of the first web exchanges. It was like going back in time when PlayerAuctions was started in 1999 as a web-based auction hosting platform for MMORPG[1] players involved in virtual asset

---

[1] Massively multiplayer online role-playing game.

trading. And in 2010 these people getting into DLT digital assets seemed so backward using local in-person meet-up groups.

Jumping ahead to the present day, the ability to bridge assets between projects is far more efficient, but not necessarily any more secure. The earliest concept of bridging DLT digital assets was conceptualized by Tier Nolan in 2013 in a paper titled "Alt Chains and Atomic Transfers." It was in 2017 that Charles Lee, founder of Litecoin, tweeted about an atomic swap of Litecoin (LTC) and Bitcoin (BTC), which are L1 assets. Those were the only classification of distributed ledger assets until 2017, but more on that in a later chapter.

In computer science, the term "atomic swap" originates from the concept of "atomicity" that refers to a transaction that is either fully executed or not at all—meaning there are no partial states with no room for one party to cheat or back out without the other party also being affected. The importance of this is to understand that the hashed timelock contracts (HTLC) Script code used to facilitate the early atomic swaps were written into the Bitcoin OpCodes, and by virtue of the Litecoin blockchain chain split hard fork from the Bitcoin blockchain in 2011, the same HTLC code existed on the Litecoin blockchain. Bitcoin Script code draws inspiration from Forth, a stack-based programming language. This Forth-like structure provides simplicity and emphasizes minimalism and efficiency. But I won't go down that rabbit hole.

As another awareness, I frequently see references in many articles to HTLCs being smart contracts, which is just a tactic of using hype language rather than a writer being technically accurate—don't fall into the hype trap. Without going into the code, I'll provide a high-level overview of atomic swap mechanisms. Two mechanisms allow the HTLC contract to function: HashLock and TimeLock.

HashLock

1. The HashLock utilizes a special cryptographic key that only the initiator of the contract can access.
2. The initiator will commit an agreed upon amount of digital asset "A" to the contract and a special cryptographic key will be generated.

3. The counterparty to the contract will receive a hash of the special cryptographic key received by the contract initiator, who will then commit the agreed upon amount of digital asset "B" to the contract.

4. Once the counterparty to the contract has deposited the correct amount of digital asset "B," the contract initiator is able to finalize the swap transaction with the special key and take possession of digital asset "B" deposited by the counterparty, and the counterparty will receive their digital asset "A" from the contract initiator.

TimeLock

The TimeLock prevents a persistent lock on the digital assets in a swap transaction by warranting the correct number of units of digital asset "A" and "B" are deposited as well as ensuring the transaction happens within a given time frame. If the contract initiator or counterparty fails to comply with the terms of the transaction, the parties to the incomplete transaction are made whole.

More about HTLC when we get to the next section on L2 channel networks.

State Channels

The previous section on L1-to-L2 contracts provides a segue into this section on state channels. In computer science, state channels are a much more significant discussion than just discussing contracts. State channels are but one purpose for locking L1 assets as a gateway to initiate off-ledger transactions that to this day largely evade the transparency constructs and heuristic service providers for tracing transactions on the L1 mainnet. However, the conversation here will be confined to the presentation of state channels to the L2 stack segment of the distributed ledger architecture. I will also note that state channels are applied in various ways across the many different architectures of distributed ledger. For example, the Lightning Network state channel is popular on the Bitcoin blockchain, whereas bridging is a more optimal application of state channels on the Ethereum blockchain. So, let's move deeper into state channels.

Before moving directly into the types of state channels, it is prudent to begin with some definitions. State channels are a model for inter-process communication and synchronization via message passing. A message may be sent over a channel, and another process or thread is able to receive messages sent over a channel. A channel system is a finite-state machine like a communicating finite-state machine in which there is a single system communicating with itself instead of many systems communicating with each other. And a finite-state machine or finite-state automaton, finite automaton, or simply a state machine, is a mathematical model of computation.

This applies to L2 channels associated with distributed ledger technology as state channel scaling solutions are off-ledger peer-to-peer methods that allow two parties to make an unlimited number of bidirectional transactions and then only post the final results to the L1 mainnet. A note about state channels, they do not require the immediate participation of validation nodes to validate transactions. State channels, in contrast, function as network-proximate resources that are integrated with the aid of an L2 contract or multi-signature method.

Channels enable the execution and validation of state changes by interested parties, which minimizes computation number the L1 mainnet network computing execution algorithms. Through this, there is a decrease in congestion, and transaction processing speeds increase (i.e., TPS). Various design methods provide two-way interactions between the L1 mainnet and state channels, resulting in off-ledger transactions. In addition to off-ledger transactions, the state channel construct is to allow transactions between users without having to interact with the L1 mainnet for each transaction and without any of the obstruction of peer-to-peer contact, as with side chains, child chains, and other L2 scaling solutions.

On the other hand, state channels function as resources near to the L1 mainnet. State channels conduct millions of off-ledger transactions every second without recording each individual transaction on the L1 mainnet. This is a major obstacle for services that provide transaction analytics, but when a transaction or series of transactions on a state channel is completed, the relevant blockchain records the final "state" of the "channel" and any related transactions with the final state on the L1 mainnet as a hash that will then be obfuscated in the hash of the entire block of trans-actions processed on L1.

Various types of state channels were noted earlier. Following is a list of some of the common types of state channels used in DLT L2 for scaling and interoperability:

- *Payment channels* are the most common type of state channels, designed specifically for handling multiple bidirectional transfer transactions between parties. As noted previously, they allow for fast and low-cost transactions by processing them off-ledger and only settling the net result on-ledger.
- *Multi-party channels* extend the concept of payment channels to support interactions among multiple participants. These channels enable complex, multi-party transactions and can be used for various applications beyond simple payments.
- *L2 contract channels* use state channels to execute and manage contracts off-ledger. These channels handle complex logic and interactions while only settling the outcomes on-chain.
- *Conditional channels* enable transactions and interactions that depend on specific conditions or events. These channels include mechanisms for conditional payments or contract execution based on prede-fined rules.
- *Hybrid channels* combine features of state channels with other scaling solutions, such as side chains or rollups (more on rollups in the next section). They aim to leverage the strengths of multiple approaches to achieve greater scalability and flexibility.
- *Bridging channels* facilitate transactions and interactions between differ-ent distributed ledger L2 networks. They enable interoperability and seamless exchanges of assets or data across diverse blockchain networks (bridges are covered after rollups in this chapter).

State channels have a conceptually simple method of locking and unlocking assets but add to the complexity of the entire architecture of the project. And as is inevitable, as the complexity of an enterprise development project's architecture increases, so goes the complexity of the underlying framework of the development plan. With this in mind, I believe it is important to provide an overview of the process to give a general understanding of state channel functions:

- <u>Channel opening</u>: Parties involved in a state channel will open the channel by locking an initial amount in a contract. This contract serves as a guarantee the asset will not be exploited by one of the parties and ensures that the channel can be used securely.
- <u>Off-ledger transactions</u>: Once the channel is open, participants can conduct multiple transactions off-ledger. These transactions are recorded only between the participants and not on the main blockchain, allowing for faster and inexpensive interactions.
- <u>State updates</u>: Each transaction updates the state of the channel. Participants exchange signed messages to reflect the new state, ensuring that all parties agree on the current state of the channel.
- <u>Channel closure</u>: When the parties decide to close the channel, a summary of the final state is recorded on the L1 mainnet. This final settlement updates the mainnet with a summary hash of the net results of off-ledger transactions and releases the locked funds according to the final state. (Refer to Figure 5.2.)

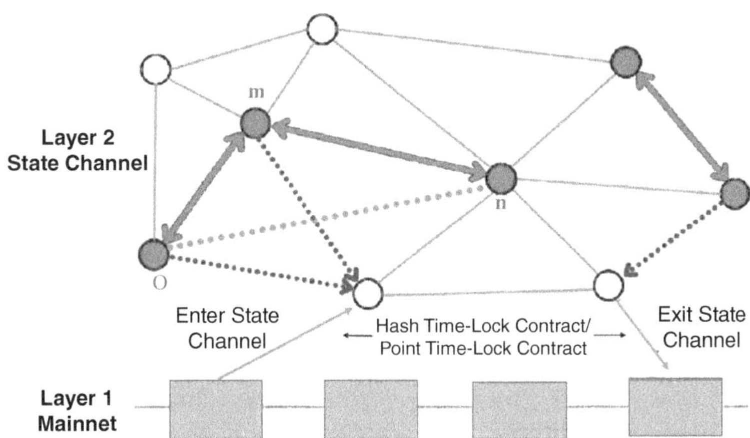

Figure 5.2 State Channel.

To conclude this section, it is important to address the advantages and challenges of state channels. The advantages of state channels are scalability, speed, cost efficiency, and privacy. However, some of the challenges are complexity, counterparty risks, and channel capacity limitations. And in the next couple of sections, I'm going dig deeper into a couple of state channel applications—rollups and bridges—given their prominent impact on the L1 mainnet scaling and interoperability as well as the L2 contract transaction processing and privacy/obfuscation enhancement.

Roll-ups

Much of the nomenclature used in the DLT L2 development space frequently comes from terms already in use by other industries or companies. For example, the term "airdrop" used when distributing DLT assets to entice a person into investing in a project, a reward to incentivize a person to complete a micro-tasks, or any number of other reasons. However, few are aware that this term originated with the military during World War I as a reference to the practice of dropping supplies (i.e., food, medicine, and equipment) from airplanes.

In current history, AirDrop is an Apple proprietary term for a wireless feature in Apple's operating systems that allows users to quickly and easily share files between nearby Apple devices.

The term "roll-up" or "rollup" has also infiltrated the DLT L2 development space. The Rollup concept in L2 was introduced in 2014. But this term rolls over, pun intended, from the mergers and acquisition industry where a rollup is when an investor, such as a private equity firm, buys up companies in the same market and merges them together, or combines multiple small companies into a larger entity that is better positioned to introduce economies of scale. This industry application of the term should help readers to better understand the application of rollups involving L2 contracts.

Precursors to rollups are side chains and child chains, which I present later in this chapter. But today's rollups look nothing like some of the early applications like child chains or side chains that also conduct off-ledger processing of transactions from the L1 mainnet for purposes of scaling.

I've read many articles circulated by industry stakeholders and enthusiasts that refer to rollups as "blockchains," but it is important to debunk the thought of rollups as blockchain, our retired term, because they are not designed with a DLT architecture or in any way provide such an infrastructure. What rollups have in common with DLT architecture is that they both have a bundle and compress mechanism to condense a

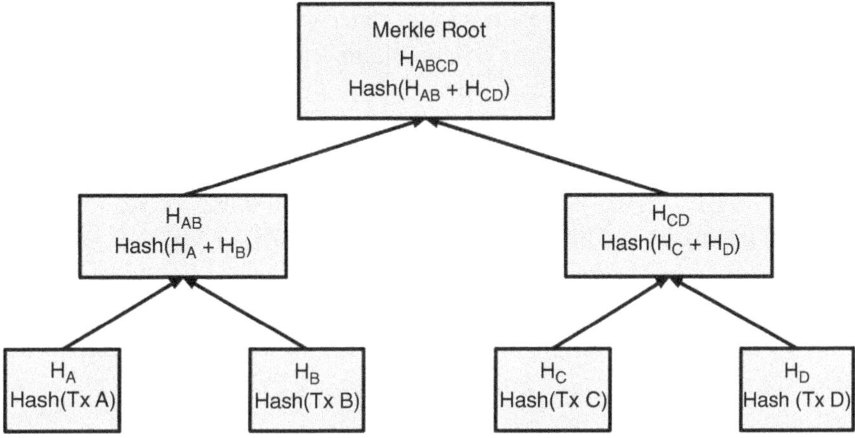

Figure 5.3   Merkle Tree and Merkle Root Hash.

group of transactions into a root hash that is added to a ledger that exists outside of the L1 mainnet. Figure 5.3 should help if there is an unfamiliarity with Merkle trees and root hashes:

I have shared the architectural primitive and various components of a DLT architecture. It has a fault tolerant network, an L1 mainnet with a data ledger as one of its components, a consensus system, messaging algorithm, and so on. However, as described earlier, rollups process transactions off the L1 mainnet, bundle them into a root hash, and periodically commit a state value of the root hash to the L1 transaction data ledger through an L2 rollup contract. The detail about the individual transactions is lost in the hash, which significantly hampers the use of heuristic tools, open-source or paid, to conduct mapping or tracing of these L2 transaction rollup bundles. This process of bundling and hashing with no consensus mechanism relies on a challenge period where users can submit fraud proofs if they believe a rollup aggregator submitted an invalid state root; this all creates a form of obfuscation that can't be undone by the heuristic analytic services once aggregated into the hash created by the L1 mainnet validation process.

A rollup is at its core an abstraction of coded that bundles transactions for off-mainnet transaction processing. As noted in the last section, rollups in computer science are classified as a state channel. Figure 5.4 shows some Solidity code extracted from a proxy rollup contract deployed on the Ethereum platform. As a note, L2 proxy contracts are quite common.

A proxy contract is an L2 contract that delegates calls to another contract, and stores state variables while delegating its logic to one or several implementation contracts. Proxy contracts allow for contract upgrades, rather than having to deploy a revised contract as in the old days, and allows function changes that are normally inaccessible to the original contract.

Again, this image of Solidity code is just a sample of what a rollup looks like; however, rollup contracts, as with most L2 contracts, frequently have hundreds to thousands of lines of code linking multiple contracts that encompass multiple functions—see Figure 5.4:

```
1   // Copyright 2021-2022, Offchain Labs, Inc.
2   // For license information, see https://github.com/nitro/blob/master/LICENSE
3   // SPDX-License-Identifier: BUSL-1.1
4
5   pragma solidity ^0.8.0;
6
7   import "../libraries/AdminFallbackProxy.sol";
8   import "./IRollupLogic.sol";
9
10  contract RollupProxy is AdminFallbackProxy {
11      constructor(Config memory config, ContractDependencies memory connectedContracts)
12          AdminFallbackProxy(
13              address(connectedContracts.rollupAdminLogic),
14              abi.encodeWithSelector(IRollupAdmin.initialize.selector, config, connectedContracts),
15              address(connectedContracts.rollupUserLogic),
16              abi.encodeWithSelector(IRollupUserAbs.initialize.selector, config.stakeToken),
17              config.owner
18          )
19      {}
20  }
```

Figure 5.4   Rollup Contract Code.

Rollups are very useful in bundling and processing transactions in an off-mainnet fashion for bridge contract transactions, called bridge rollups. Bridge rollups are helpful to bridges in a similar way of scaling for the L1 mainnet because the bridge entry points can become a chokepoint causing transaction congestion just like vehicle traffic at rush time involving physical bridges.

As described earlier, batches of newly executed transactions are in the form of a highly compressed new state root hash that is then committed, validated, and stored on the L1 mainnet along with any transaction processed on the L1 mainnet. Figure 5.5 shows a simple flow of the rollup process from the rollup to the L1 mainnet.

There are currently two basic types of rollups: ZK rollups and Optimism rollups.

Optimism rollups batch transactions, compress, bundle, and post the state root to the L1 mainnet. The rollup contract maintains a historical record of state roots, but at the time of posting to the mainnet, it is not

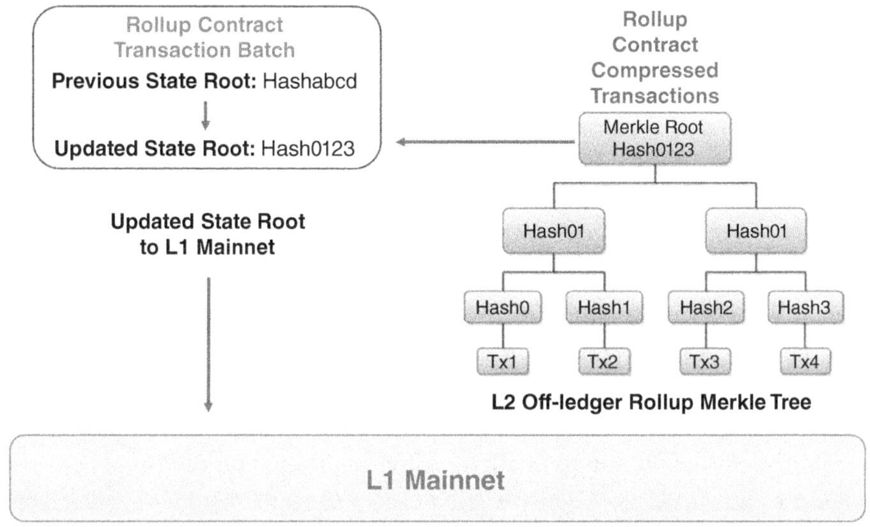

Figure 5.5 Simple Flow of the Rollup Process.

actually validated that the transactions have been executed correctly—i.e., optimistically posting the new state root. So, if it is discovered that a batch has an incorrect state root has been saved to the optimism rollup contract, a fraud-proof is generated. The fraud-proof includes a proof of pre-state root, proof of new state root, and the proof of the executed transactions.

The fraud-proof is posted to the rollup contract, and the rollup contract verifies the proof and compares the result to its state root. If the fraud-proof cannot be verified, the contract rolls back the batch and all the batches after it until it reverts to the last known valid batch. A fraud-proof duration is 7 days, which requires users to wait approximately a week to withdraw their assets from an Optimism rollup contract.

While more widely adopted than the more secure ZK rollups, some challenges of the Optimism rollup are that they are centralized, prone to manipulation from the centralized developer control, not very user friendly, L1 scaling is limited due to transaction verification data commitments back to L1, and users are responsible for their own security.

So, where Optimism rollups work on an "innocent until proven guilty" methodology, ZK rollups can be described as having a "don't trust, verify" methodology. ZK is short for zero-knowledge, as in zero-knowledge proofs. ZK rollups verify state change validity cryptographically.

The core infrastructure of a ZK rollup has two parts to it: the on-chain contracts and the off-chain virtual machine. In the on-ledger contracts, ZK rollups are operated by L2 contracts. ZK rollups can bundle thousands of transactions in a single batch and execute them on the L2 contract. The main contract stores rollup transaction bundles, tracks deposits, and monitors state updates coming from the ZK rollup. Another verifier contract is used to validate the ZK proofs submitted by producers. The off-ledger execution engine of ZK rollup is responsible for the computation and storage of transactions and channel state. And the ZK contract produces a validation proof to confirm the correctness of the processed transactions. And finally, the contract commits the hash transaction bundle summary as a ledger entry to the L1 mainnet.

Some of the ZK rollup challenges are that they require complex cryptography, they can be expensive, subject to manipulation from centralized developer control, and limited to simple L2 contracts.

Bridges

Ethereum, deployed in 2015, was the first DLT platform to provide an enhanced L2 contract enterprise development environment. As noted earlier with user adoption, the developer adoption of DLT increased, L2 contract development environments proliferated (e.g., Arbitrum, Solana, Cadano, BNB, Polygon, Algorand, Tron, Hedera [a DAG ledger architecture], and the list goes on). This led to what new projects scaling projects like bridges. Some of the first bridges were introduced by NEAR and Syscoin in 2020. Bridges are sometimes called cross-chain bridges, but this is a rather nonsensical term, factually and technically, because a bridge links different DLTL2 tiers —not the L1 mainnets that contain the data ledger. So, bridges are in fact L2 bridges that allow users to transfer or communicate token assets and information between different DLT L2 tiers. Like most L2 developments, the processes of ridging are off-ledger, i.e., bypass the mainnet, and do not record transactions on the L1 mainnet. Only the locking or burning of token assets moving between the L1 mainnet and L2 bridge contracts, as well as the subsequent minting contracts associated with a burn or lock that invoke a respective ledger entry. There are several processes in an L2 bridge that leave no footprint on the

L1 mainnet that include validator action approvals, which exist in their own L2 P2P network signing and attestation to a bridge message, API transaction details, and the developer web user interface (UI) requests, to name a few. The ability to monitor the L2 bridge process is through the use of subgraphs (a graph that is a subset of another graph) as well as developer platforms that observe the L2 bridge in real time. Figure 5.6 is a simple diagram that I trust will provide a simplified visual context of the bridge flow.

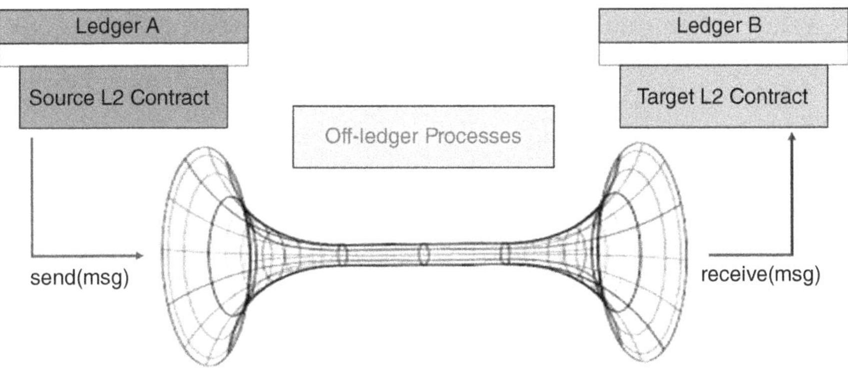

Figure 5.6 Layer-2 Bridge.

As an over simplified summary of the L2 bridge processes: assets in an L2 contract on DLT "A" on one ledger are locked or burned. Then the bridge communicates/messages the lock or burn of an L2 token asset to DLT "B", and an equivalent value of a different L2 token asset is minted by the receiving DLT L2 contract.

One of the first L2 bridges to be developed is the Avalanche–Ethereum bridge (AEB) launched in 2021 by utilizing ChainBridge, a modular multi-directional bridge framework to move ERC-20 and ERC-721 tokens between Ethereum and Avalanche. It has made multiple changes since this early deployment, but it provides some context to the early start of L2 bridging.

There is now a plethora of L2 bridges that exist in the L2 stack of many DLT networks that exist such as BNB, Base, Polygon, Tron, Solana, and others that allow for movement of L2 token assets between their DLT L2 tier stack.

Bridges are typically DLT project specific (e.g., Avalanche-Ethereum bridge) for simplified contract construction, but it is possible to integrate multiple bridge applications through web-interfaced Distributed Applications (DApps; more on DApps in the next section). To expand on the previous overview of a bridge, there are general message passing (GMP) bridges. The L2 bridge has the capability to lock and burn L2 token assets in addition to passing messages or arbitrary data that permit developers to call functions on other DLT networks. And GMP provides users the ability to swap assets across supported DLT networks in fewer steps and without multiple platforms and wallets. These L2 bridges messages can provide a plethora of metadata for investigations.

Another important aspect of bridges is that there are permissioned and permissionless bridges. Bridges are not always readily accessible to all users. That is to say a "permissioned bridge" refers to an L2 contract designed to facilitate the transfer of L2 assets between different DL platforms, but with restricted access only to authorized users. A "permissionless bridge contract" allows any user to transfer respective distributed ledger assets across specific networks without requiring prior verification or approval, essentially like participating on a permissionless DL network where anyone can participate. As in the instance of permissionless and permissioned DL user access.

To conclude on the topic of bridges, it is germane to understand bridges are often misunderstood by users in regard to their vulnerabilities, cost to use, and code flaws that allow for exploits that are taken advantage of by cybercriminals. One of the highest dollar value exploits occurred on the Solana Wormhole bridge in 2022. The attack exploited was the result of an unpatched Rust L2 contract in Solana involving the use of a deprecated, insecure function to bypass signature verification that was manipulated into crediting 120,000 ETH. While the details of the exploit are fascinating, the short version is that the bad actor made a contract to wrap 120,000 ether in Solana, but instead extracted the minted wrapped tokens and immediately converted them to ether coins on Ethereum using the Solana Wormhole bridge. This exploit was all due to the deprecated signature bypass not properly verifying the original 120,000 ether, which were actually never deposited.

In addition to security flaws in the underlying L2 contracts that allow bad actors to exploit user assets, bridges also face counterparty risks from bridge validators colluding to steal assets passing through the bridge, subjecting users to exploits in the form of censorship, rug-pulls, and other nefarious acts. Bridge users also face financial risk from bridges that use wrapped token assets to mint official versions of an asset and exposing users to exploits like the Wormhole example provided. And there are yet unrealized risks as bridges are still in a nascent stage of development and uncertainty of bridge performance in different development applications such as rollups in L2 and distributed applications in L3.

Oracles

It is important to interject oracles into the conversation at this point because oracles are essential to the functionality of many L2 contracts. Many times, when I introduce oracles during conversations about L2 contracts, people will typically get a strange look on their face because their minds immediately go to Oracle, the technology DB software company.

Without oracles, L2 contracts would be completely limited to L1 mainnet data, which is very limited, in order to keep the data ledger minimized for storage and network messaging of the data ledger. Although oracles are not part of the infrastructure, i.e., an architectural component, of a DL, they are integral to providing L2 contracts the ability to ingest off-ledger data and extending the utility and value of L3 distributed applications—more on distributed application (DApps) in the section on Layer-3.

In the L2 tier of the DLT stack, an oracle is an L2 contract that specializes in providing data feeds to L2 contracts, making off-ledger data sources available to L2 contracts. This is necessary because smart contracts cannot, by default, access information stored outside the ledger network. For example, prediction markets rely on oracles to provide environmental data from sensor readings, satellite imagery, and advanced ML computations that are used to validate user predictions, and L2 contract exchanges (DEX) use oracles to acquire off-ledger digital asset pricing information that comes from external sources in order to settle trades. And there are many other use cases involving oracles, presently and in future developments, that I will not expand on in this book. My objective here is to delve into providing a better understanding of how oracle contracts work.

Oracles are programs. And an oracle program will source, verify, and transmit information stored in web backend or other sources of digital data that reside anywhere outside of the DL network necessary for the specific data needs of a smart contract running on a DL's L2, as noted earlier. In addition to "pulling" off-ledger data and broadcasting it to an L2 contract, oracles can also "push" information from the L2 contract to external systems, e.g., unlocking an IoT connected lock once the user sends a fee via a DL transaction such as Ethereum.

Oracles differ based on the source of data (one or multiple sources), trust models (centralized or decentralized control), and system architecture (immediate-read, publish-subscribe, and request-response). Categorizing oracles is important for professionals to understand based on the operational direction of the oracle feeds, where the oracle is retrieving information from, what type of data are being retrieved, and the security of information touched by the oracle.

So, oracles retrieve external data for use by L2 contracts (input oracles), send information from the distributed ledger L2 contracts to off-ledger programs and applications (output oracles), or perform computational tasks that support L2 contracts (computational oracles).

Following is a basic categorical list of oracles:

- Hardware-based oracles are where individual contracts need to interact with the real world. They are designed to obtain information from the real world and make it available according to the needs of smart contracts. Such data are provided by other devices used to read the data (e.g., barcode scanners). In this case, oracles play the role of a translator that translates the obtained information into a language understandable by smart contracts.
- Software oracles interact with web-based information sources that then send the data to an L2 contract. The data come from a variety of databases, servers, or websites accessed through APIs or web scraping. Their advantage is that they transmit information in real time, thanks to a constant connection to the Web. They are one of the most popular oracles.
- Input oracles transmit information from the outside to smart contracts. Such an oracle informs the smart contract of what information has been recorded by an external sensor.
- Output oracles, acting in an inverse direction to an incoming oracle, are ones that send data or command from the L2 contract to off-ledger systems. This can include informing a banking network to make a payment, telling a storage provider to store the supplied data, or pinging

an IoT system to unlock a car door once the on-ledger rental payment is made.

- Single node oracles means there is a single point of failure. And if there is a failure, the oracle will not be able to receive or send data to or from an L2 contract. In addition, single sourced oracles have risks because the effectiveness of the execution of a given L2 contract depends entirely on the third-party and they are exposed to exploits or attacks subject to data manipulation. This results in the L2 contract having faulty data that cannot be reversed and potential permanent loss of use assets.
- Distributed oracle networks (DON) avoid the risks of single node oracles by sourcing data from multiple oracle nodes. A DON combines various oracle node operators and multiple reliable data sources. A DON makes it possible for an L2 contract to send queries to multiple oracles to determine the validity and accuracy of the data sought as precisely as possible.
- Bridge oracles (aka GMP- General Message Passing) can read and write information between different distributed ledger networks. Cross-DL L2 contract oracles enable interoperability for moving both data and assets between blockchains, such as using data on one blockchain to trigger an action on another or bridging assets cross-chain so they can be used outside the native blockchain they were issued on.
- Compute-enabled oracles are a new type of oracle becoming more widely used by L2 contract applications. They use secure off-ledger computation to provide services that are impractical to do on-ledger due to technical, legal, or financial constraints. This can include using Chainlink Automation to trigger the running of contracts when predefined events take place, computing zero-knowledge proofs to generate data privacy, or running a verifiable randomness function to provide a tamper-proof and provably fair source of randomness to smart contracts.
- Contract-specific oracles are built specifically to a particular contract. They are time-consuming and expensive to maintain and implement; however, they are ideal for situations where the data from a real-world event needs to be verified and cannot be used for other purposes.
- Human oracles are used when an oracle must rely on human input. This can be as simple as a multiple-choice quiz or a user typing in a phrase. It is with these types of oracles that fraud and falsification of information are prevented.

Side Chains and Child Chains

I'm covering side chains and child chains in the same section because the structure objective is the same despite some minor differences in architectural design, which I will distinguish a little later. Side chains and child chains are L2 off-ledger structures. While they are often described by nonexperts as independent L2 "blockchains," they are not DL full-stack independent data ledger networks. While these data chains maintain a data ledger in L2 projects, they often have dependencies on the L1 mainnet infrastructure in their objective of providing scaling by off-loading L1 transactions to L2 to reduce L1 congestion. This is similar to what was discussed in the section of rollups.

As with other L2 technologies, there are significant off-mainnet processes that obfuscate transaction details on the L1 mainnet; however, L2 off-mainnet transactions are sometimes accessible involving side chain/child chain using data ledger explorers. But there remains a limited transparency of what takes place on the L2 child chain and side chain, and there is also significant centralized control over the mechanics of what takes place. And this is again an important aspect for professionals in all industry sectors to grasp because heuristic conclusions are more limited in this environment and require different heuristic rules than what is used for, say, the Bitcoin mainnet. Side chains and child chains are touted as independent, but they are still rudimentary in the robustness of their architectural components, leaving processes with cybersecurity vulnerabilities. In addition, misinformation about the infrastructure, like being a Layer-2 blockchain, creates a false sense of security for users. The lack of transparency and the structure's transaction obfuscation relative to the L1 mainnet, I have suggested over the years that disclosures should be required by developers in a prospectus format in terms plainly explained to potential and current investors and users alike. In a later chapter, I the introduce the topic of DLT SROs (self-regulatory organization) that would ensure the L2 environment is much safer for users into the future.

Also, many find it confusing when untangling these L2 child chain and side chain structures. They are often incorrectly referred to as "blockchain" type architectures layered on a "blockchain." It should be clear after discussing the architecture of each and showing they are truthfully part of the L2 stack infrastructure that they are agile structures but have a limited capability as an L1 mainnet scaling solution. It is also notable that an L1 mainnet can support multiple L2 side chain and child chain structures. So, here we go.

Side Chains

Side chains are more independent of an L1 mainnet than child chains, but they have interoperability with the L1 mainnet through a two-way peg. This allows the light architecture of a side chain to operate more independently of the more complex and operationally intense components utilized by the underlying L1 mainnet. However, structure security is often maintained by the mechanism being incorporated into the design of the side chain's architecture as in the case of zones in the hub-zone alternative structure. This is critical to understand because the robustness of the security design of the L2 side chain may be overlooked due to the attention paid to the more independent nature of the side chain or overlooked due to the robust architecture of the L1 mainnet. Figure 5.7 shows a graphic representation of the relationship between the L1 mainnet and the L2 side chain.

A note about the side chain architectural designs, even as L1 mainnet have different design topologies around transparency and privacy, the same is true of side chains. Some of the basic side chain architectures include design features discussed in a previous chapter, such as federated,

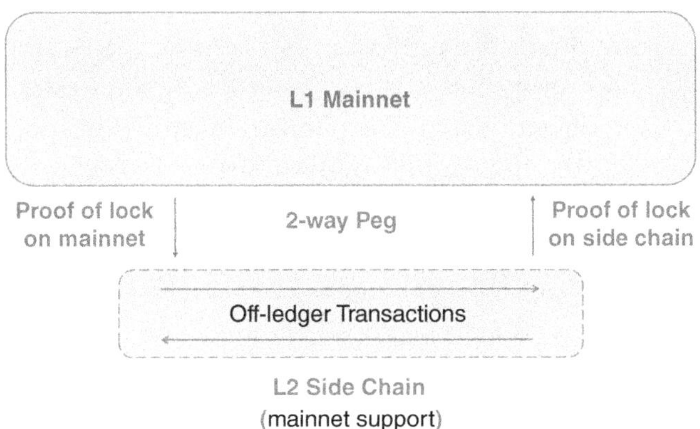

Figure 5.7   Side Chain Flow Diagram.

permissioned/permissionless, private/public, and of course a proprietary customized variation can be introduced by developers of side chain projects depending on the needs of the side chain use case involved.

As noted earlier, side chains are light versions of the L1 mainnet that direct transactions off-mainnet. Side chains periodically record their state value to the L1 mainnet ledger, and this is managed by an L2 side chain contract. This is for the verification and integrity of the off-mainnet data of the side chain. It is executed using a state commit with a periodic Merkle tree commitment scheme, where only the root of the tree is posted on the L1 mainnet; hence, there is a level of obfuscation of the L2 transaction data that heuristically makes it difficult for services to analyze transaction data. It is notable that these commitment schemes are designed so that a party cannot change the value or statement after the committed. That is, commitment schemes are cryptographically binding in the ledger component. It is interesting to note that the concept of commitment schemes was first formalized by Gilles Brassard, David Chaum, and Claude Crepeau in 1988.

A prominent example of a side chain is Polygon. Polygon (formerly Matic Network until 2021) is a side chain constructed on the L1 Ethereum mainnet as part of the L2 stack. Polygon transaction processes differ from the Ethereum-compatible mainnet and have the capability to return them to the primary Ethereum L1 mainnet after processing. This method reduces the burden on Ethereum by moving L1 mainnet transactions to the Polygon side chain that has a lighter transaction processing burden and speeds up the transaction process and thereby decreases transaction costs.

It is also important for professionals to know that side chains frequently introduce an exclusive digital asset (sometimes referred to as a native asset) for operational and economic incentive purposes. Staying with Polygon, when ether (ETH) transactions are moved to Polygon for processing, ether is locked, and an L2 contract mints an equivalent value of the Polygon (POL) ERC-20 tokens (formerly MATIC). Inversely, when Polygon transactions are committed to the Ethereum L1 mainnet then MATIC tokens are burned and ETH unlocked.

The POL token contract, for those interested in viewing the ERC-20 token contract, is at Ethereum address 0x455e53CBB86018Ac2B8092F-dCd39d8444aFFC3F6 (former MATIC contract address is 0x7D1A-fA7B718fb893dB30A3aBc0Cfc608AaCfeBB0) and transactions of the POL token are viewable on etherscan. With that noted, mapping and tracing MATIC and POL tokens across L1 and L2 on Ethereum can be very difficult, and these addresses change with each platform that supports this, or any, ERC-20 token asset.

It is worth noting that the Polygon process flow just outlined is because ETH cannot be transferred to a Polygon plasma chain; L2 mechanisms cannot support L1 assets. But the L1 ether coin asset can be represented on the Polygon side chain by locking ether and engaging an L2 contract (Poly contract address: 0×7ceB23fD6bC0adD59E62ac25578270cFf1b9f619) that will mint a wrapped ether token on the Poly side chain.

Child Chains

As noted earlier, child chains and side chains have a common objective: to provide transaction scaling for the L1 mainnet. But the child chain architecture and mechanisms are quite different from side chains, making child chains uniquely dissimilar. Child chains are essentially scaled down copies of the parent L1 mainnet and are more tightly integrated into the mainnet than a side chain resulting in the expression "child-parent" relationship, with the "child" network entirely reliant on the "parent" mainnet and deriving all of its assets from the mainnet—unlike side chains.

However, like side chains, child chain design handles transactions outside of the L1 mainnet (i.e., off-ledger) and periodically commits a state value to the L1 mainnet. Child chains can define their own asset, which can

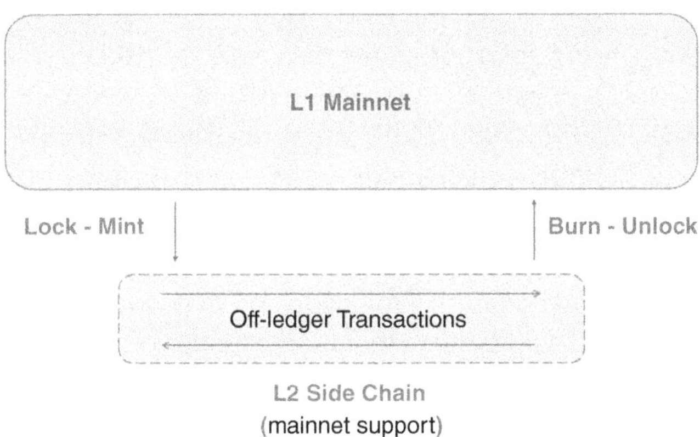

Figure 5.8 Child Chain Flow Diagram.

be exchanged with the mainnet through a mint-lock and burn-unlock relationship with the parent L1 mainnet. Figure 5.8 shows a graphic representation of the relationship between the L1 mainnet and the L2 child chain.

Layer-3 (L3)—Distributed Applications Layer

I will begin by debunking the hype behind Layer-3 as a wonderland of mystery and magic that exists to create an all-new web environment. Gavin Wood, Ethereum cofounder and Polkadot founder, coined the term "Web 3.0" in 2014. This concept was introduced by Gavin Wood in a 2014 blog post titled "DApps: What Web 3.0 Looks Like" in which he explained his vision for a "decentralized online ecosystem based on blockchain." It has since been shortened to "web3" and the concept behind the term gained interest in 2021 from enthusiasts, digital asset intermediary stakeholder companies, and venture capital firms. However, the concept of web3 is rooted in a significant amount of misinformation. And Ethereum developers stopped support of the web3 interface as of March 4, 2025.

From a technology perspective, there is a lot wrong with how the web3 concept continues to be hyped, and I'll break it down. And supporting this is the developer of the World Wide Web, Timothy Berners-Lee. Sir Timothy Berners-Lee speaking at the Web Summit in Lisbon on November 4, 2022, said: "It's a real shame in fact that the actual web3 name was taken by Ethereum folks for the stuff that they're doing with blockchain. In fact, Web3 is not the web at all."

First, the internet is not the web. The current version of the internet, what we call the internet, is the successor of ARPANET that was launched by the Dept. of Defense's (DoD) ARPA (now DARPA) in 1969 and decommissioned in 1989. The current internet was deployed in 1990 and is based in TCP/IP, which are the protocols that allow for computers to connect and communicate. However, the World Wide Web (or Web) introduced by Sir Timothy Berners-Lee in 1991 is based on HTML for structure, CSS for styling, and JavaScript for dynamic interactivity. The WWW has evolved up its own technology stack of growing from the layer of static web pages in the 1990s, to the current layer of the more interactive, app-like experiences that have followed. Berners-Lee is active in developing the next layer, Web3 if you will, originating as an MIT research project, and is now being developed by Solid, led by Berners-Lee as cofounder of the startup. He is engaged in an open-source strategy to reinvent the web through new decentralized, privacy-minded tools to move the next web environment away from the tech giants like Alphabet, Microsoft, and AWS that control the web and web content today.

So, with the realization that DLT web3 is not the web but a web interface, that brings us to L3. The following must be realized to move on: the Web is not the internet, and the internet is not the Web; they are entirely separate and distinct structures. And the problem here is that when Gavin Wood coined the term Web 3.0, the concept behind it is to change the structure of the internet. Do we see the problem here?

DLT uses the internet as its base layer, L0, to support the networking of nodes. And at the other end of the DLT stack, L3, the L2 contracts are interfaced through L3 internet distributed nodes to the web.

To summarize for emphasis, DLT does not create or introduce a new web or web3. Is DLT using the existing TCP/IP technology of the internet in L0, and the same old HTTP/CCS/JS web to interface L2 contracts through L3 applications. And to close the circle, the HTTP/CSS/JS web structure exists on Layer-3 (application layer) of the internet technology stack—i.e., the web needs the internet, the internet does not need the web. The web is a human friendly way to interact with networking systems. In the same way that the web requires the internet, it is DLT the requires the internet and the web.

So, what do L3 Distributed Application (DApp) deployments have in common with the web3 concept? The commonality is a community of followers that have aggregated the two under the same core notion of decentralization, user-controlled experience, and free from single points of control. And this presents a new problem because DApps are under the control of the developer or entity that benefits from the fees generated by the application code. Also, understand that the L3 application DApp tier is literally a technology layer of web tools to interface a DApp to a website (not the internet) that is also not under the control of the user or the DApp developer. The internet and web have a synergistic relationship just as DLT has a synergistic relationship the internet and the web.

So, to summarize, Layer-3 is the fourth layer of the DLT technology stack and it represents the space where developers use specialized Layer-3 utilities to interface a Layer-2 contract to a website. This enables a user to interact with a Layer-2 contract without needing to have specialized knowledge of DLT technologies to directly interact with a Layer-2 contract.

As a final note on DApps and cybersecurity, DApps present unique cybersecurity challenges and opportunities, requiring proactive security measures to protect users and assets from vulnerabilities and attacks. Developers frequently lack the knowledge or expertise to implement web-facing security measures. Additionally, Layer-2 contracts, which, if flawed, can be exploited or breached through the DApp web interface. These are many aspects that professionals are not aware of in associating with DApps in Layer-3.

In closing out this chapter, I trust that has provided new insights as well as a better understanding of the technology of DLT architecture, alternative structures, and the technology that underpins making it possible for DLT to exist.

Chapter 6

Digital Currency in the Context of Currency and Money Systems

I am beginning this chapter with a quote from one of my favorite economists, which goes back days of my early days as an undergrad, Friedrich August von Hayek, Austrian-British economist and author (1899–1992): "I don't believe we shall ever have a good [monetary system] again before we take the thing out of the hands of government, that is, we can't take them violently out of the hands of government, all we can do is by some sly roundabout way introduce something that they can't stop." According to Hayek, instead of a national government issuing a specific currency, use of which is imposed on all members of its economy by force in the form of legal tender laws, private businesses should be allowed to issue their own forms of currency, deciding how to do so on their own.

This speaks quite loudly to the early introduction of the first digital currency, e-cash, in 1990 by Dr. David Chaum followed a couple of decades later using these digital currency algorithms with the convergence of technologies under the umbrella of DLT. The digital currency revolution is rooted in the concepts of computer science and cryptographic methods developed by David Chaum in the late 1970s.

This chapter will focus on the convergence of digital currencies with distributed ledger while providing some of the historical underpinning that set the stage for many of the current day distributed ledger digital assets. But before moving on, as a financial economist and computer scientist there is always a caveat: 2.5+ million DLT assets in circulation are lumped under the flawed heading of crypto or digital currency with less than 1% of these 2.5+ million assets containing code as a digital currency.

As I begin, I believe it is important to touch on the topic of money versus currency from an economics perspective rather than simply attempting to build on the naive paradigms as they are used to make a case for digital currencies as a currency or a monetary system—it varies based on what one is trying to prove. The remaining digital assets fall into the classification of noncurrency assets and typologically fall into any number of categories that will be covered in an upcoming section.

I have taught banking and currency, economic game theory, and principles of money and currency for decades at several universities. The common denominator I find in student surveys, which is not atypically from what I find among investors, bankers, and investment advisors that post on the web, is the lack of knowledge that results from conflating the principles of money with the function of currency. So, let's discuss the differences.

Money vs. Currency

As I share with grad students in class, the topic of money and currency must start with the quantity theory of money (QTM). The QTM proposes that an increase in the supply of currency in a money-based system decreases the marginal value of the function currency. In other words, when monetary policy allows a supply of currency to increase, with all else being equal (ceteris paribus), the buying capacity of one unit of currency decreases.

Money is a broad term that defines an ideal and intangible concept that articulates a system of value transfer that makes the exchange of goods and services sustainable, i.e., an economy. Many have difficulty embracing the theory of money because of bias that has been engrained into their thinking for years or decades. But let's use our critical thinking method and explore the history of the early economist who first defined money.

Money

William S. Jevons (1835–1882) was an English economist and philosopher who made significant contributions to economics by driving the move from classical economics to neoclassic economics. His many contributions are in the areas of marginal utility theory. He was the first economist to create index numbers, and he influenced the use of statistics and econometrics in social sciences, foreshadowed logical empiricism, and pioneered computing with the "logical abacus" that was an early example of logic machines. But from my perspective as a financial economist, Jevons is the first to define the functions of monitary systems for economics.

In 1875, Jevons published a classical work: *Money and the Mechanism of Exchange*. In his book, he defined money systems as having four functions:

- Medium of exchange: When a money system is used to intermediate the exchange of goods and services, it is performing as a medium of exchange. Thus, it avoids the inefficiencies of a barter system: the inability to permanently ensure "coincidence of wants," which is when two parties each possess an item the other wants or needs, and they agree to a direct exchange without any medium of exchange.
- Common measure of value:[1] Money provides a standard, numerical monetary unit of measurement of the market value of goods, services, and other transactions.
- Standard of value (aka standard of deferred payment): A money schema can be used as a widely accepted way to value debts, allowing people to buy goods and services now and pay for them in the future, essentially enabling borrowing and lending activities by providing a consistent unit for future payments. It is considered one of the key functions

---

[1] Unit of account became the replacement term in the late nineteenth and early twentieth centuries.

but has been left out in modern economic textbooks. This is due to the U.S. abandoning the gold standard in 1971. Since then, the U.S. dollar has been a fiat currency, meaning its value is not backed by gold or any other commodity, but rather by the "full faith and credit" of the U.S. government. This abandonment of the gold standard, known as the "Nixon shock," ended the international convertibility of the dollar to gold effectively ending the Bretton Woods system, which had linked global currencies to the U.S. dollar, which in turn was convertible to gold. The "payable to the bearer on demand" clause on Federal Reserve notes was removed in 1963, and the ability to redeem pre-1963 notes for gold or silver ended in 1968, marking significant shifts in how the dollar functioned as a standard of deferred payment.

- Store of value: A money system must be reliably saved, stored, and retrieved, and in all probability be usable as a medium of exchange when it is retrieved. There are those who hold that the value must also remain stable over time; however, that is a characteristic of a currency discussed later.

In economics, one will commonly define currency using these functions of a money system which is incorrect and this will be discussed later.

The US Federal Reserve defines a money representation (i.e., a currency) as any financial instrument that can align with the functions of monitary policy. It is with this introduction of "financial instruments" in this definition that I will transition to our discussion on currency.

Currency

Money and currency are frequently used synonymously; however, I trust that we understand that they are quite different. The financial instruments previously mentioned collectively refer to the actual instruments that comprise the model money supply of an economy. In other words, the money supply is composed of financial instruments, i.e., currencies and other financial instruments, within an economy that are available for purchasing goods or services.

The distinction here is that a money system defines four functions in planning policy around an economy, while currency is the minted application of the ideals around the functions of money. Currency, in economics, has characteristics that have been introduced over the decades by economists to ensure a currency can support the functions of a money schema. Unfortunately, they incorrectly associate currency with the functions of money within an economic framework outside of barter.

To review, the functions of money are a medium of exchange, a unit of account, a standard of value, and a store of value. And to fulfill these various functions, a currency standard is created, and a currency is minted, which will likely include many of the following characteristics of what a circulating currency should have. These currency characteristics have been taught by economic professors since my earliest days, beginning with my first undergrad degree:

- Durability: able to withstand being repeatedly used
- Fungibility: one unit of currency is viewed as interchangeable with another
- Portability: can be easily transported and transfered to others
- Divisibility: divided into smaller units of value
- Uniformity: all versions of the same denomination must have the same purchasing power
- Acceptability: everyone must be able to use the currency for transactions
- Scarcity: the quantity of a currency is constrained or restricted
- Stability of value: currency in circulation ensures values remain relatively constant
- Inability to counterfeit: a currency should not be easily duplicated
- Recognizability: a currency should have attributes so counterfeits can be easily identified

My assessment is that the teaching of the money functional characteristics has been largely lost in the curriculum at institutions of higher learning along with the understanding of how monetary versus financial institutions function. Including this training in curriculum at all levels of learning would help students to become smarter consumers, borrowers, lenders, and investors.

It is important to note that there is no currency in circulation today that perfectly aligns with the functions of the money illustrated in the diagram in Figure 6.1.

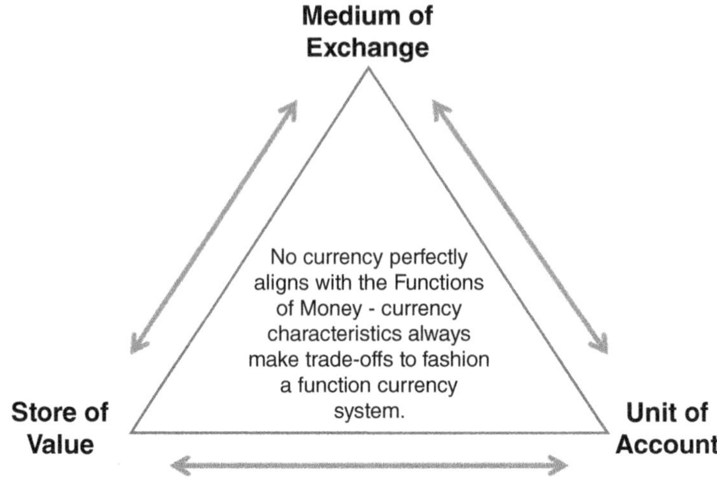

Figure 6.1   Functions of Currency.

Creating a currency is, in general, controlled by a government's central bank. This puts financial management of its currency under the control of the country's government, which determines currency characteristics to be employed and how the nation's currency will be managed to conform to the various currency characteristics. However, I will add that many under-developed countries I have visited have nongovernmental forms of currency; consequently, local currencies are prevalent and may have existed for centuries and change across localities. I have also visited developed countries where the exiting government has simply adopted the currency system that has been in place for centuries, long before the current government was even in power. So not all currencies are introduced by a government decree. Suffice it to conclude that no currency perfectly fits all of the ideals of being fully inclusive of all of the functions of a monetary system. And this is what separates a monetary schema from a circulating currency.

Some of the various types of physical items that are used as currency are commodities in the form of precious metals, shells, beads, grain, etc. A currency, as Jevons noted, can be representative currencies, trade tokens, and paper notes. Known in some jurisdictions as fiat currency (i.e., government issued), its worth is not derived from any intrinsic value, but instead only has value given to it by the government that issues the currency. A fiat currency may also be declared a legal tender—anything that is recognized by law as a means to settle a public or private debt or meet a financial obligation.

As a second generation American, it was fascinating as an undergrad to study the economic and financial system history of the United States. The new American dollar replaced the British pound as the official currency of the new United States when the Continental Congress met in New York on July 6, 1785, following the ratification of the Treaty of Paris on September 3, 1783, when Great Britian acknowledged the sovereignty and independence of the United States. It was during the second session of the United States Congress that the Coinage Act of 1792 established a national mint to be located in Philadelphia. Congress chose decimal coinage in parts of 100 and set the US dollar (USD) fractional parts (half, quarter, eighth, sixteenth). This Act also established the silver dollar as the unit of currency in the United States and declared it to be lawful tender.

Having spent over a decade in the US military following my first round in university, not anticipating there would be many more rounds to come, I had the opportunity to travel the world. I developed quite a collection of currencies from across the globe, some of which are no longer in circulation in their respective countries. Ultimately, I found myself at the US Dept. of the Treasury working with digital currency and other digital assets. And with that, this brings us to digital currency. I love going down the path of digital currencies—digital currency broadly and digital currency associated with DLT networks. So, let's go.

Digital Currency

As painful as it may have been going through the discussion on the function of money and characteristics of currency, I trust that it laid the foundational understanding and provided an appreciation for the distinction between the functional concepts of a money model and the practical deployment of a currency, with its characteristics, managed by the central bank within a monetary policy schema.

As I present digital currencies in general, having worked in the US Treasury Department for 20 years, I have been exposed to so many discussions on whether a digital currency is money, which it is not and neither is a dollar, or if it is a currency. It is unfortunate that I repeatedly find references to noncurrency digital assets being discussed in the context of a currency, which further confuses the foundation of determining the value of digital currency in use case models within a central bank's monetary policy. This frequently results in contention that snowballs into misunderstandings and misinformation on the classification of digital assets within an economy. It is important to note that broadly referring to all digital assets as crypto-currency or just crypto is not all helpful in these discussions because not all distributed ledger digital assets are a digital currency. The lack of knowledge about the core technologies underlying digital currency, and not having a universally accepted categorical classification of digital assets, is in large part what prevents digital currency from being broadly accepted. DLT also has developers who introduce vulnerable systems, allowing bad actors to take advantage of this relatively ill-informed and inexperienced consumer and poorly framed regulatory environment. As exemplified in this quote from Henry Thomas Buckle (1821–1862), an English historian, author, and sometimes called "the Father of Scientific History": "Society prepares the crime; the criminal commits it."

The discussion about digital currency has led the contentious conversation about central bank digital currency (CBDC) versus privately held digital currency. And the misunderstandings I addressed earlier have led to a hot debate by those who rail against a CBDC, but are fine with the central bank being holding the cryptographic key of a digital currency in the form of a reserve account on behalf of a government. Even I tend to be confused by those who take opposite positions on both sides of a digital currency framework that have essentially the same outcome. Whether the government creates the digital currency and circulates it as fiat in lieu of, or alongside, a physical fiat, or the government begins taking control of a private digital currency system that has a public facing ledger that the government already monitors doesn't logically make sense. Actually, this starts to set a pattern by which a government issues decrees where a digital currency that has a limited supply, could begin to look like the Franklin Delano Roosevelt (FDR) 1933 confiscation of gold from citizens when the US government needed more gold. Do we not see the limited digital currency supply issue? Especially as governments all over the world, and this includes many states within the United States apart from the federal government, are moving toward having a bitcoin reserve fund. There is a limited supply of bitcoin, and I see a version of the future where governments acquire control of a private digital currency. This is something that many are advocating for but are repulsed by a CBDC. The outcome is the same—the government is in control of the digital currency.

In the last US election cycle, a prominent topic was creating a bitcoin reserve fund that would be held by the US Federal Reserve. The reasoning was that in its capacity as fiscal agent of the United States, the New York Fed is directed by the US Treasury Department to manage the foreign currency reserves held by the Exchange Stabilization Fund (ESF). However, a bitcoin reserve fund might end up being controlled by another US department under new legislation. Time will tell!

So, despite support or objections for bitcoin as a function of money, it is irrelevant because the Bitcoin network architectural design was for bitcoin to act as an alternative currency, not a money system. In fact, the UTXO algorithm was introduced into the mainnet so that bitcoin transactions would mimic cash transactions; this was something I addressed in the section on architectural design. Thus, the store of value and other functions of money arguments go out the window involving bitcoin because the discussion should involve the characteristics of a currency: durability, fungibility, portability, divisibility, uniformity, acceptability, scarcity, stability of value, inability to counterfeit, and recognizability.

Again, note that no currency embodies all of the characteristics of a currency. Look at the Fed notes, paper and coin, that circulate as US fiat legal tender currency. Does it perfectly align with all the functions of money, much less meet all of the characteristics of currency?

My objective in pointing out these facts is to give a framework for professionals to determine when a digital asset is a currency or has some other use case. And when a discussion involving the validity of a digital currency transpires, it will lead to a discussion founded in fact about the characteristics of currency rather than devolve into conflict based in conjecture. I will be discussing the tokenization of RWAs in the form of synthetic fiat (aka USD pegged token; there is no technology basis in support of a nomenclature terminology for stablecoin) in a later chapter.

I'm going to move away from the historical economic aspects of digital currency, and transition to a technology perspective on digital currency. I have spent too many years working in government policy discussing the function and characteristic aspects of digital assets so it was a little too easy to go down the road we were on. What is important here is that that there is an understanding of the technology sustaining digital currencies to develop better policy, laws, and compliance decisions. And it's not going to be helpful long term to regulated digital currency as crypto because the government has been attempting to regulate the use of cryptography since the early 1980s, and this is perhaps another excuse for government regulators to gain a foothold in that effort.

If DLT digital assets are going to be respected as a digital currency or an asset class in the investment industry, it will require forming a universally accepted taxonomical hierarchy, which will establish a foundation for risk assessment models. The technology underpinning DLT digital currencies, and other DLT digital assets, provides the basis for development of a taxonomy model. I developed a taxonomy mode during one of my postdoctoral studies a number of years ago, but the model has withstood the test of time, and I will share it a little later. But developing models like this requires grasping the nuances of the technology underpinning digital assets.

Why? Because not every digital asset on a DLT stack is minted in the same way; they do not use the same technology as they reside in different layers of the DLT stack. In addition, the intended use case of each digital asset is often different by design, so it diverges outside the realm of being part of the very small share of digital assets that exist as a currency.

I trust the critical thinking mindset will have kick in when considering the following matters. It is meaningfully insignificant to use the term "crypto" which originates from the Greek word kryptós, which means "hidden" or "secret." I trust that "a lightbulb turns on" as to why those who are not advocates of digital assets hold to the thinking that only criminals use "crypto"—because for most people the term "crypto" implies secrecy.

There is an inconsistency in associating DLT digital assets with the term crypto, especially for those who are conducting DL analysis, or examinations are a fool's errand because cryptography makes something secret. The reason is that, if distributed ledger transactions were actually cryptologic (i.e., hidden) then there would be no need for ledger analysts because there would be nothing to find. Because these assets are not hidden is why I can develop and deploy AI clustering algorithms to identify links and patterns allowing for heuristic (not forensic) assumptions to be developed.

Another inconsistency in referring to DLT assets as "crypto" but on the opposing side DLT is touted as providing transparency. How can the asset data ledger be transparent while the digital asset is hidden? If it is hidden, how does the L1 mainnet follow the asset transactions? How do criminals find and steal the asset if it is hidden? Calling a digital asset crypto just comes across as inconsistent nonsense because the transaction algorithms have never supported an asset being hidden. What is hidden is the private cryptographic key of the sender and receiver and, on some DLs, the metadata of the transaction. Of course, if I'm referring to DLnetworks like Monero and Zcash.

The first use of the slang term "crypto" came in 1989 when Wei Dai, in his paper on b-money (www.weidai.com/bmoney.txt), mentions the crypto-anarchist movement of Tim May who died in 2018. Dai's b-money was intended to be an anonymous, distributed digital currency system; however, it was never officially launched. B-money introduced many of the same features of distributed ledger associated digital currency in circulation today. It was after Dai's concept of b-money that media picked up on the term and introduced "crypto-currency" that later was joined and shortened to "cryptocurrency." The question on the use of cryptocurrency was raised in a 2009 Satoshi email in regards to replacing "Digital P2P Cash." Of course, we know that the whitepaper used the term electronic cash.

In the Bitcoin white paper, cryptography or cryptographic are not used in relationship to the bitcoin asset. And in the Introduction section is reads: "What is needed is an electronic payment system based on cryptographic proof instead of trust, …." This specifically points to the fact that digital currency is not cryptographic at all. Cryptographic "proofs" secure transactions between two willing parties without the need for a trusted third party.

However, in 2014, when the Ethereum white paper was published, it used terms like "crypto-fuel" in a reference to ether, "crypto-commerce" to allude to a use case involving L2 contracts, and "crypto-asset" as opposed to cryptocurrency. This has evolved into today's vernacular that anything associated with DLT and digital assets are simply referred to as "crypto." There is more cryptography in an encrypted email than there is in any DLT asset or L2 contract, which also does not have any cryptography. It may be astounding to some that an encrypted e-mail is not referred to as "crypto-mail" (my attempt at humor), but it hopefully emphasized the message.

Regardless of how it was started, DLT digital assets do not contain cryptography nor are they protected by cryptography. The cryptography in DLT only protects the digital asset transaction and the transaction is not the asset. I guess the next book will be titled *If It's All Crypto, Why Isn't It Safe?* Moving on.

Of course, intermediaries introduce an entirely different component of obfuscation—defined as "to be evasive, unclear, or confusing"—but in the context of transparency and cryptography, a critical thinker will conclude that the terms "crypto" with digital assets and "transparency" in data ledgers are diametric opposites. I trust exploring this realization is exposing some truths that are mostly a covered up in attempting to convey that digital assets are more secure than what the technology says they are.

The origin of digital currencies really starts with David Chaum who wrote the earliest papers on the development of digital currency transactions using cryptographic proofs as a security method for electronic transactions.

Question: Why were cryptographic transaction proofs so important in the 1970s and 1980s when David Chaum was developing cryptographic proofs?

It is because financial data breaches didn't begin when companies began storing data digitally in the 1990s. In fact, data breaches have existed for as long as individuals and companies have maintained records and stored private information in digital form. It was in 1971 that IBM partnered with the banking and airline industries to develop an international standard for magnetic-stripe credit card data storage. But before computing became commonplace, a data breach could be anything as simple as viewing an individual's medical file without authorization or finding sensitive documents that weren't properly disposed of. Still, publicly disclosed data breaches increased in frequency in the 1980s, into the 1990s, and public awareness of data breaches began to rise in the 2000s.

It was also during this period that digital virtual currencies were already popular. The multitude of virtual digital assets, which utilize a very different technology than that of DLT digital assets, existed nearly four decades before the development of the first distributed ledger associated digital currencies and were prominent in online gaming, airline carriers, hotel franchises, grocery store loyalty programs, and more. And just as with data theft, virtual currencies could be easily stolen by bad actors or taken away by the game developer without any consent or proof of two willing participants agreeing to the transaction. But it is also significant that, until the 1990s, virtual currencies only had worth within a closed network. For example, in gaming, the game's virtual currency could only be used to acquire skins, weapons, land, buildings, and leveling up. However, in 1999, PlayerActions began as one of the first trading platforms for virtual currencies and other virtual assets for gamers to trade and exchange. My focus here is making a distinction in the technology, but the US dollar (USD) value in global Real Money Trades (RMT) in the virtual asset secondary markets is in the billions annually, and that is on top of the half trillion USD in gaming revenue for online gaming.

Virtual currencies are not exempt from fraud and theft. It was in 2018 that I received a request to support a $10 million dollar Microsoft virtual currency theft that achieved a 2020 conviction, resulting in a prison sentence and restitution.[2] And in 2020, Nintendo reported that more than 300,000 accounts had been compromised through an account take-over (ATO) attack. After the Nintendo ATO, there was an uptick in the conversion of Nintendo assets to v-bucks (the virtual currency in *Fortnite*). The use of virtual currencies continues to grow, especially with the incredible interoperability of virtual currencies across the spectrum of industries in that virtual currencies transact seamlessly from hotel to casino to restaurant to airline to retailers to banks. The risks of gaming platform virtual currencies and communication networks are a national security concern and this was highlighted by the Director of National Intelligence (DNI) in late 2023 in an NCTC memo.[3] The Federal Bureau of Investigations (FBI) and Dept. of Homeland Security (DHS) have raised similar concerns involving virtual currency gaming platforms. However, I will note that virtual currencies in other platforms are also used to commit fraud as I have personally been engaged involving the use of virtual currencies issued by hotels, airlines, and casinos used in bribery and money laundering. So, my warning to financial crime and investigative professionals is to guard against tunnel vision by only considering DLT digital assets in financial criminal activities.

Digital currencies were introduced in the 1990s, beginning with DigiCash's e-Cash deployed in 1990 founded by Dr. David Chaum. In the

---

[2] US Attorney's Office. (2020). Former Microsoft software engineer sentenced to nine years in prison for stealing more than $10 million in digital value such as gift cards [Press release]. https://www.justice.gov/usao-wdwa/pr/former-microsoft-software-engineer-sentenced-nine-years-prison-stealing-more-10-million

[3] Joint Counterterrorism Assessment Team. (2023). First Responder's Toolbox. Available at: https://www.dni.gov/files/NCTC/documents/jcat/firstresponderstoolbox/144s_-_First_Responders_Toolbox_-_Terrorist_Exploitation_of_Online_Gaming_Platforms.pdf

following years, there were hundreds of digital currencies issued that were using cryptographic transaction methods. It is notable that e-Cash was deployed in 1990, the same year the new TCP/IP internet was deployed to replace the retired ARPANET. The deployment of e-Cash was the result of nearly a decade of research and development of cryptographic protocols introduced by Chaum. One of the many papers he authored is titled "Blind Signatures for Untraceable Payment" published in 1983.

It is not difficult to understand why Chaum is acclaimed as the "Father of Digital Currencies," having developed the original protocols and cryptographic algorithms as well as the first-to-market digital currency services. And to demonstrate Chaum's contributions to the future development of digital currency, following is a short list of papers he authored:

- "Computer Systems Established, Maintained and Trusted by Mutually Suspicious Groups" (1979)
- "Untraceable Electronic Mail, Return Addresses, and Digital Pseudonyms" (1981)
- "A New Paradigm for Individuals in the Information Age" (1984)
- "Multiparty Computations Ensuring Privacy of Each Party's Input and Correctness of the Result" (1988)
- "Untraceable Electronic Cash" (1988)
- "Undeniable Signatures" (1989)
- "An Interactive Signature Scheme" (unpublished)
- "A Provably Secure and Fast Message Authentication Scheme" (unpublished)
- "Minimum Disclosure Proofs of Knowledge" (2011)

It is significantly notable that Chaum's 1982 Berkeley dissertation, "Computer Systems Established, Maintained, and Trusted by Mutually Suspicious Groups," is the first known proposal for a distributed transaction data ledger, which contained every element found in Bitcoin L1 mainnet with the exception of the Proof-of-Work (PoW) validation mechanism. But then, the PoW consensus mechanism wasn't introduced until 1993. However, the proposed vault system lays out a plan for achieving consensus state between nodes, chaining the history of consensus in blocks, and immutably time-stamping the chained data. The paper also lays out the specific code to implement. In Chaum's introduction of the digital currency, e-Cash, he introduced several cryptographic algorithms, like the Blind Signature and Mix Networks, and addressed the Dining Cryptographer's Problem. The Blind Signature algorithm needs no explanation, but a bit more on the Mix Networks and Dining Cryptographers Problem.

Chaum published the concept of Mix Networks in 1979 in his paper "Untraceable Electronic Mail, Return Addresses, and Digital Pseudonyms." Mix Networks are routing protocols that create hard-to-trace communications by using a chain of proxy servers known as mixes, which take in messages from multiple senders, shuffle them, and send them back out in random order to the next destination, such as another mix node. This breaks the link between the source of the request and the destination, thus making it more difficult for bad actors to trace end-to-end communications. Furthermore, mixes only know the node that it immediately received the message from, and the immediate destination to send the shuffled messages to, making the network resistant to malicious mix nodes. Perhaps this sounds somewhat familiar when discussing mixers, tumblers, and Tor. A caveat to mixers and tumblers because many people use the terms synonymously: They are completely different methods of obfuscation and not just synonymous terms. I am not covering heuristic investigative methods in this book, but this is something for analysts, legal and private investigators, compliance professionals, and policy/law makers to keep in mind. Now, on to the Dining Cryptographer's Problem.

In cryptography, the Dining Cryptographers Problem studies how to perform a secure multi-party computation of the boolean-XOR (Exclusive OR) function. Chaum first proposed this problem in the early 1980s and used it as an illustrative example to show that it was possible to send anonymous messages with unconditional sender and recipient untraceability. Anonymous communication networks based on this problem are often referred to as DC-nets where DC stands for "dining cryptographers." Chaum coined the term Dining Cryptographers Network, or DC-net "The dining cryptographers problem: unconditional sender and recipient untraceability").[4] As a side note, the Dining Cryptographers Problem stems from the scenario of three cryptographers gathered around a table for dinner. The waiter informs them that the meal has been paid

---

[4] Chaum, D. (1988). The dining cryptographers problem: Unconditional sender and recipient untraceability. *Journal of Cryptology,* 1, pp. 65–75. https://link.springer.com/article/10.1007/BF00206326

for by someone, who could be one of the cryptographers or the National Security Agency (NSA). The cryptographers respect each other's right to make an anonymous payment but want to find out whether the NSA paid. So, they devise a two-stage protocol to solve what is called the Dining Cryptographers Problem.

It may be of interest and is reasonable to credit others who developed digital currencies that were introduced from 1990 to 2006. Here is a a short list of some of the prominent digital currency payment systems and exchanges beginning with E-gold (founded by Dr Douglas Jackson in 1996), Bit Gold (founded by Nick Szabo in 1998), Beenz (founded by Charles Cohen in 1998), PayPal (originally named Confinity and founded by Peter Thiel and Max Levchin in 1998), Flooz (founded by Lamine Cheloufe in 1999), GoldAge (founded by Arthur Budovsky in 1999), and Liberty Reserve (founded by Arthur Budovsky in 2006). All this was overshadowed by the government's war on the public dissemination of cryptography, known as the "Crypto War." Another event that served to overshadow digital currency adoption in the 1990s was the market and business driven enthusiasm of web-based e-commerce with the deployment of the WWW in 1991 and the launch of the first website in 1992. But what developed following the House passage of the E-Commerce Act in 1992 is what is called the Dot Com era (1997–2003), which peaked on the NASDAQ in 2000,. The culmination of these two events led to the death of all digital currency projects by 1998, with e-Cash as the last to collapse, and ironically the first to market in 1990. In a *Forbes* post in 1999, Chaum stated: "As the Web grew, the average level of sophistication of users dropped. It was hard to explain the importance of privacy to them."

Digital Asset Taxonomy, Typology, and Topology Insights

From a taxonomical perspective, a conversation must begin by discussing the technology of L1 as coin assets and L2 as token contract assets. It is worth noting that there is a prevalent misconception that DLT architecture requires that the infrastructure include an imbedded digital asset, which can't be farther from reality. DLT networks

There are many distributed ledger architectures, permissioned and permissionless networks, without a digital asset. The intended design purpose of DLT was to essentially function as a "distributed secure messaging ledger." In that context, a number of DLT projects currently exist with use cases that include inventory tracking, supply chain management, drone swarm communication, first responder communication systems, and bank-to-bank deposit settlement.

It wasn't until 2009 that an embedded digital asset component converged with a DLT architecture. It was the Bitcoin payment network architecture that was the first to converge an entrenched digital asset element called bitcoin for the purpose of providing a safer currency payment system alternative for digital transactions. And that was just the beginning of what was to come. The bitcoin asset was not the first digital asset to be associated with a cryptographic ledger and was certainly not destined to be the last. What came next was a myriad of digital assets minted in different layers of the DLT stack and the taxonomies and typologies, not just the topologies, expanded rapidly.

As I begin to break down the taxonomy, topology, and typology of digital assets, there are some required definitions because these terms are often used incorrectly. Starting with digital assets, in computer science, a digital asset is any type of data that exist digitally, can be identified, and has value. Examples of digital assets include text, images, audio, video, animations, documents, spreadsheets, logos, websites, and I'm quite certain that this list can be expanded well beyond this page. However, I believe the construct is clear—a digital asset isn't just oriented to mean currency. The focus for this book will be digital assets associated with DLT and virtual assets (i.e., centrally controlled assets associated with gaming platforms and other non–DLT alternative currency systems).

Following are familiar terms used when classifying and categorizing objects within a system:

Taxonomy: A practice and science concerned with naming, circumscribing (defining), and classifying. Typically, there are two parts to it: the development of an underlying scheme of the unique characteristics making it possible to organize items into a consistent hierarchy.

Typology: The study of various traits, or the systematic types of something according to their common characteristics and refers to the study of classifying things based on categories, essentially analyzing and grouping things based on a shared characteristic.

Topology: With its roots in math, it's the study of objects that can be stretched and moved while points on the object continue to stay close to each other. Two objects are equivalent if you can make them resemble each other by stretching, bending, or twisting them; thus, the constituent parts are interrelated.

The application of typology and topology can be a little confusing, so I want to clarify: Typology is about categorizing based on grouping, while topology is about analyzing based on the ability to be bent without changing their fundamental structure.

I've developed these models using scientific methodology during one of my postdoctoral studies in the economics involving digital assets many years ago. While I have kept the components of the models updated, it has required very minor adjustment as new developments have been introduced into the respective digital asset environments, and so the models have withstood the test of time and remain true over the years. I will also note that there have been many who have attempted to depict the relationship between different digital assets, but they typically come to the crypto nomenclature. And none have been scientifically developed using taxonomy, topology, and typology methods as these models have.

Taxonomy

Figure 6.2 is the taxonomic graphical representation for digital assets focused on the broader scope of all digital assets that currently exist.

Note that the graphical model representation in Figure 6.2 encompasses the aspects of the definition of taxonomy provided earlier: naming, circumscribing (defining), and classifying by utilizing an underlying scheme of distinctive technology used, use case categories, tiered stack deployment, and other defining characteristics to organizing assets into a reliable hierarchy.

The first level scheme applied to the topography is that of the underlying technology. Because virtual assets have a different underlying technology from DLT assets, that becomes the first major fork for classification. Further divisions delve into layers, coding, use case, and function.

My model clearly makes the distinction between DLT assets and virtual assets, for good reason: they are completely different technologies.

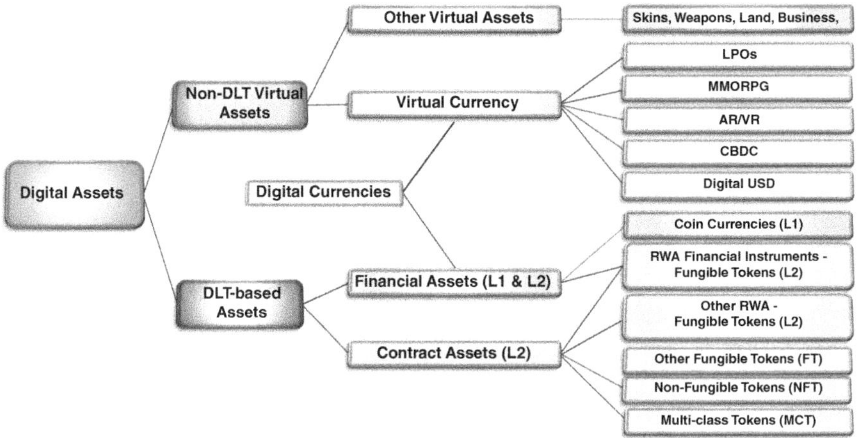

Figure 6.2 DLT Digital Asset Taxonomy.

The term "virtual" is often used in the context of "Nearly," "Almost," or "Close to, but not quite." For example, I frequently see sentences such as: That person virtually won the race. We spent virtually all day shopping. The stadium was virtually empty by the time the game ended. I remember virtually everything he said. That illness is virtually unknown in this area.

However, in computer science, "virtual" refers to not physically existing as such but made by software to appear to do so. For example, there is no code for the currency as there is for DLT digital currency. A virtual currency exists only because it is stated that it exists, such as the game developer, and it is simulated as a balance value in a software accounting environment. This is very different than distributed ledger associated assets, which have code and the code to mint the asset is visible to be viewed by anyone who has an interest.

In the courses I teach, grad students receive a kinesthetic learning environment that utilizes coding labs to enhance their experience and provide a deeper grasp of this point in the difference between virtual digital assets and DLT assets. Grasping this perspective that this initial division in digital assets is necessary for professionals in all fields in order to appreciate the need to taxonomically divide these assets in the manner when building policy, conducting heuristic or investment analysis, or following investigative leads. I have personally led investigations that have gone down the path of the conversion of virtual assets, to gift cards, and then used to acquire L1 DLT assets that were converted into L2 assets. Ultimately, the DLT digital assets were converted into USD, real estate, and vehicles, thinking they had hidden the trail. It made the heads of attorneys figuratively spin (or should I have written "virtually") when showing the evidence I had gathered supporting what had happened. The government won the case but was hampered by poorly written federal and state laws and policy because state and federal laws do not exist for the theft of virtual currency as stolen property.

Typology

Moving to typology, I use the model in Figure 6.3 to demonstrate a typology hierarchy based on categorical classification made in the taxonomy. I elaborate on the typology of coins and tokens, but I believe the graphic in Figure 6.3, developed at the same time as the taxonomy model in my grad courses. It has proven to help students obtain a clearer understanding of the model concept through a visualization.

In this model, I isolate the typology around the common characteristic found in DL assets. But then I bring to everyone's attention the fact that these digital asset categories are unique by the layer where they are located within the DLT stack. And because they exist in different layers,

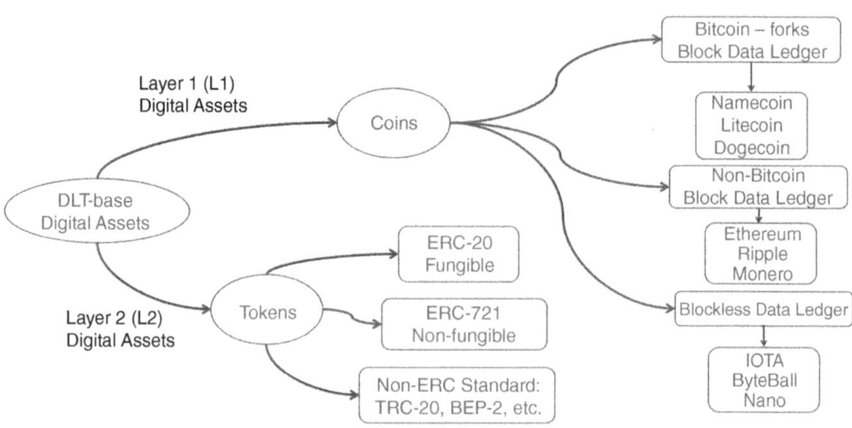

Figure 6.3   DL Associated Digital Asset Typology.

the digital assets also have unique attributes regarding different transaction boundaries, functionality, and interoperability in this short list of category classification differentiation.

I have finally arrived at the topic of topology of DLT digital assets. Here I will use my topology model for L2 token assets. These are assets that are minted in L2 contracts rather than L1 coins minted through a consensus system. As a refresher, the definition of typology is the study of objects that can be stretched and moved while points on the object continue to stay close to each other, which is why topology is divided by layer. In topology, two objects are equivalent if you can make them resemble each other by stretching, bending, or twisting them; thus, the constituent parts are interrelated—these are the L2 token digital assets in Figure 6.4.

Topology

While coin assets have a topology, tokens are particularly interesting to demonstrate how L2 contracts will stretch and bend a token standard, or even develop a new token standard, to accomplish the intent of a developer. Figure 6.4 displays an overview of token topology.

It is particularly notable that L1 DLT digital assets are digital assets bound to their respective mainnet, which is why they are typographically categorized as a "coin."

But in 2014, with the startup project of the Ethereum platform, the bounding issue changed with the enhanced development of Ethereum's

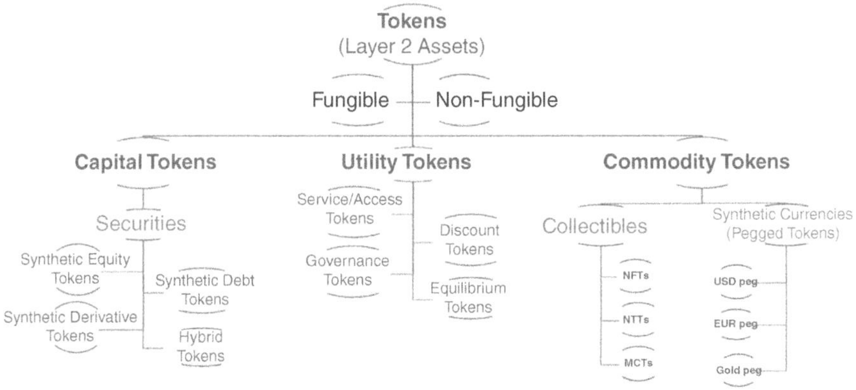

Figure 6.4 Token Topology.

L2. However, with the enhanced L2 contract stratum introduced by Ethereum developers, which is lacking in the Bitcoin infrastructure, users became acquainted with the concept of being able to create their own token assets by employing an L2 contract, which allowed user flexibility because tokens don't require a private in contact-to-contract calls—i.e., L2 token assets are not bound to their respective mainnet like L1 coin assets. The term "token" became the conventional nomenclature as designated in the Token Systems section of the Ethereum white paper.

And it is with this new introduction of an enhanced L2 that required the taxonomic distinction of DLT digital assets begins, but it never happened, so I've take the opportunity to add clarification to digital asset through some of my work on the topic. This is a significant and key distinction that influencers, evangelists, law enforcement investigators, private investigators, policy and law makers, regulators, investment advisors, and compliance professionals need to get right. Why? They are rooted in two different technologies and, as such, have different minting procedures, transaction methods, use case scenarios, cybersecurity concerns, distributed ledger stack associations, and interoperability capabilities.

Professionals embracing this knowledge on the taxonomy, typology, and topology of DLT digital assets will add value in risk assessments, identifying necessary resources for heuristics, and better understanding of the transaction paths of different assets.

I trust this was a helpful discussion on digital currencies specifically and digital assets generally.

Chapter 7

Governance Tenets of Distribution, Democratization, and Decentralization (G=D³)

In this chapter I am taking on the misunderstood governance tenets (i.e., a position held as part of a philosophy, religion, or field of endeavor) that are associated with DLT. I can't begin this chapter, however, without establishing the need for learners to adopt a mindset of critical thinking, which is what I do with graduate students who enroll in my courses, and government employees that I have been contracted to support involving technology-oriented education and advanced investigative heuristic and forensic support. The teaching of critical thinking in academia has been largely dismissed and removed, which is why I make the point of establishing the ground rules of thinking critically in research, problem-solving (another lost academic topic), and learning.

In this chapter I am unpacking the actual meaning of the terms in DLT in the context of distributed network ledger governance. To begin, the tenets of governance can have an influence on the design of the architecture of a distributed network ledger system, but these tenets are not intrinsically a technology, nor can they be a function of the code in the programming of these thousands of projects that currently exist. And for this reason, I debated whether to include this discussion on these governance tenets in this book. However, because of the extensive use of these governance terms in describing distributed network ledger technology, I ultimately determined that clarity in this area is necessary, just as I do when teaching grad students aspiring to develop intelligent designs as DLT architectural engineers.

To go on this climb, it is important to put on their critical thinking hats as I noted earlier. And to do that, following is my crash course on critical thinking. Critical thinking is a process invoked by an individual to aid in decision-making, problem-solving, and objective evaluation/analysis that empowers individuals to question social or community norms, and uncover their underlying assumptions, philosophical ideology, and potential harms to ultimately foster independent and fact-based decisions.

For professionals involved in investment decisions, policy development, law enforcement investigative analysis, technology development, and the list goes on, critical thinking is a necessity.

Critical thinking and problem-solving courses were required in course curricula throughout my academic career. And, although I didn't always appreciate what I was learning, I discovered it to be invaluable in many of my courses, such as business development, behavioral economics, international finance law and policy, cryptography, architectural engineering, data security, and cybersecurity. So, by diving into some of my course resources on critical thinking that I now teach to graduate students, the following information encompasses the mind attitude that is needed in one who wants to learn because critical thinking is the process of identifying and analyzing the research of available "facts" and "evidence" involving a subject matter or hypothesis test by questioning assumptions and preconceived philosophies that allow feelings or opinions (i.e., bias) to affect the outcome of when making determinations or decisions as a further emphasis on what I wrote in the prior paragraph.

Because I have raised the topic, I believe it is important to present a few of the core principles and criteria of critical thinking (in no particular order) to align the base of information as well as provide an understanding of the parameters of critical thinking that some may not be familiar with:

- Identify your biases on the topic.
- Research: ask questions of qualified experts, not self-professed experts.
- Practice active listening.
- Analyze your research.
- Develop your logic and reasoning.
- Problem-solve.

Problem-solving is the most important skill that critical thinkers can possess because problem-solvers are able to identify that there is, first of all, a problem, and then go on to analyze the problem, research the problem, and continually learn through solving problems.

Rest assured, I am not committing this chapter to critical thinking by any means, but it is my compulsion as an educator that is forcing me to provide these basic critical thinking principles that I trust will also serve as a teaser to conduct some additional research into critical thinking and explore courses.

In critical thinking, it is paramount to absorb and grasp the principles just listed to be open-minded about what I will unpack in this chapter as well as move toward being a life-long learner. What I raise as necessary corrections in thinking in this area of technology isn't unlike attorneys who are very protective of the legal vocabulary and are usually not shy about correcting others on the proper use of legal terminology. Having attended law school, served for several years as an adjunct professor at a law school, and continuing to guest lecture at law schools in law courses on asset and risk management, I can say I understand the attorney mindset to protect legal terminology. And as a professor teaching distributed network-ledger architectural engineering to grad students, I emphasize the accurate use of terms related to technology to reduce confusion and misconception, not to mention the consequence of losing credibility as a professional. Some students resist and push back on the implication of accuracy versus using the terms people are familiar with. My response is that all people need the opportunity to be in an upward trajectory on their learning curve, and if you want to stay at the level where most people are, then you're better off being a politician.

As a critical thinker, words matter. And many times people use words that are inaccurate because they don't know any better. Or perhaps words are used incorrectly because of groupthink influence. But more often, it is because it is an attempt to sound smart. For a speaking engagement topic on technology and fraud, I put together a collection of ways that people use terms whose meaning and origin they often have no real concept. This is the list I presented:

- Heavy-hitters in remote calls these days use terms like "bandwidth" and "signal to noise." These are terms that come from electrical engineering.
- Instead of bias, the term "over-index" is frequently used, which comes directly from statistics.
- "Mission creep" is a military term originally used to describe US involvement in the Somali civil war.
- "Exponential growth" is obviously from math, although most of the line graphs people casually call "exponential" in meetings are actually polynomial.
- My favorite, and by far the weirdest, is "light cone." It's a physics term (meaning "all of the light emitted from a point in space") that smart-seeming people use to mean "full extent." Probably the most pretentious use I've heard came from Sam Altman who dropped "light cone" in a sentence during a TechCrunch interview, "If OpenAI cracks AGI, it could capture the light cone of all future value in the universe."

I closed that slide in the presentation with, "May you find all the bandwidth you need to titrate your distractions and seek signal in the noise today."

So, thinking critically is not only about how something is said; it is also about what is said and the terms used to say it. And as I go into these terms involving the governance principles in DLT, the facts will likely go against a tide of bias; however, my desire is that a more accurate perspective about DLT governance will be realized with respect to distribution, democratization, and decentralization. And in addition, accept the intellectual tools to explore these terms in the context of their roots in economics, enterprise management, and computer science.

My motive here is simple—to bring integrity, credibility, and a framework of risk management into DLT when presenting the legitimate use of digital assets and the practical use case applications of DLT. Unfortunately, for the past decade and a half, the vast majority of professionals that I have worked with in the federal government carry the view and belief that these technologies are all designed to anonymize their identity and for bad actors to perpetrate fraudulent investment scams or schemes by introducing meme assets and structure pump-and-dumps utilizing the distributed networks like DLT and off-ledger capability. As a certified fraud examiner and retired federal agent, I suppose one could conclude that this is a pompous ethics discourse, but I trust this discussion will bring light to the importance of governance in DLT architecture. And how governance in DLT is articulated is of utmost importance. So, with that, I'll begin with outlining the principal tenet of "governance" in DLT.

Leslie Lamport, who was introduced in the first chapter, is widely recognized as a key figure who established foundational concepts in distributed networks and computing, and who is often referred to as the "Father of principled distributed computing" due to his significant contributions to protocols that enable computer systems to cooperate and avoid errors in distributed environments. Lamport developed crucial concepts for the "logical clock" model and "happened-before" model that came together in the ordering of events which are fundamental to understanding causality and provide the context for the "binary code of governance" models utilized by distributed systems. And his work laid the groundwork for designing reliable distributed algorithms, particularly in areas like consensus systems and mutual exclusion. If the necessity for rules of governance was realized back in the days of Lamport (1970s and 1980s), it is significantly more important that this same realization prompt urgency in development of governance standards be established sooner than later.

A foundational generalized definition for "governance" will follow, but it is important to explain that governance has contextual implications that introduce various definitions, depending on the characteristics of the governance environment. By way of example, in financial economics, governance is defined as the system of rules, processes, and institutions that guide economic activity. It includes how economic policies are created, put into action, and monitored. Economic governance affects investment and financial decisions and helps maintain stability and economic growth.

And although many distributed system projects have financial and economic goals, governance scenarios found in distributed network-ledger are sometimes complicated, they are diverse, and compel transparency, e.g., entity/developer corporate governance, governance policy involving the distributed network, and data ledger algorithmic governance.

This brings me back to laying out a general definition of governance: the overall framework of processes, functions, structures, rules, laws, and norms born out of the relationships, interactions, power dynamics, and communication within a system. And with that definitional foundation, it is fascinating to look at development projects and their governance structure from an organizational management perspective. With the "G"—governance—in my DLT governance formula of $G = D^3$ being define, the first "D" governance tenet I will address is Distributed.

Tenet 1: Governance in Distributed Systems

Governance in distributed networks is misunderstood and is not often given the attention deserved. I provided a definition of a distributed network system in the context of computer science in a previous section, but I am repeating it here again for easy reference: A distributed system is a collection of independent nodes working together across a network to achieve a common goal, sharing resources and data in a unified system, with each node performing a specific part of a larger task and communicating with other nodes to coordinate their actions in determining a common state. Essentially, it's a coordinated system of electronic devices with a governance framework where processing power and data are distributed across multiple machines rather than confined on a single machine.

Note, however, that a distributed system only exists in a dichotomous state—either it is a distributed system, or it is not. Even a network with only three nodes is considered distributed, while any less than three nodes is not a distributed network. I always have to chuckle when I read or hear people talk about distributed networks in the context of centralized or decentralized systems. The reason I am humored is because node distribution is not about ownership or control, but whether the distributed network has a network of nodes that meet the standards of being a distributed network. Nodes in a distributed network are centrally controlled by the declarations of ownership by a university, a corporation, or an individual. So, it is highly likely that, even if the node is donated, there is a person or entity that owns and controls the node or group of nodes. Which is why a distributed system requires a governance protocol to be deployed in order to keep humans out of the node's decision-making processes. Governance in distribution determines the rules that all of the nodes in the network will follow, regardless of ownership, which results in the independence of the node to perform under the applied rules (i.e., independent by virtue of not being under the active control of ongoing human intervention). If a node is malicious and under the control of a human actor and not following the governance protocols of the distributed network, then we are back to the Byzantine Generals Problem laid out by Lamport and the distributed network governance protocols will override the malicious node. An example of distributed network typologies that are broadly categorized as distributed network systems include data storage, messaging, computing, ledgers, filesystems, and applications. These were discussed in an earlier section.

I will further note that the level, or range, of distribution of a network is by no means an arbitrary or subjective measure. However, this raises the critical thought into an examination of how a distributed network might be measured for the level of distribution. Network distributions are all too frequently misaligned on control factors such decentralization and centralization. The technical and foundational principles of a distributed node network structure are that it consists of a collection of processes that are spatially separated, they do not share a common memory, but they communicate with one another by exchanging messages and are all controlled by a common governance framework.

A distributed network can be calculated using long-standing mathematical methods such as the Gini coefficient. Another metric of measuring the level of distribution is the Nakamoto coefficient; however, due to the method being relatively unproven, I will only present it as an alternative metric. The Gini coefficient was developed by Italian statistician Corrado Gini, who built on the work of American economist Max Lorenz and published his work in his 1912 paper titled "ariabilità e mutabilità" (English: "Variability and Mutability"). In economics, the Gini coefficient, also known as the Gini index or Gini ratio, is a measure of statistical dispersion intended to represent the income inequality, the wealth inequality, or the consumption inequality within a nation or a social group, and it is presented as a ratio with values between 0 and 1 that is converted to a percentage. In the context of distributed computing systems, the Gini coefficient is used as a metric to measure the inequality in workload distribution across different nodes or processing units; essentially, it indicates how unevenly tasks or computations are distributed, with a higher Gini coefficient signifying a greater imbalance where a few nodes handle a significant portion of the workload while others remain relatively idle.

The question to be asked here is about the mention of the significance of data ledger structure is in the governance of distribution. I will restate a point that I made when discussing data ledger architectures, which is, data ledgers are not a distributed, decentralized, or democratized system—data ledgers are a record that the nodes commit data to and they will then disseminate the ledger across the entire network, thus, a distributed ledger. How that happens is outside of any function of the data ledger and is defined by the governance protocol. And the data ledger is simple a ledger of transactions protected by the governance protocol as executed and enforced by the distributed node network. So, what we have is the convergence of a data ledger structure with a distributed node system as a portion of the entire DLT architecture that many naively call the block-chain, but may in fact, not even be based on a block data structure. Rather, it may be DAG, Radix, or a hybrid of these different data structures.

Data ledgers don't necessarily require a governance framework because they exist primarily as a ledger receiving hashed data. But distributed networks and distributed computing are far more complex systems that require a planned orchestration of activities between the nodes as well as integrating how the messaging mechanism that provides communication between the nodes will support the network. Therefore, they require a governance framework (i.e., a set of rules) to coordinate all these activities.

But understand, the convergence of distributed network and the data ledger that form the construct of the distributed network-ledger infrastructure requires a far more complex governance framework. In addition, this distributed network-ledger architecture requires a completely different set of governance rules than what a distributed network alone has. In a simple computer science characterization, distributed network-ledgers are more complex than a simple distributed network environment because a distributed network-ledger architecture must provide the infrastructure and algorithms that instruct nodes on how to validate data, message, and store data in a distributed manner without the requirement of a third party.

In a non–DLT environment, data are kept on servers maintained outside of the network. This, I trust, provides a new insight into the complexity of architecting a DLT design.

The third-party aspect, i.e., outside of the DLT infrastructure, provides a principal takeaway—developing a distributed network means removing third-parties and introducing "independence," or a form of self-governance, into the infrastructure. However, this is still on decentralization as I will cover in a later section.

The quest for distributed networks began in the 1970s, and the quest for achieving optimal distribution of data ledgers has achieved new milestones. But pause for a moment and ponder this question: How many of the distributed network-ledger projects that currently exist **do not** have some level of reliance on third-party participation or interaction?

Bitcoin has become dependent on third parties, such as centralized exchanges, so it can be traded as an alternative investment rather than fulfilling the white paper architected design of being a payment network. And the distributed node network that once existed as a network of users today has become far less distributed with the majority of node hashing power residing with just a few node pools.

I trust it is interesting to learn that the governance algorithms on the Bitcoin network that define how transactions are executed, verified, and validated by the distributed node network have declined in distribution and are not so democratized. There are governance algorithms that attempt to ensure immutability of the data secured in a data ledger (i.e., data blocks linked through hash pointers), but as the node network becomes less distributed that becomes less assured.

This concludes what is a very brief discussion that explains the need for governance in distributed networks, but it describes the necessity of distribution as one of the tenets in the governance framework DLT governance. And now it is necessary to move on from distributed network governance to governance in democratized systems.

Tenet 2: Governance in Democratized Systems

I consider it a challenge to take on governance in democratized systems in the context of DLT architecture because DLT projects seem to be less distributed, but also less democratized with only those that can afford to be in the system being the ones that control the system. However, it is worth the effort to bring a broader understanding of governance in democratization to the surface as one of the chief intentions for the introduction of distributed systems dating back to the 1970s. Also, I believe this section will bring information to the discussion on democratization as an important governance tenet in the $G = D^3$ formula, as well as reintroduce democratization as one of the primary objectives in DLT and the governance rules into the mainstream conversation, which is nearly absent in current mainstream discussions. And it should be at the forefront of nearly every legitimate DLT project use-case explanation.

Perhaps the reason that democratization is missing from the mainstream conversation is the lack of standardized, authoritative, and respected formal education programs acquired by those entering the distributed network and data ledger space. Regardless of the cause, the impact is that a very important component of the distributed network/data ledger governance structure is missing in DLT projects. Literally, many are being shut out of adopting DLT projects simply due to the cost, which is often the argument levied against the traditional system.

If one considers the concept of democratization, it is a governance tenet that implores providing access to the masses. And this is clear in the general definition of democratization, which is "the action of making something accessible to everyone."[1] Specifically in technology and business, democratization is the process of making technology more accessible and easier to use for a wider audience and that includes making technology more affordable and providing more access to marginalized communities. If I zoom in with a focus on DLT, I can define democratization as the concept of spreading power and decision-making authority across the network of all users as well as delivering every participant an equal voice and ability to contribute, rather than relying on monocratic dominance. The argument for the era of globalization has been characterized by the democratization of technology, democratization of finance, and democratization of information. Technology has been crucial to the finance and information democratization processes by facilitating the expansion of access as well as changing the way that people view and access their finances and data. However, the counterargument is that this is just a process of massification—i.e., more people can use banks, technology, and have access to information, but it does not mean there is a democratic influence over its acquisition of production. And this perfectly describes what is happening in DLT projects.

From a technology or business perspective, the word "democratization" exists as a conspicuous divergence from the colloquial use of the term "decentralization" applied to DLT in an attempt to capture

---

[1] *Concise Oxford English Dictionary.* 12th ed. Oxford University Press, 2011.

democratization. And it fails in large part because the projects are neither democratized nor decentralized despite the narrative to the contrary. This is why democratization is such a very important inclusion as a tenet of governance in distributed network ledger design.

Democratization is a challenging governance doctrine because it isn't something that exists in the code (i.e., DNA) of DLT. To advance democratization in a project, whether it involves an L1, L2, or L3 project, components such as accessibility, affordability, user-friendly UIs, user open-source collaboration, inclusion of democratic processes not based on position or wealth, and providing education/training for users will determine the degree of democratization.

Some of the key beneficial aspects of democratization in distributed network applications are the following:

- Distributed Governance (discussed in last section from a network perspective): Decisions involving the applications are made through a consensus system among users, where each participant has the opportunity to contribute to the project's decision-making process rather than relying on a single leader, governing body, or foundation. Is this what really happens?
- Fault Tolerance: No single node or third-party can collapse the project (i.e., no single point of failure); therefore, the project can continue to function even if some nodes are compromised, offline, or network threats. However, many projects cease to exist and can shut down operations when it is deemed by the project's developer authority regime – these clearly do not employ governance protocols based on distribution, democratization, or decentralization. This often happens when an exploit of a project occurs. A short list of examples include Base's largest L2 exchange; LeetSwap announced a pause in its operations due to fears of a potential exploit in 2023; Consensys' Linea briefly halted block production after a $6.8 million Velocore exchange exploit in 2024; L2 exchange XT.com abruptly suspended withdrawals, citing a wallet upgrade and maintenance but it turned out to be a $1.7 million in suspicious transfers in 2024; and there are many more examples. These look more like vulnerable technology services run by conglomerates rather than DLT distributed, democratized, independent structures.
- Reduced Censorship: Democratized projects in distributed networks make it more difficult for any single entity or third party to control

information flow or prevent access to project information. While networks are supposed to be censorship resistance, there are potential avenues for censorship, such as sequencer control or RPC manipulation. A malicious sequencer could potentially reorder or censor certain transactions before they reach finality, although this is a design risk. A specific example is Sony, which implemented a strict policy at the RPC level to censor early tokens they deemed "unapproved." This policy resulted in users receiving a "forbidden" response when interacting with blocked contracts.

So, it shouldn't be a stretch to recognize that independent autonomous "democratized applications" require certain governance rules in order to maintain democratization; however, the governance rules of decentralization are infrequently incorporated into the operation by leadership of the project.

Now, with the governance tenets of "distribution" and "democratization" firmly in place, I will move to the third governance tenet of "decentralization" as it applies to distributed network ledger projects.

Tenet 3: Governance in Decentralization

The governance tenet of decentralization is at its core a problem of miscommunication. The miscommunication is much like what is used in social engineering schemes, which are designed to lure a person into doing something they wouldn't otherwise consider doing. Decentralization was originally conceptualized in the framework (not infrastructure) of the Bitcoin white paper for what the original developers wanted the network to be, but the term is now just a standard label slapped on any project deployed within a DLT network.

Using decentralization as a descriptor of a project's design appears to be more of a lure to attract users under the premise that ownership, authority, revenue sharing, and control of a DLT project is spread among the users. This message of decentralization are spread throughout project marketing and media promotional content, but it is usually nowhere near what happens in actuality.

The use of the term "decentralize" in the context of a DLT project is inconsistent with the etymology and context as defined in lexica. To illustrate, the following is an example of a definition I have consistently observed being circulated across various web and print channels explaining decentralization by various projects, DLT platforms, third-party stakeholders in the DLT sector, and those that are supposed educators of DLT: In the context of cryptocurrency, centralization refers to a system where a single entity or authority controls the entire network, while decentralization refers to a system where control is distributed among multiple nodes.

Although the explanation correctly defines "centralization" as being under the control of a central authority, it completely misses the target when providing an explanation of the dichotomous position of centralization as decentralization. They are inaccurately instructing that decentralization is a distributed node network. This is factually a false statement. As I wrote in the section on the governance tenet of distribution, a distributed node network is a network of autonomous computers (aka nodes), which has nothing to do with centralized or decentralized decision-making control of the project. Stated another way, a distributed network of nodes is still distributed regardless of whether the entire network of nodes is controlled by a single entity made up of n number of individuals; they are still distributed, which has nothing to do with decentralized decision-making. The tenet of governance in distributed network ledger projects is about who has the decision-making control of the project. Is it a central entity making decisions on behalf of the network, such as the developers or foundation or a few of the prominent node operators (i.e., centralized control) versus the decision-making spread across the entire network of users (i.e., decentralized control)?

A study of the etymology of the word "centralized" denotes that the contradictory position of centralized is decentralized. Used as a prefix in English, "de-" (with its origin in Latin) carries the meaning of "away from or down from," as in "de-centralize" is a change "away from" centralize. However, for full disclosure, the prefix "de-" is used with other words in English that can take on the meaning of "down to the bottom," as in "de-construct," which in this context means "to tear down." As a note of awareness, I am using hyphenation as a visual emphasis to provide emphasis for the analytical distinction being made and it should not be construed as the accurate spelling of the words in the preceding sentence.

Centralized, as the opposite state of decentralized, has a rather interesting origin in the context of decentralized governance in distributed network ledger systems. The word "centralization" came into use in France in 1794 as the post-Revolution French Directory leadership created a new government structure, and the word "decentralization" came into usage in the 1820s according to Vivien Schmidt, author of *Democratizing France*.

Defined in technology, decentralization is the process by which the activities of an organization, particularly those related to planning and decision-making, are delegated away from a central, authoritative group and given to smaller factions within it.[2]

And like the other governance tenets discussed, they exist as a dichotomy. As such, the governance dichotomy configuration involving decentralization exists in either a state of centralization or decentralization, which is unlike the tenet of governance in democratization that is either democratized or autocratic. The obvious deconfliction required is between distributed network ledger technology governance concerning democratization and decentralization that always appears when framing the attributes of projects in this space.

I want to emphasize that my objective in writing this book is to bring an educational component to clarify the technological, not philosophical, infrastructural components of DLT as opposed to initiating a discussion about semantics or word play. I believe an objective analysis using the factual application of etymology removes the semantic or work play argument and focuses on the technology. And it may be apparent that applying lexical standards in this technological field, as it is in other fields of technology and other professional fields like law, should significantly affect the use of prose in providing accurate and transparent descriptions and disclosures of DLT platforms about the project, how the project benefits a user, how fees and revenues are earned by the project, distribution of those fees to users (if any), and the overall governance structure of the project, to list a few. But simply describing the platform or project as decentralized should be unacceptable to users and professionals in all sectors.

In my decades of experience in civil and criminal law enforcement, this technology has been attacked as being developed for the purpose of committing nefarious activities, as is the case with a number of government attorneys I have opposed in their bias on DLT. And with this mindset, it introduces a guilt before proven guilty approach to law enforcement and prosecution. What I have advocated in favor of for

---

[2] *Merriam-Webster Dictionary*. Continues *Merriam-Webster's Collegiate Dictionary*, 11th ed. (first published in 2003). Continually updated at https://www.merriam-webster.com/.

many years is the formation of an SRO that monitors how platform and project operate and promote themselves, as is done in the traditional securities markets for marketing of financial instruments under FINRA (Financial Industry Regulatory Authority), which is an SRO. But enough on policy.

At this point, it should be abundantly clear that there needs to be a massive shift in the use of terminology in association with the marketing of L1, L2, and L3 projects. And decentralization should not be perceived as a barrier to civil or criminal action because it is well known that the majority of L2-L3 projects are not decentralized. However, the inaccurate use of "decentralization" in marketing and promotional statements has led to the assumption they can't be touched.

I consistently use in my courses examples of L2-L3 projects even before the deployment of the project that are promoting a false narrative about what they clearly can't provide any evidence of, like decentralization, democratization, or even distribution. They use redundant hype terms to describe the project as decentralized and "self-executing" and deployed on a network of nodes making the project impervious to developer control, or have the ability to manipulate the code or censor users. There are also communications involving terms signifying a hands-off or arm's length principle in the promotion of meme-tokens or other digital asset projects, suggesting that the developers don't benefit from the profits generated by the project. I've yet to actually come across a project where this is what is truly taking place other than perhaps the Bitcoin network where the fees and subsidies go to individuals who can afford to purchase and operate validation nodes (aka miners).

As an expert witness in many federal prosecutions and grand jury cases, I have successfully presented as evidence that I have present to prove willfulness and intent to promote fraudulent behavior. This is because I have been able to make the case from the point to these governance tenets and the project code, and the etymology of the words used in promoting and marketing. This alone does not provide a clear path to conviction, but it has gone a long way towards being able to clearly articulate an in-depth understanding of architectural engineering and how they converge within a project.

Unfortunately, when it comes to understanding governance in conjunction with technology, what has developed and propagated is a DLT groupthink social collective that inaccurately markets and informs about decentralization as if it were part of the code. But decentralization is a concept and cannot be coded into the infrastructure of a project. Even platforms that have voting systems have to provide the construct outside of the DLT architecture or code. Some projects introduce a DAO (Decentralized Autonomous Organization) as a method of voting and sharing revenues (aka dividends) from their investment in a project. However, there are DLT systems, like the Bitcoin network, that have no system for voting on soft forks or hard forks. It is essentially done through a forum of those who operated validation nodes, and those providing the most hashing power to the network have a louder voice in the decision-making process of code changes.

The ideal of "decentralization" tends to be used as an initial attraction to garner attention and attract users to adopt a digital asset or sign-on to using an L2 project or L3 app. And many users and observers admit that the marketing hype is successful in enticing a potential user to take a look. But what often lures adoption is a promise of initial and subsequent airdrops. And then there is a promise of more airdrops to further entice users into acquiring more of a digital asset or becoming a regular user of a projects services. Note that these airdrop distributions are not part of a self-executing contract algorithm; they are part of the organization governance that is centrally controlled by a DAO, foundation, or developer group. These promotion methods are created and implemented to enhance revenues in a best-case scenario or defraud in a worst-case scenario. Either way, this is not an example of decentralization.

Decentralization signifies a system or network where decision-making is distributed among multiple participants with the aim to reduce reliance on intermediaries and enhance transparency and resilience.

The irony to highlight is that the legacy Bitcoin payment network developers envisioned a system where everyone could participate in Bitcoin block validation, which is written in the abstract of the Bitcoin white paper. It was originally designed to provide all users an equal opportunity to validate blocks using their existing laptop hardware equipped with CPU and GPU processors, and, most importantly, no user could control or monopolize the hashing power required for block validation—an example of decentralization. And the concept of decentralization is why the lead developer of the Bitcoin payment network has to date never been identified.

The decentralization of the Bitcoin payment network has significantly eroded since its deployment in 2009. A case in point, validation node pooling (i.e., mining pools) was introduced in 2010, when Slush launched the first mining pool, Slush Pool. In 2010, a user on the BitcoinTalk forum named Slush noticed that validation nodes (aka miners) could improve their probability of validating a block, and thus earn the block subsidy, by joining forces. Slush Pool was the first pool on the Bitcoin payment network based in the Czech Republic.

As a result, more pools were formed and introduced. And to entice users to join their pool, mining pools developed formulas for how a block subsidy would be allocated to the individual users who contributed hashing capacity to the pool. In time, the pooling formulas and transaction fees from those operating the validation equipment that the formulas have become standardized and are essentially coded into code that governs the Bitcoin transaction algorithm.

However, as the Bitcoin network grew, those running validation hardware (i.e., nodes) had to invest more in computing power to get meaningful rewards. By 2010, pool operators pushed users who wanted to validate blocks from using CPU (central processing unit) to GPU (graphic processing unit) hardware. But then around 2013, corporate pools were adopting faster and more expensive ASIC (Application-Specific Integrated Circuits) that cost significantly more than most users could afford. This was not done by a "vote"; the transition to ASICs happened organically within the large node operators as the Bitcoin base code does not have a governance system for voting.

Currently, pool operations are now primarily composed of centrally owned organizations like Foundry, AntPool, ViaBTC, F2Pool, MARA Pool—in order of market share at the time of this writing[3] as the Top Five centralized organizations controlling 80% of the entire Bitcoin network, and just under 50% are controlled by the Top Two pool operators.

The legacy Bitcoin payment network was originally the only network designed and built without a profit motivation, but even that has changed in the last decade. It has now been mixed with such projects as ordinals and inscriptions, which results in a massive strain on an infrastructure that was never architected for that use case. And with an application to distributed

---

[3] Hashrate Index. "Bitcoin Mining Pools Comparison." https://hashrateindex.com/hashrate/pools Hahsrateindex.com.

network governance, fees increased dramatically after the deployment of runes and ordinals on the Bitcoin network. I'm not going to go down the path of the digital asset economics or the code and technical aspects, but I will assess the deployment of these assets from a governance angle.

One of the major principles that requires emphasis is related to "decentralization": It does not have a transference property as in mathematics. In mathematics, the "transference" principle refers to the technique used to extend results from one mathematical system (like real numbers) to another (like hyperreal numbers or a different model). A distributed network ledger system is distributed by nature of its construction under a specific architectural engineered design, but it is not inherently decentralized. If a platform or project is controlled by an entity or group, to whatever degree that might be, it is not decentralized. However, that same platform or project can be distributed because of its connection to the location design of the distributed components. This contrasts with centralization/decentralization with the existence/absence of a central authority or point of control by an entity, group, or team.

As I close out this chapter, I believe it is important to set the record straight on these tenets of governance ($G = D^3$), if for no other reason than to educate users, many of whom are being deceived by the misinformation that is communicated through various channels.

I am not oblivious to the fact that some people just don't care about the facts underpinning the technology and economic model implications on how distributed networks transmit information about ledgers that provide transaction information of digital asset units, or the transaction process is cryptographically secured. But most people in the United States didn't seem to care about what was in their food until the 1970s and 1980s, which serves as a good example related to this technology. And in 2025 there is a resurgence in this movement of integrity in the food supply and manufacturing, but it has expanded to medicine.

In my personal observations of the events related to food technology as a teen growing up in an agricultural/ranching area of the United States during the 1970s and 1980s, it seemed previously the public essentially put their trust in the US Department of Agriculture (USDA) and Food and Drug Administration (FDA) that communicated that the food supply in the US was safe. It wasn't until 1990 that the Nutrition Labelling and Education Act (NLEA) and the Organic Foods Production Act (OFPA) were signed into law that required a groundbreaking requirement for food manufacturers to place food labels on items that list the most important ingredients in an easy-to-follow format and set uniform standards for organic producers. At the time of writing, it is interesting that 30 plus years later, in the United States, food safety is again an issue.

Perhaps the time has come to bring this same type of initiative to DLT. I have spent years working within the federal government contributing to policy and guidance development. Following my "retirement" from government, I have had many interactions as an academic with lobbying groups and developer communities to determine the interest in creating a self-regulatory organization (SRO), and not just from the perspective of trading digital assets. There is a significant need for a development standards approach to L2 and L3 involving contract use-case and vulnerabilities standards, Dapp cybersecurity standards, asset development standards, and DEX exchange standards to list a few that have been on my list. Formation of an SRO has the potential to curb the push for government regulation and go a long way in formalizing standards across all projects to adopt conformance of standards for privacy, security, accessibility, social impact, and many other characteristics, including the use of a consistent lexicon of certain terms as I have outlined in this chapter. But it could also go a long way in providing credibility to this space rather than always being referenced as a "wild west" environment.

Intermediary stakeholders are already under the control of government jurisdictions across the globe. Suggesting an SRO governance structure is clearly better than a government attempt at regulation, And I trust it is apparent from this discussion that DLT projects are not decentralized; they are run just like any traditional startup, small business, or corporate enterprise, something for stakeholders to ponder and consider. And an SRO should consist of only the "BIG" company stakeholders in DLT. It needs to include those with innovation and technology expertise within the economic and computer science fields—this is what represents the very nature of "decentralization."

Chapter 8

Trends in Use Cases and Convergence with Other Technologies

It is undoubtedly obvious without writing about it that the convergence of DLT with other technologies like AI, IoT, XR, and PQC is creating new opportunities for data management, security, and efficiency across various industries, including finance, supply chain, and healthcare.

However, dwarfing the convergence of technologies is the global conversation currently taking place in the use case of DLT L1 coin assets (e.g., BTC, XRP), L2 contract token assets (e.g., USDC, RLUSD), approval of Exchange Traded Funds (ETF), and the synthetic L2 token asset markets involving the tokenization of Real-World Assets (RWA) or In Real-Life Assets (IRLA) such as securities (debt and equity), fiat, commodities, and derivatives (securities and commodities).

So, I will close out this book by focusing on these topics. Many professionals likely find it challenging to keep up with the flow of developments in the prominent technology fields, which seems like a daily occurrence, and in separating the hype of what they can do today, much less, from the realistic developments of these technologies into the future. So, jumping right into this, I'm going to start with a topic that is garnering significant attention as I'm writing this chapter.

Digital Asset Reserve Funds

I am watching the live signing (March 6, 2025) of an Executive Order (EO) by the US president that allows the federal government to take digital assets currently owned by the federal government (i.e., owned means forfeiture is complete and not in the status of seized and the EO plainly list the statutes). Part of the EO reads: "Bitcoin that was finally forfeited as part of criminal or civil asset forfeiture proceedings or in satisfaction of any civil money penalty imposed by any executive department or agency."[1]

I am not taking a position on whether this is a good idea; although I have some thoughts from the economic perspective, but what I believe is that in this moment of anticipation and exuberance, many are not thinking clearly about the long-term economic outcomes for the Bitcoin community nor considering the founding concepts of why digital currencies were originally introduced. My favorite economist, F.A. Hayek (1899–1992), whom I quoted previously, made this statement during a 1984 interview, "...take the monopoly of issuing money from government. I'm convinced we shall never have good money again so long as we leave it in the hands of government."[2] Unfortunately, Hayek passed before Bitcoin's inception, but in his book *The Denationalisation of Money*, he argued for nothing short of stripping the state of its monopoly power of money itself. The ultimate objective of the denationalization of currency

---

[1] "Establishment of the Strategic Bitcoin Reserve and United States Digital Asset Stockpile." 2025. The White House. March 7, 2025. https://www.whitehouse.gov/presidential-actions/2025/03/establishment-of-the-strategic-Bitcoin-reserveand-united-states-digital-asset-stockpile/

[2] CraigShipp.com. "Friedrich August von Hayek predicting Bitcoin in 1984 A Sly Roundabout Way." https://youtu.be/CBIidtaUCzs?t=53

advocated by Hayek was related to monetary policy independence from political interference with the basic idea that the possibility of banks issuing different currencies would open the way to market competition.

So, would Hayek like bitcoin as currency? I never met Hayek, but as a side note, he conducted the interview containing the quote the year I graduated with my first undergrad degree in economics. But I think he would have encouraged what it represented as well as the extent to which it takes currency supply out of the hands of the state as a way for individuals to transact peer-to-peer, permissionlessly, and stateless. Stateless—this prompts a second question.

Would Hayek like bitcoin as a reserve currency? Hayek's idea was that currency issuers would be interested in keeping the value of their currencies stable, and by contrast, bitcoin is now only a toy for inventors and governments controlling it by hoarding it under the guise of a reserve fund.

The first digital currency payment network was introduced by David Chaum in 1990. It was to introduce privacy in the age of personal data theft from collected credit card data and of the e-commerce revolution, all of which was kicked off with the newly introduced internet deployed by DARPA the same year. And of course, I will not forget the subsequent version of a digital currency payment network. Bitcoin introduced a merged technology architecture that included distributed networking technology and encrypted data ledger structures building off of "Chaum's failed attempt," as quoted in a Nakamoto email during the development of the Bitcoin payment network. It has not actually given rise to the launch of a next generation version of alternative private payment network to remove intermediaries, centralized ownership and control, and government censorship. So, just as Nakamoto claimed Chaum's attempt at privacy had failed, I suggest the evidence and trending direction is that Nakamoto's attempt to achieve decentralization (i.e., removing centralized control and ownership), privacy, removal of intermediaries, and prevention of government censorship has largely failed as well, especially in light of recent government actions. Hayek would likely come to the same conclusion.

In the last few days I have witnessed the introduction of US Senate bill S.954: to establish a Strategic Bitcoin Reserve and other programs to ensure the transparent management of bitcoin holdings by the federal government, to offset costs utilizing certain resources of the Federal Reserve System, as well as other purposes. It was introduced to the Senate

Committee on Banking, Housing, and Urban Affairs by Senator Cynthia Lummis on March 11, 2025. The bill was also sponsored by Senator Cynthia Lummis with Senators James Justice, Tommy Tuberville, Bernie Moreno, Roger Marshall, and Marsha Blackburn signing on as cosponsors of the bill. And in addition to bitcoin, additional DLT Layer-2 digital token currencies have been suggested like XRPL and USDC.[3] This is also noted by law firms like Anderson P.C. in a report writing, "A parallel Treasury-managed stockpile will custody other digital assets (e.g. Ethereum, XRP, Solana, Cardano per administration statements) that have been forfeited to the government."[4]

During the two decades that I was working with the federal government concerning DLT asset guidance, policy review, investigative support, and education, I observed nearly two dozen bills introduced into both chambers (i.e., House and Senate) of the US Congress. And to date, none have passed by the House of the Senate in order to go to POTUS (President of the US) for signing. But as in the past, many advocates, influencers, and evangelists in the digital asset space are extremely optimistic and driving lobbying efforts to ensure that S.954 is passed. But many questions arise that have no clear answers:

- Is this only going to benefit bitcoin investors?
- How is this going to benefit the US government?
- Are there protections to prevent the government from being incentivized to conduct administrative forfeitures similar to FDR's EO 6102 action in 1933 for the purpose of removing the constraint on the Federal Reserve from increasing the US dollar supply during the depression?
- How will putting hundreds of thousands of bitcoin under the control of the federal government, state governments, and any number of internation governments impact the Bitcoin payment network that was architected as a safer alternative payment system over the traditional financial, banking, and credit card system? Or has Bitcoin essentially failed in its intended purpose and design?

---

[3] The text of the bill at the time of writing is available at https://www.lummis.senate.gov/wp-content/uploads/BITCOINAct.pdf.

[4] P.C. Anderson. "Bitcoin as a Strategic Reserve: Policy, Legal, and Compliance Implications. April 17, 2025. https://anderpc.com/insights/bitcoin-as-a-strategic-reserve-policy-legal-and-compliance-implications

- What other DLT ledger Layer-1 and Layer-2 assets will the federal, state, and international governments potentially acquire and take over ownership of in addition to bitcoin?
- What if a federal administration that doesn't have a favorable view of these digital assets is elected? Will the current EO be dismantled resulting in an indiscriminate or systematic unloading of digital currencies by the government?
- How will this government ownership and control over certain digital assets impact development and innovation involving DLT architecture and digital assets? How many new synthetic versions of the USD might come as a result if there are no guardrails on who can issue a USD token currency?
- Will government engagement and ownership influence developers to innovate for the singular purpose of driving the government's agenda over social betterment?
- Will governments taking over major portions of certain popular Layer-1 and Layer-2 assets have the ability to then censor or manipulate consumer behavior by expanding and contracting the supply (i.e., economic behavioral manipulation)?

There are so many other questions, but these get the conversation started.

As a financial economist, digital asset economist, DLT architectural engineer, CEO/CTO of a technology startup, and professor, I am asking stakeholders promoting government control over swaths of Layer-1 and Layer-2 assets: What is the driver behind the enthusiasm for government ownership and control of private, open-source, nongovernment minted digital currencies; and what do they envision as the short-term and long-term outcomes—positive and negative? The detail in their response is the personal and business enrichment it will deliver through the anticipated increase in the value of assets that governments decide to acquire. However, the supply-and-demand curve doesn't typically work for the Layer-2 assets with unlimited minting supplies like ether, which is an L1 coin asset.

I will historically note that, not too many years after the launch of the Bitcoin payment network, I was asked by an executive who I reported to in the federal government how one could go about "turning off or shutting down" the Bitcoin "blockchain." The question was limited to the topic of the bitcoin asset because it was the only asset widely circulated at that point in time. However, my trend analysis noted that more Bitcoin archetypes would follow, just like what took place in the early era of virtual currencies when I observed the virtual currency trends that occurred during the evolution from one to two player consoles to VR MMO (Massively Multiplayer Online) and RPG (Role Play Gaming) landscapes. This was driven by improvements in the VR technology and expanded into the IRL (In Real Life) VR economies that introduced platforms like Second Life (SL) with its Linden Dollar (L$/SLL) launched in 2003.

In the 1990s I witnessed the birth of a plethora of the first digital currencies existing in code, not virtual, that were transactionally secured by sender and receiver being verified cryptographic proofs—the first use of cryptography in conjunction with a digital currency. That came to a conclusion toward the end of the 1990s as a result of what is called the "Crypto War." In this case, crypto did not refer to the digital currency; it was a period where the government did not like the open use of cryptography because it was perceived as a national security threat. It is apparent these cycles keep repeating as we see similar issues with different technologies today (e.g., AI and quantum computing).

By 2008, cybercrime involving bad actors operating in Second Life had escalated, and I participated in many domestic and international investigations involving gaming. Today there are far more options for bad actors using the messaging and value transfer possibilities within MMO such as MOBA (Multiplayer Online Battle Arena), RTS (Real-Time Strategy), and FPS (First Person Shooter) games. And while cybercriminals took advantage in the form of ATO (Account Takeovers) and currency laundering that I had trained many federal agents about, law enforcement and government regulators never understood that technology and the off-game exchanges continued to operate and provide liquidity to VR assets. All the while, regulators and policymakers continued to call them "closed-systems," but traded openly on the surface web, despite the game developers' EULAs (End User Licensing Agreements). Other evidence that I have provided over the years in working with policymakers is the existence of VR currencies and asset trading platforms like PlayerAuctions. com, launched in 1999 and still operating today, and VirWoX (the acronym for Virtual World Exchange) launched in 2007 and closed in 2020 due to cited regulatory pressure after adding BTC to its list of exchange assets. Following a two-month training for US federal analysts, agents, and executives on VR gaming, VR environments, mapping of various VR worlds, use of VR currencies (the real virtual currencies) in laundering and terror financing, and a number of other matters of investigative techniques and digital forensics. In addition, I contributed to a working paper published by INTERPOL in January 2024 on the same topic. And it seems not so coincidental that the CFPB (Consumer Financial Protection Bureau) put out a warning to banks in April 2024 about the risks of video game and fraud.[5]

In light of government actions against digital currency platforms in the late 1990s, which reference David Chaum's 1995 launch of the company Digicash, which was being referred to in emails with the domain name of "satoshi," I began to follow the new economic trend and document it in the early 2000s. The Bitcoin payment network ushered in an entirely new convergence of several computer science technologies, i.e., distributed computer networking and node messaging, data ledger encryption, cryptography, and digital asset transaction procedures. Again, the concept of digital currency, like bitcoin, was not new because digital currency cryptographic transaction platforms had already been launched going back to the early 1990s. But the common link in digital currency systems between David Chaum's early efforts and the Nakamoto deployment nearly 20 years later was the necessity for data privacy in financial transactions to protect from cybercrimes (due to weak cybersecurity measures taken by transaction intermediaries) and government censorship. Do these sound like current day themes?

Intermediaries are still one of the major current day points of vulnerability for digital asset exploits (e.g., Buybit and Coinbase as recent examples). And I find irony in people calling for government control and essentially begging the government to buy up bitcoin, which is contrary to their belief that DLT assets should be free of government control. And yet it is this group that rejects instituting DLT and digital asset sector SROs to self-regulate the space.

But returning to my response about "flipping the off-switch" on the Bitcoin "blockchain" payment network, I wrote an informal internal brief explaining several options ranging from lowest to highest degree

---

[5] Cameron Emanuel-Burns. "US Personal Finance App Monarch Raises $75m Series B." Fintech Futures. www.fintechfutures.com/2024/04/cfpb-publishes-new-report-highlig hting-risks-related-to-financial-transactions-in-video-games/.

of success. I wrote that if a government wanted to attempt to turn off and deconstruct a distributed network ledger system (what government familiarly referenced as shutting down a blockchain), one approach would be to flood the node network with their own nodes in the form of a Sybil Attack, a cyberattack where an attacker (entity or individual) directly or indirectly controls a significant number of nodes (Sybil nodes) with the goal of tricking honest nodes into believing that the Sybil nodes are distinct and separate with the aim of undermining the entire network. This was the least likely option to be chosen, so it was the first on the list, but it met the primary objective of collapsing the mainnet network. I explained that targeting and collapsing the validation node network would stop any further blocks from being formed, thus new mints of BTC, and it was unlikely that the nascent project would recover, which was CPU supported at that time. My analysis on the degree of success was low in large part due to the resource requirements and the lack of expertise in conducting such an operation. Now, if the perception is that I'm crazy and this was a stupid idea, several years later in 2015, Chanalysis was forced to defend itself after allegations that its surveillance tactics had disrupted the Bitcoin network. Three Bitcoin Core developers, Wladimir van der Laan, Peter Todd, and Gregory Maxwell, say that Chainalysis' actions amount to a so-called Sybil attack on the Bitcoin network. Moving on.

But at the other end of the probability of success spectrum was an operationally viable tactical move based in a game theory matrix analysis; the move was to quietly begin acquiring the entire limited supply of bitcoin as it comes into circulation using stealth key management tactics and hold (e.g., sell in auction or exchange for USD) all forfeited BTC. Perhaps that internal brief of buying up bitcoin finally made its way into the right hands after 15 years. Or maybe they figured it out on their own, but I doubt it. It is simply a case of the government typically being 10–15 years behind because we find that this is what the government is doing in creating a BTC reserve fund—it is buying up bitcoin. It may not be to necessarily control the supply at this point, but into the future that might change. Moving on.

I'm not going to examine the legislative and policy issues concerning governments buying up and holding (aka HODL[6]) a reserve of the limited

---

[6] The origin of HODL dates back to 2013, when a user with the pseudonym GameKyuubi posted a now legendary message titled "I AM HODLING" on the BitcoinTalk forum.

supply of bitcoin (e.g., US federal government, US states, and various governments around the globe). But without a doubt, this will remove Bitcoin from circulation and held like US gold at Ft. Knox. And by reducing the supply, one might argue that it makes bitcoin more valuable; however, it also significantly reduces the liquidity of bitcoin within the network. Reduced liquidity means that there is less bitcoin available for all users, and it causes significant delays in exchange transactions, but that alone would not significantly affect the valuation of bitcoin. However, the lost interest due to delays and loss of liquidity would likely shift interest to other assets, and this would cause a decline or even a potential collapse of the network. Other impacts of reduced liquidity include the following:

- Price Volatility: Low liquidity increases price shifts with even small transactions resulting in significant movements.
- Slippage: Executing large orders can result in significant price discrepancies (slippage) due to the lack of buyers or sellers at the desired price.
- Higher Costs: Low liquidity often results in having wider bid-ask spreads, meaning the difference between the price you're willing to pay (bid) and the price someone is willing to sell (ask) is larger, increasing the cost of trading.
- Reduced Confidence: Low liquidity can deter new participants and established market participants, as the uncertainty and difficulty of trading can erode confidence.
- Manipulation Risks: Smaller markets are more vulnerable to price manipulation by large players.
- Barriers to Exit: Selling assets in low liquidity environments can be difficult and result in additional liquidity in an already stressed market.
- Economic Disincentive: Reduced liquidity results in disenfranchising network participants and resulting in a move to alternative digital assets of which there are over 2.5 million Layer-1 and Layer-2 in circulation with the major, however, generated by Layer-2 contracts.

It is important to grasp that bitcoin as a reserve currency likely cause BTC to be classified as a near-money asset changing the measures currency supply as well – the implications of this are well beyond the scope of the book. These are financial assets that are highly liquid but not as immediately usable as cash or demand deposits, such as savings accounts, money market funds, and short-term government securities—i.e., non-fiat currency assets that can be converted to fiat currency. The US Federal Reserve defines the concept for testing liquidity in the development of monetary policy in regulating currency supply by the Central Bank in M1, M2, and M3 analysis. Examples include savings accounts, money market funds, certificates of deposit (CDs), short-term government securities (e.g., Treasury bills), and liquid foreign currencies.

To conclude this section, I will note the impetus to include other distributed network ledger digital assets as a reserve fund. Less than 0.0004% of the 2.5 million Layer-1 and Layer-2 DLT assets are designed as a currency for transfer of value across networks or for in-network fees (e.g., bitcoin (BTC)/Bitcoin Network—L1 coin, USDC (Circle)—L2 token, USDT (Tether)—L2 token, RLUSD (Ripple Labs)—L2 token, ether (ETH)/Ethereum Platform—L1 coin, SOL—L2 token/Solana Platform, ADA—L1 coin/Cardono Platform). As such, the most significant implications of bitcoin, or other assets that might be included as a future reserve asset, are multifaceted and pose the risk of volatility to existing owners of the asset as well as imposing new and unintended regulatory burdens that were never built into the governance framework of being a private currency rather than being part of government held synthetic fiat currency reserve assets, which will likely lead to a shift in global financial power.

It is interesting to contemplate that the future BTC holdings by the US federal government alone will be between 5% and 10% of the complete supply of bitcoin. This calculation represents a very simplified version of elements that make up the current total supply of 19.8 million BTC to demonstrate the estimate of a 5–10% potential government holding of BTC.

I'll begin by subtracting the estimated 20% of unrecoverable BTC (as in, my ex-girlfriend threw away the hard drive with my BTC wallet folder on it[7]). Supporting my estimate is a report by Ledger in a 2025 article on Ledger Academy.[8] The amount of remaining BTC is: current

---

[7] Escher Walcott. "Man Says Bitcoin Fortune Was 'Buried' in Garbage Dump by His Ex." https://people.com/man-says-bitcoin-fortune-buried-landfill-now-buying-back-8789 754#:~:text=James%20Howells%20from%20Newport%2C%20Wales,January%2C%20 according%20to%20the%20BBC

[8] Vineet Nair. "How Many Bitcoin Are Lost? Ledger." Ledger Academy. https://www.led ger.com/academy/topics/economics-and-regulation/how-many-bitcoin-are-lost-ledger

minted supply of 19.8 million $\star$ 20% = 3.96 million (assuming there are no future losses of BTC), plus the 1 million BTC (200,000 BTC/yr for 5 years with a minimum holding period of 20 years) to be acquired under a proposed bill discussed by Representative Nick Begich in a press release on March 13, 2025, using Federal Reserve discretionary surplus funds up to $6 billion/year, plus the current 200,000 reported forfeited BTC owned by the federal government as reported in the executive order to be transferred to the reserve fund. That equals 7.3% of all bitcoin currently in circulation: (19.8M BTC in circulation − (19.8M BTC $\star$2 0% unrecoverable)) − 1M BTC potentially to be acquired − 200K BTC currently in US ownership under forfeiture laws = 14.6M BTC. I am conservative using 21 million BTC, which is the current annotated total supply of BTC in the Bitcoin code, because there is assumed purchasing that will take place over 5 years and that brings the total supply closer to 21 million BTC. So, the computation is 14.6M BTC/21M BTC = 6.8% owned and controlled by the US federal government. I have also not factored future forfeitures into this computation under the assumption that future forfeitures of BTC owned by the federal government through legal proceedings will be used as an offset to the 200,000/year BTC purchase acquisition proposed in the congressional bill, which remains an unknown. And for purposes of this computation to support the 5–10% US federal holdings, my computation purposely does not consider the holding of BTC by US states and global governments and foreign jurisdictions that own and control holdings of BTC, so that percentage could easily double or triple on a global basis for all government holdings. In private treasuries and ETF holdings, the combined holding of BlackRock and Strategy equals approximately 6% of all BTC currently minted. In private holdings, the Top 4 wallets hold 3.5% of BTC minted with the next 93 wallets holding 14% leading to the Top 97 holding 17.5% of total BTC currently minted. It is notable that only approximately 5.7% of BTC remains to be minted.

When all is done, relatively speaking, the US federal government will likely end up owning a significant portion of bitcoin that is minted.

A couple of last points on the minted supply of bitcoin. Everyone, and I do mean everyone, states or writes that there can only ever be 21M bitcoin minted. In fact, that is in the code. But what many do not realize is that Bitcoin network developers have been rewriting the code for more than a decade. It took just one developer to change the Bitcoin code to deploy Ordinal and Inscription, which enables messages to be scripted into a sotashi (the smallest divisible denomination that is 10^{-8} of a bitcoin unit) thereby rendering them nonfungible. All of this happened without consent of the entire Bitcoin community.

Adding code for Ordinals, Inscriptions, and Runes was possible through the Taproot code introduced by Greg Maxwell in 2018 and added to the Bitcoin network code in 2021 as a soft fork. There is no voting on these changes because the Bitcoin network has no governance framework (DLT governance is discussed in Chapter 7) for voting on code changes, so it is determined primarily by the prominent developer and largest validators.

Then in 2023 Ordinal code was deployed with Runes following in 2024 (to coincide with the block subsidy halving). This code was introduced by developer Casey Rodarmor. Initially there was curiosity, intrigue, and excitement with a frenzy of users going wild calling them the NFT of Bitcoin—until users discovered the downside.

Block validators (aka miners) were consulted and agreed to support the deployment by supporting the validation of these unique satoshi units. And of course, validators agreed because they stood to profit from the deployment. And that is the downside of Ordinals that users didn't catch. Adding inscriptions (metadata) to a satoshi meant it was going to cost more to validate, and this meant higher fees on Ordinal transactions. This was a potential financial windfall for validators being able to increase transaction fees. Did it pay off?

A quick overview of the financial economics following the deployment of the Ordinal project shows that when the number of users surged to inscribe Ordinals on the Bitcoin network, it drove up the transaction fees as expected to compete for the limited byte space in a block. In fact, the data from ledger analytics evidenced that the average transaction (TX) fee on the Bitcoin network jumped from approximately \$2/TX to more than \$20/TX within a 2-day period from May 23, 2023, to May 25, 2023, which persisted. By December 2024, Bitcoin ledger analytics revealed that companies that operated validation nodes received a record \$9.97 million.

Ensuring that the sequence of events dots are connected, a developer changes the code on the Bitcoin network with no vote from users, only the approval of the validation node operators to accept the code. This resulted in users on the Bitcoin network paying just under \$10 million in additional transaction fees. This is why I again raise the need for published governance protocols by each DLT project. However, bitcoin.org makes the following statement on its website: "Then… who controls Bitcoin? Bitcoin is controlled by all Bitcoin users around the world. Developers are improving the software, but they can't force a change in the rules of the Bitcoin protocol because all users are free to choose what software they use."[9] So, Bitcoin users beware.

It is not my objective in any way to demean or degrade the foundations or developer organization hierarchy created around these projects; however, I believe there is a social and community obligation for honesty, integrity, and transparency in providing clear reporting of the governance systems ($G = D^3$) in clear language that users can understand. So, the next time an ad, white paper, or marketing piece touts a "user focused" governance system, professionals from across the industry stakeholders need to look under the hood to determine the architectural design and research the organizations and foundations associated with the project.

Now I will circle back to the 21 million bitcoin supply thesis I presented earlier on increasing the supply. First, I believe I have provided solid evidence that the Bitcoin network code can be changed as the most frequently stated objective to my thesis that I introduced to cohorts back in 2019. The base code has been augmented in the past, and more is coming in the form of several new BIPs (Bitcoin Improvement Proposal) that have been submitted in 2025. I am following one in particular that supports my thesis and that I will discuss in a moment.

Second, Bitcoin is not fulfilling the purpose of its architectural design as a digital payment system. Its present use case is hoarding bitcoin, or stockpiling if you will, as a store of value, which necessitates increasing the supply significantly, or risks users no longer having access to obtaining bitcoin. An extreme example: if there were only 1 BTC and one person owned it with no intention of selling, but nine other people would also like to own it, the outcome is that nine people go without. From a financial economic perspective, I see this as a hoarding of wealth among those who can afford to acquire large quantities of the asset and hold it, thereby creating a concentration of wealth among a few. As I laid out the data on the current distribution of BTC earlier,

---

[9] https://bitcoin.org/en/about-us#:~:text=Bitcoin is controlled by all, choose what software they use.

more than 34% is already being held by approximately 1% of users. The governance protocols are not in place on the Bitcoin network to prevent hoarders, despite the white papers, claimed objective being a payment network. So what is the solution? Increase the supply of bitcoin in the Bitcoin code.

When I first raised my hypothesis that the number of bitcoin will have to increase, the responses were you can't just change the code from 21 million, and this was rebutted as ludicrous and impossible. However, the paradigm of "only 21 million coins that can ever be minted" is false, and I'll demonstrate.

The <GetBlockSubsidy> is what calculates the maximum subsidy a validator node can claim. However, the Bitcoin code contains a constant called <MAX_MONEY>, which is set at 21 million bitcoin, but this is more of a safety check than a strict limit. All the Bitcoin code (legacy and changes) is viewable for anyone who has a desire to view it.[10] Nakamoto addressed in various writings that fees would eventually replace subsidies, and fees have already been programmed into the Bitcoin legacy code. This is essentially developers acting as a central bank, kind of like adjusting interest rates.

Given the tunnel vision and bias that many have, their conceptual idea is that a developer just changes 21 to let's say 42 with a few key strokes. However, that would break the system; it must be done more subtly through a backdoor. Well, that is exactly what is happening, and now the reveal that supports my hypothesis: it is BIP-177. It proposes replacing a "satoshi" (SAT) with "bitcoin" (BTC) as the system's base unit—by the way, the satoshi unit was named in honor of Satoshi Nakamoto. BIP-177 was introduced and authored by John Carvalho, CEO of Synonym and officially entered BIP status in December 2024.

Proponents of BIP-177, Jack Dorsey is one of those proponents, argue that the practice of representing small bitcoin values in decimals causes unnecessary confusion. Current code defines one Bitcoin as 100,000,000 satoshis, which is what makes bitcoin divisible. That goes away under this BIP. It is more like the traditional equities market: an investor cannot acquire fraction shares of a single stock; that's why mutual funds and other investment vehicles exist.

---

[10] https://github.com/bitcoin/bitcoin/tree/v25.0/.github

What BIP-177 proposes is something like a stock split. At $100,000 per BTC, 1 SAT equals $0.001. If BTC hits $1 million, 1 SAT would be worth $0.01. BIP-177 suggests adjusting the base unit to reflect the nonnegligible value of the base unit, i.e., get rid of the SAT like the US Treasury recently got rid of the penny.

Under the new rules of BIP-177, 0.0001BTC will be replaced with 10,000BTC. This method of abolishing the SAT in this manner increases the supply of BTC, like a stock split increases the number of stock shares available for distribution. Of course, as with a stock split, the value of each share drops by the ratio of the split, but now more shares are owned so the overall value of the combined shares is the same as before the split. So, now that I have established my credibility that when I was teaching that the number of bitcoin is not static and can be changed, I am vindicated and will move on to the next trend in digital assets.

Tokenization of Real-World Assets (RWA)/ In Real-Life Assets (IRLA)

Token development began a significant rise in 2018, especially in respect to tokenization of Real-World Assets (RWA) and In Real-Life Assets (IRLA) with the introduction of the Ethereum ERC-721 token standard deployed in Layer-2 contracts. Although many perceive the RWA and IRLA tokenization market as a recent development, tokenization has now been in existence for over 10 years.

To provide some context, tokenized RWAs most frequently refer to the tokenization of tangible and intangible assets such as good will, carbon credits, agricultural commodities, precious metals, real estate, securities (debt and equity), nuclear material, fiat, and other such real-world assets. IRLAs, on the other hand, are typically tokenized tangible and nontangible collectible items or items that can be tokenized to be retained as a collectible such as concert tickets, photographs (digital or print), and music. Some may recognize that some of the items in the IRLA list were popular as NFTs (non-fungible tokens), which were primarily named as NFT after the NFT ERC-721 token standard to create a tokenize many assets that were mass productions of assets that were not often multiple reproduction of the same asset as in the case of songs where thousands of

NFTs were created for the same song. So, within the category of IRLA, it can include FT (fungible tokens) as well as NFTs.

Many are not as exposed to these two categories, and as such, the majority of web search results for IRLs deliver outcomes only for RWA; however, I am starting to observe more publications including IRLAs as a distinctive group, but there are also articles that make reference to an RWA and IRLA as being synonymous. Because these terms have no basis or origin in a specific technology other than being represented by a token minted by a Layer-2 contract, it is not something to get particularly concerned over. However, I do find it provides a clean distinction between general references to a financial asset (i.e., RWA) versus a collectible asset (i.e., IRLA).

From an economic trade and market efficiency perspective, I perceive that the tokenization of RWAs, which in academia are also referred to as synthetic assets, will be the next major digital asset evolutionary event. However, tokenized RWAs predate the current trend; they just weren't called tokenized RWAs back then. But the value of tokenized RWAs, like synthetic fiat, has been around, and the initiative is permeating the focus in the development of entirely new markets and digital marketplaces where these token assets can be purchased, traded, and sold. Following on I will focus on several prominent synthetic asset groups within the RWA category.

Synthetic Fiat

J.R. Willett is credited with the idea of asset-pegged digital currencies in 2012, which is the foundation for Layer-2 tokens pegged to fiat. J.R. Willett is an early post–Bitcoin network deployment developer who published the paper titled "The Second Bitcoin Whitepaper" in 2012 and was the first to introduce the concept of a trusted development layer on an established trustless distributed network ledger. And at this point in history, the only one was the Bitcoin network ledger, as the newly chain split hard fork of Litecoin was only a few months old.

Willett's white paper hypothesizes utilizing the Bitcoin network ledger as the base procedural mainnet for deployment of a development layer for anyone to develop new digital currencies using new rules. If this rings bells and sounds like the Ethereum platform, it should be noted that

Ethereum was not the first network ledger system with a Layer-2 concept and the Ethereum founders learned from Willett's white paper and subsequent deployment. It was in 2013 that Bitcoin received its Layer-2 component with the launch of what Willett dubbed MasterCoin and later rebranded as the Omni layer in 2015.

The Omni layer functioned as a protocol layer built on top of the Bitcoin network ledger infrastructure for creating and trading custom built digital assets as well as providing an interface for the new digital currencies project to settle and record transaction metadata on the Bitcoin ledger that is distributed across the Bitcoin node network. A graphical representation of this concept looks like the graphic in Figure 8.1.

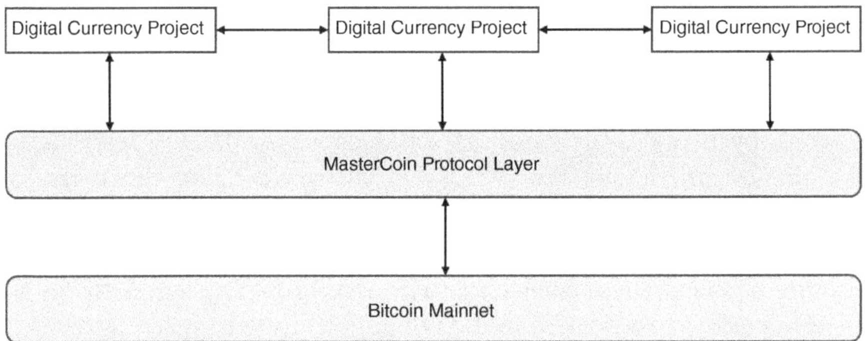

Figure 8.1   Bitcoin Node Network.

As noted in Willett's white paper, a Layer-2 solution was developed for the following primary reasons: (1) to avoid competing with the bitcoin currency and diluting its influence, (2) to avoid adoption momentum of bitcoin, (3) the Omni Layer would have the effect of increasing bitcoin's value, (4) providing interoperability, and (5) no permissions would be required from the Bitcoin network stakeholders to add this layer.

So why does any of this matter and what does it have to do with the topic of RWA fiat tokenization (synthetic fiat)? Great question, and here is the answer: The first RWA tokenization of a fiat began in 2014 with the introduction of Tether (USDT), pegged to the US dollar (USD), founded by Brock Pierce, Reeve Collins, and Craig Sellars; it was the first Layer-2 USD pegged token asset. I remember when Tether was initially launched as "Realcoin" in July 2014 but was later rebranded as "Tether" in November 2014 to avoid confusion and association as a Layer-1 coin asset.

But wait, there's more. It is notable that another USD pegged digital currency, called BitUSD, was launched in 2014 on the BitShares network mainnet (the first to adopt Delegated Proof-of-Stake as a consensus mechanism). BitShares network ledger was deployed in 2014, preceded by ProtoShares that was launched in 2013 by Larimer, was cofounded by Dan Larimer (developer of DPoS), Charles Hoskinson (cofounder of Ethereum and Cardono), and Stan Larime. The cofounders of BitShares (Larimar, Hoskinson, and Larime) authored the white paper titled "A Peer-to-Peer Polymorphic Digital Asset Exchange" published in 2013 and outlining the architecture of the BitShares concept and infrastructure.

The BitUSD digital currency was deployed as a Layer-1 coin on the BitShares distributed network ledger and attempted to compete with the Bitcoin network ledger, which is what the Omni layer wanted to avoid, as well as provide interoperability between different digital assets. However, several aspects of the BitShares network ledger provided features that the Bitcoin network did not, but I will hold back from detailing those features, as interesting as they might be. However, I will highlight what I mentioned earlier: BitUSD was a Layer-1 USD pegged coin collateralized by another digital asset; whereas Tether is a Layer-2 USD pegged token that is touted to be collateralized by USD, but both were launched in 2014.

It was in late 2013 that the term "stablecoin" started appearing in media articles. While there isn't a single person universally credited with coining the term "stablecoin," J.R. Willett is considered as coining the concept of asset-pegged digital currencies with his MasterCoin protocol white paper mentioning this concept in 2012. Today, tokenized RWA fiat pegged assets are Layer-2 contracts using certain code for token standards specified and controlled by developers of the platform on which the token contracts are deployed. These tokenized RWA fiat pegged assets are frequently and erroneously referred to as "stablecoins." It is important to note that these pegged assets fluctuate in value against their pegged assets (aka de-pegging). As noted by the Kraken centralized digital asset exchange in 2024: "Shifts in supply and demand may push the price above or below the peg, especially when combined with a lack of transparency or loss of confidence. Counterparty performance, which may be affected by financial, operational, legal, or regulatory challenges, adds further complexity."

Over the years that I have been monitoring and collecting data on trends in the adoption and use of RWAs by institutions and individuals,

2024 has continued the longer-term trend of increasing adoption. For many investment and market analysts, the major focus is on unit price and market capitalization trends; however, most of my trend analysis over the past decade has been oriented toward the use of digital assets in cybercrimes and bank failure digital asset key storage. I have focused my analytics on transaction volumes in conjunction with USD pegged tokens. USD pegged tokens are an asset that I frequently monitor along with developments in synthetic securities (L2 tokens pegged to traditional equities, debt, and derivative instruments), USD tokens, synthetic EUR tokens, and synthetic gold tokens. Tokenized RWA shares in art (physical) and real estate (retail and commercial) are a fairly niche sector from a technology perspective, but it is an area. Transaction volume trends were, and still are, important to monitor because they provided me with insights on information gathered for civil and criminal investigations and the transactional trends are significantly more descriptive than using currency-based volumes involving nefarious actors moving value through various types of L2 contracts and L3 web UI applications. But trends analysis has become more difficult since 2018, which at the time essentially included USDT in 2014, and USDC launched in 2019 in collaboration with Coinbase. At the time of writing, there are 234 synthetic fiat tokens, and these synthetic fiat tokens are collateralized by various assets such as other digital assets, fiat, short-term financial instruments, commodities, and sometimes there is no collateralization.

A brief overview of the capitalization and transaction trends of synthetic fiat tokens demonstrates the growth in adoption. At the beginning of 2021, the market cap of synthetic fiats was $62.7 billion, but the transaction volume of these synthetics was $1.1 trillion. The market cap of synthetic fiat was only $24 billion at the beginning of 2019.

At the close of March 2025, the market cap of synthetic fiat had grown to $231.7 billion while transaction volumes, at the same point of time, reached $27.6 trillion. To add perspective on the volume, for the fourth quarter of 2024, the transaction volume of the major synthetic fiat digital currencies was just under $10 trillion. However, Mastercard and Visa posted fourth quarter USD transaction volumes of approximately $6.5 trillion combined. It might be of interest to point out that more than 50% of the synthetic fiat token transactions are executed on Ethereum's Layer-2 contracts.

The phrase "pegged tokens" is a literal elucidation of a token minting by an L2 token used to represent the value of another asset. A pegged token references either a real-world asset (e.g., USD, real estate, gold, etc.) or another digital asset (e.g., bitcoin, ether, etc.). However, the colloquial term commonly used is stablecoin, but many do not grasp the imprecise nature of this term.

Their term stablecoin is not attributed to any single individual, but the concept is rooted in the ideal of why BitUSD was deployed in 2014, discussed in a prior chapter, was to provide an alternative digital asset pegged to USD as an alternative to the more volatile assets, prominently bitcoin, that were available at the time. However, the concept and application of the term stablecoin has evolved over time and is used in reference to tokens pegged to other digital assets. As an example, a number of distributed exchanges in L2|L3 use the term stablecoin to categorize wrapped tokens—a 1:1 representation of an L2 token with an L1 coin like wrapped bitcoin and wrapped ether tokens.

Given the polynomial growth in adoption, it shouldn't be surprising the big four and top tier banks are attempting to take advantage of this synthetic fiat craze. However, banks believe that policy and regulatory requirements mandate that they develop their own proprietary networks for issuing synthetic fiat, but that view has dissipated under the current administration in the United States. This has prompted JPMorgan Chase to deploy what they have dubbed their Onyx platform, and they are taking advantage of data ledger, distributed computing, distributed networking technologies, and the Layer-2 token contract tier to create options for tokenizing USD bank deposits to reduce transactional processing cost and the friction in the financial system of moving currency across the globe.

I have broken down the entire Onyx architectural framework for certain bank regulators who I have been contracted with. However, with my security clearances in mind, I don't have the freedom to provide the information in the book. What professionals should grasp is that the scope of activity not often discussed is in relationship to the proprietary permissionless DLT environment, which is quite significant in banking and financial services.

Unfortunately, these architecture DLT designs are often dismissed as illegitimate by those that hold firm to permissionless-only DTL. But per-missioned access, or lack of it, has no basis in defining DLT in architectural engineering.

The hypocrisy in this notion of the purists that insist the "only" legitimate DLT network is permissionless are willing to dismiss the centralized projects deployed on permissionless platforms and accept intermediaries that DLT is designed to eliminate in the name of interoperability and convenience to increase adoption. The Point: Do not dismiss these permissioned systems because they are a legitimate design aspect in distributed networking. Permissioned DLT use cases are as relevant to the expansion and adoption as government and regulated financial institutions are bringing unprecedented authority to custody digital assets, interact with them on permissioned DLT projects like Onyx, as well as use synthetic fiat and other digital assets within proprietary permissioned DLT networks.

Another myth to debunk is the association of the term stablecoin as an exclusive reference to a token pegged to USD. The term is actually used very loosely within the larger community of DLT platform developers and users.

It is for this reason that a colloquially manufactured term like stablecoin should not be construed to be an asset class.

In the remainder of this section, I focus on tokens pegged to fiat currencies, such as USD, EUR, and other government issued currencies, which fall into a class of "synthetic fiat." A synthetic fiat (or fiat pegged token) is a digital token purposely minted pegged to a currency issued by a government. Interestingly, synthetic fiat approaches crossing a line into forgery (aka counterfeiting). What mainstream synthetic fiats lack is the intent to deceive under the statute Title 18 USC § 471: "Whoever, with intent to defraud, falsely makes, forges, counterfeits, or alters any obligation or other security of the United States, shall be fined under this title or imprisoned not more than 20 years, or both."

I want to take the opportunity, having worked in the development of policy in digital assets with chief counsel at Treasury, to point out that I have always cautioned against the use of loose and broad terms used in DLT development communities, which typically lack clarity. Lawmakers and regulators using vague idiomatic slang terms (e.g., stablecoin and crypto) when fashioning laws and guidance often fail in fulfilling the desired outcome of setting guardrails that will provide safety for users. However, my caution has always been largely ignored as evidenced by the continued use of slang terms in current bills.

Professionals should take note of several cautionary caveats involving synthetic fiat. These assets do fluctuate in value. Although they may not be as volatile as nonpegged digital assets, they do have valuation fluctuations, and there are analytics firms that track synthetic fiat token peg volatility.

Sometimes these fluctuations are influenced by issues with their underlying collateralization. USDC, within hours following the failure of Silicon Valley Bank (SVB), lost its peg to the US dollar. It wasn't until the next day that I learned, working on bank failure with FDIC, that Circle (owner/issuer of USDC) had a uninsured depository account of $3 billion dollars that were collateral for the USDC token in circulation, which was published in a number of open-source documents.

Significant events in the synthetic fiat sector can also influence peg volatility. This was evidenced in mid-2022 with USD pegged token projects that began to see substantial volatility in pegs due to peg collapse led by Terra's UST USD pegged token. At the time, UST was one of the few that managed their collateralization with an algorithmic. The de-pegging was largely attributed by many sources to a failure in the algorithm managing the peg; however, the true culprit behind the de-pegging involved the assets collateralizing UST, which was primarily made up of the Terra governance token (LUNA). As a result, the algorithms were not able to compensate for withdrawal demands that were causing a collapse in the value of LUNA.

I trust this discussion has provided a couple of insights on the following: (1) synthetic fiat are pegged L2 tokens and not a Layer-1 mainnet coin asset as suggested by the term "stablecoin"; (2) synthetic fiat have unique volatility factors that can't be ignored or dismissed as encompassed in the term "stablecoin"; and (3) synthetic fiat are minted and modeled using code employing a type of token standard in L2 contracts, issued and controlled by companies, not decentralized as often touted (i.e., management and decision-making spread across users).

There are countless recorded instances of a synthetic fiat token issuer pulling back or censoring individuals involving transactions, or any other token for that matter.

I mentioned collateralization earlier in this section, and it is worth detailing with some additional information. There are three recognized forms of collateralization for pegged tokens: fiat collateralized, digital asset collateralized, collateralized by a commodity, or perhaps no collateralization at all (not recommended). Some sources include algorithms as a category of collateralized pegged tokens. One such example is: "Algorithmic stablecoins are a unique breed, distinct from the others as they do not rely on collateral. Instead, they use algorithms and smart contracts."

This is a very inaccurate statement because algorithms in computer science are defined as a set of well-defined instructions designed to solve a particular problem or perform a specific task. And that is what algorithms do in collateralized pegged tokens. They programmatically manage the collateralized assets to ensure the pegged token maintains the specified peg. With the introduction of Augmented Narrow Intelligence AI bots, there are alternatives to pure programmed algorithms that included AI or human managed supported by AI analytics. Regardless, using an algorithm to maintain the peg is not in any way a method of collateralization, it is a method of managing the pool of assets that collateralize the pegged token.

Researching the assets collateralizing the pegged token and how the assets are managed in maintaining the peg are both important facets for professionals to research.

I will wrap up the topic of synthetic fiat by analyzing some of the provisions in the proposed US Congressional legislation on "stablecoins."[11]

This first point is that there is no language in the bill that requires an L2 contract developer of a pegged token to provide the level of clarity or disclosures on proof of reserve audits, types of algorithms (if any), income generated from financial instruments used to collateralize the pegged token, a reporting requirement or framework for immediately reporting of a de-pegging event as well as a public disclosure notice, or a mandate for a cybersecurity review prior to deployment of the pegged token contract and regular subsequent security reviews. All of these should be minimum requirements specified in the bill.

Second, as discussed previously, the term "stablecoin" is lossely applied to many types of wrapped versions in the DLT developer and user communities. There are 575 instances of the use of the term stablecoin in the bill, and the phrase repeatedly used throughout the bill in every occurrence with stablecoin is "payment stablecoins," which further broadens

---

[11] Andrew Olmen et al. "Congress Moves Forward on Stablecoin Legislation: The US Senate Banking Committee Approves the GENIUS Bill." Mayer | Brown. March 17, 2025. https://www.mayerbrown.com/en/insights/publications/2025/03/congress-moves-forward-on-stablecoin-legislation-the-us-senate-banking-committee-approves-the-genius-act

the use of the term stablecoin and introduces ambiguity about the technology that can be used to deploy what Congress has termed a "payment stablecoin." In other words, a "payment stablecoin" can be deployed within a VR gaming platform outside of a DLT architected platform. But that goes back to my earlier comment that the term "stablecoin" needs to be retired.

In addition, the proposed legislation requires issuers to maintain reserves backing their payment stablecoins on at least a 1:1 basis with overcollateralization allowed. Acceptable reserves would include US coins and currency, deposits with Federal Reserve Banks, demand deposits at insured depository institutions, Treasury bills, notes, or bonds with a maturity of 93 days or less, certain repurchase agreements, reverse repurchase agreements, and money market funds. Reserves could be tokenized or held in their "natural" form according to the current version of the bill at the time of writing.

As a financial economist, this has the potential to create what I hypothesized in one of my post-doctoral papers where I address "digital runs" in reference to tokenizing gold assets as an alternative currency to government issued currency (e.g., USD or EUR). My research focused on the impact on the supply-demand implication of USD in circulation in the face of an alternative currency. Tokenized gold, as a tokenized RWA, collateralized by gold acquired and held by a third-party, could essentially replace the USD as a functional currency choice. This bill does not allow for gold as collateral, but it does take currency, short-term bonds, and notes out of circulation.

A digital run can result in a bank run. For those not familiar, and I realize I am dating myself, a bank run is when customers of a bank or financial institution withdraw their USD deposits en masse. And as more people withdraw their deposits, the probability of bank default increases, which prompts fears resulting in more people withdrawing their bank deposits.

A digital run involves a bank run on limited fiat resources driven by alternative currency options. Without going deep into the economic theory, the fundamental economic principle of limited currency resources, or "scarcity," means that resources are finite while human wants and needs are potentially infinite, forcing choices and trade-offs in resource allocation. Thus, alternative currency demand for synthetic USD pegged token assets (i.e., stablecoin in the legislation) can force a significant demand for USD fiat in exchange for synthetic USD prompting bank customers to withdraw USD deposits, or other types of USD accounts held at a financial institution. This action essentially decreases the supply of USD in circulation and is used to acquire, what the bill terms payment stablecoins. The increase of payment stablecoins in circulation requires collateral to be increased and collateral has to be held at a financial institution in a ratio of at least 1:1. The difference is that deposits at a financial institution have a less than 1:1 reserve requirement for normal deposits. Currently, the reserve requirement on US banks is set at 0.0% as of February 2025. This change was made following a reduction to 0% effective March 26, 2020, which eliminated reserve requirements for all depository institutions.

Anything above a bank's reserves is generally available for lending to small businesses, issuing mortgages for purchases of homes, etc. And the loan is repaid, with interest, to the financial institution (i.e., investments). This is why banks are often referred to as "currency creators," because they expand the supply of currency in circulation by using deposits of customers to make loans to other customers, which then become part of the overall money supply.

However, collateral deposit of payment tokens would likely not be available for lending. By allowing a financial institution to lend collateral, it would risk creating a de-pegging scenario—not enough USD to cover requests for liquidation of a payment token. This is basically what happened to UST. And at the same time, USD is taken out of circulation because it is no longer available for lending, so the supply of USD declines (tied up in collateral accounts of payment stablecoin projects). This will likely impact the tightening of lending and increase long-term interest rates. There are a number of economic consequences that are real and varied. I have yet to see any economic models on the impact in the face of demand for an alternative currency that ties up deposits presented by congressional members to date as this bill is pushed through the Senate. I will note that consumer spending is not impacted; it involves deposits and lending by financial institutions.

The GENIUS Act does state that "It shall be unlawful to represent that payment stablecoins are backed by the full faith and credit of the United States, guaranteed by the United States Government, or subject to Federal deposit insurance or Federal share insurance." However, the payment stablecoin tokens are not insured, and there is no provision in the bill that requires a payment stablecoin token issuer to secure adequate insurance. I am speculating that a payment stablecoin issuer would indemnify the holder with funds out of the collateral deposit account, but the bill does not specify and should be a required disclosure on how a payment stablecoin token issuer would indemnify a holder who had their tokens stolen while stored on the issuer's platform. If the token is held in custody by a CEX, then it would fall to the intermediary exchange, but if the custodian is a bank, then there are no insurance options for indemnification.

I was engaged with FDIC specifically related to digital asset and DLT at banks before and during the record-setting bank failures in 2023. In fact, I forecasted a significant rise of first quarter 2025 bank failures in an October 2022 report—6 months before the Silvergate Bank self-liquidation in March 2023. This event sparked by a massive run on the bank, with customers withdrawing $8.1 billion in just one quarter in response to the FTX collapse.

Factors that I cited in October 2022 as indicators of potential bank failures involved issues involving two large centralized digital asset exchanges. The first red flag indicator for a possible bank failure would come if there were to be a major disruption in FTX operation. FTX, launched in mid-2019, had rapidly risen to dominance as the No. 3 centralized digital asset exchange by exchange volume by 2022 and was being run by a small group of 30-somethings, inexperienced adults spending a lot of time meeting with prominent members of Congress and contributing significant amounts of cash to party campaigns. In addition, Binance held a large portion ($2.1 billion) of FTX's utility token (FTT) in a transaction for FTX to buy back its equity holding from Binance. In a dispute between FTX and Binance, Binance was threating to sell off its holding of FTT, which would likely plummet FTX in bankruptcy. Finally, there had been some significant losses suffered in 2022 by Alameda Research, a sibling company of FTX and trading firm, and Sam Bankman-Fried was serving as CEO of both.

The second red flag indicator came from Binance, the No. 1 global centralized digital asset exchange, and was completely separate from the feud with FTX. Binance was named in a US Securities and Exchange Commission (SEC) complaint of 13 charges filed on June 5, 2023, with the US District Court for the District of Columbia, demanding a jury trial. The SEC's filing raised concerns about the audit of Binance. US and highlighted difficulties in ensuring the company was fully collateralized. The filing further alleged that Binance had used BAM Trading Services, the entity managing Binance.US, for unlawful purposes.

What do these bank failure red flags that I identified have to do with synthetic USD? Banks were holding billions of dollars of collateral reserves of USD pegged tokens. In the case of FTX, addresses attributed to Alameda's known wallets were the largest pegged token depositors and sources of liquidity to all FTX's known wallet addresses, accounting for 10% of Tether transfers and 30% of USDC transfers on the exchange. As to Binance, the Binance USD (BUSD) USD pegged tokens were being issued by Paxos on behalf of Binance. In November 2022, BUSD had reaching a peak market capitalization of $23.5 billion. In January 2023, Bloomberg reported that the BUSD peg "was often undercollateralized between 2020 and 2021." As a result, BUSD's market cap experienced a severe decline, and market cap dropped by $3.8 billion by June 2023. The market cap decline was further fueled by a regulatory intervention by the New York Department of Financial Services (NYDFS) directive that directed Paxos to cease minting new USD-pegged BUSD tokens. The impact was an abrupt shock that caused the circulating supply to shrink from $16.1 billion to $12.7 billion.

As operations began to fall apart at FTX and Binance in 2022, it led to massive withdrawals from Silvergate Bank, culminating in self-liquidation in March 2023, as noted previously. But with the initiation of the FTX fraud prosecution moving into 2023 and the continued regulatory pressure and subsequent SEC prosecution filings against Binance and other centralized exchanges (e.g., Coinbase and Ripple Labs), there would be more bank-related issues during 2023. During 2023, there were five bank failures, including the notable failures of Silicon Valley Bank, Signature Bank, and First Republic Bank, which were among the largest in US history. The complete list and time of 2023 bank failures are as follows:

- Silicon Valley Bank (SVB): Failed on March 10, 2023
- Signature Bank: Failed on March 12, 2023
- First Republic Bank: Failed on May 1, 2023
- Heartland Tri-State Bank: Failed on July 28, 2023
- Citizens Bank: Failed on November 3, 2023

I want to draw attention to the failure of SVB, which was closed March 9, 2023, by the California Department of Financial Protection and Innovation and turned over to the FDIC. The closure resulted from a bank run triggered by concerns of financial stability. This marked the second-largest bank failure in the United States since the collapse of Washington Mutual in 2008. While SVB did not have custody of any digital asset keys, SVB banked several prominent digital asset companies. There was $3 billion of uninsured deposits at SBV that constituted a portion of the reserve funds for a major USD pegged token issuer.

Concerns about fractional reserves at the bank prompted investors to divest their holding to the USD pegged token and result in a de-pegging of the pegged token currency until the FDIC was subsequently able to provide assurances for all SVB deposits. This assurance to protect all SVB depositors, including those with uninsured amounts like the collateral of the pegged token issuer, the FDIC, along with the Treasury and Federal Reserve, invoked a "systemic risk exception" and transferred all deposits, both insured and uninsured, to a newly created bridge bank, ensuring that all depositors would be made whole. While there has been some research that has explored the systemic risks of USD pegged tokens (payment stablecoin by the bill) and their reliance on traditional banking, there has been limited focus on how banking sector shocks affect digital asset markets.

The March 11, 2023, collapse of SVB highlighted the critical dependence of USD pegged tokens on the traditional US banking system for their reserves and highlights the intensifying systemic risk within the financial landscape and synthetic token currencies.

I will simply wrap up noting that I have only scratched the surface of why this is not smart legislation. Contributions to legislation need to be inclusive of academic technologists and digital asset economists with real-world experience on how the RWA synthetic is capable of threatening the economic and financial security of a country. And the voices included in regulatory discussions need to go beyond the enthusiastic lobbyist with cash to contribute to campaigns, or industry heads that have made significant fortunes as intermediaries in a DLT that is designed to eliminate intermediaries. Here again is a perfect opportunity to advocate for both a Digital Asset SRO as well as a DLT infrastructure SRO to reduce the repeated use of the paradoxical and contradictory conflict of interest advisory to a legislative body that clearly has inadequate information or knowledge about DLT and digital asset, much less involving the regulation of AI technologies and the growing quantum wave that is coming. Legislators and administrators need less advice from conflicted individuals and special interest.

Synthetic Securities

To continue with tokenization of RWAs, I will transition to securities with a detailed focus on equities in the securities market and somewhat more limited coverage in respect to debt securities. I began lecturing and teaching on the RWA tokenization of securities in 2017, and one of my first speaking engagements on the topic was for the Blockchain Council in a 2019 session addressing RWA tokenization.

Synthetic equities, the tokenization of real-world shares of publicly traded companies on traditional market exchanges, are gaining the attention of investors—digital asset investors and tradition stock investors. It should be of interest to most that there are currently 80 synthetic RWA synthetic equities that have tokenized shares of Tesla, Alibaba, Amazon, Pfizer, Moderna, Beyond Meat, and PayPal, just as some examples.

The RWA tokenized synthetic equities offerings have been growing significantly over the past 8 years, although this growth has been very much under the radar of regulators and legislators. While politicians have been particularly focused on synthetic fiat, tokenized financial assets, or synthetic securities, have moved from pilot to at-scale deployment unnoticed with adoption yet to be widespread. The attraction for many is the unregulated component, of course. During this quiet phase of deployment, traditional financial institutions have been putting infrastructure and capabilities in place right under the nose of regulators and legislators who do not see the explosion of synthetic securities coming because they are certainly not currently organized by providing relevant supervision or proposed regulations to guide developers in configuring rules.

Synthetic securities are primarily gaining momentum due to the recognized efficiencies of cost and established distributed network ledger environments that are converging the continuing developments in Type-1 ANI (Artificial Narrow Intelligence), AI in the form of LLMs (Large Language Models), and agentic environments, i.e., systems that can act autonomously to make decisions and take actions to achieve specific goals without constant human intervention, which eliminates the need to train a human employee on how to use a separate desktop deployment of agent bot software like Salesforce, Chat, DeepSeek, etc. This is a really high-level and an oversimplification of the sophistication it takes to integrate these processes and systems. I am well versed in it, and I have been advising on a couple of such projects for more than a year now, but the overarching principle is clear—the traditional financial market industry complex is antiquating the coming wave by integrating the technology. But with this enhanced sophistication of converging ANI agents with distributed network data ledger technology, the adoption of synthetic equity trading is the next natural step in the evolution in the securities industry. Backtracking to synthetic fiat for a moment, margin accounts and purchasing fiat securities becomes a seamless integrated process alongside settlement of fiat security acquisitions. Do you see the future? Well, it is here in the present with early developments beginning in 2020.

So, is all of this really significant? When reviewing 2024 data on the USD valuation of the global equities market, of which the United States makes 60%, there is $124 trillion invested in equities globally. From my perspective, this is significant, indicating that there is a massive market in which synthetic securities can participate to introduce efficiencies that industry participants are requesting.

Diving a little deeper into the existing market environment where synthetic assets live, the entire globalized L2 contract and L3 web interfacing of those contracts that are oriented toward financial services produced $20.48 billion based on the L2|L3 analytics from Grand View Research, and they project the Compound Annual Growth Rate (CAGR) to be 53.7% from 2025 to 2030. Business Research Insights reported in a March 2025 analysis and forecast that synthetic securities (debt and equity) trading in 2024 was $5.6 billion. Synthetic equities represent nearly 60% of that value. And a McKinsey estimate suggests that the market capitalization across asset classes could reach $2 trillion by 2023, excluding asset classes such L1 assets (e.g., Bitcoin (BTC), ether (ETH), and other Layer 1 assets) and synthetic fiat assets (e.g., USDT, USDC, and other fiat pegged token assets).

It is important to bring some attention to the distinction in the exchange environments in which traditional and synthetic equities are traded. So, with that primer, traditional shares of publicly traded companies are exchanged on established market exchanges like the NASDAQ,

NYSE, London Stock Exchange, Shanghai Stock Exchange, KOSDAQ, Canadian Securities Exchange, or any other exchange out of the approximately 80 different exchanges established in countries globally. And each exchange has its own set of rules created under the established laws of the country in which the exchange is located.

And on the flip side, synthetic equities or stocks are very different from traditional exchanges, and they are often outside the regulatory control of a country's securities regulators; however, as I outlined the technology in prior chapters involving the union between Layer-2 contract|Layer-3 application web interfacing components. As part of merging contracts with web interfaces, there are often third-parties that are engaged to provide some legitimacy on the handling of the traditional shares. For example, an RWA tokenized synthetic equity for Amazon (AMZN) issued by FTX makes the disclosure that CM-Equity is the custodian of the shares of Amazon that collateralize the synthetic shares. CM-Equity is regulated under German securities laws as a financial institution permitted to custody the traditional shares. However, CM-Equity is outside of the L2|L3 exchange platform for trading the synthetic shares, and there is no mention of FTX being licensed or regulated under the securities laws of any country. Hence, trading of the synthetic shares, as well as the DEXs, continues to be largely unregulated by any standard. Some of the top L2|L3 synthetic stock and stock derivatives trading platforms include Synthetix (SNK) and SytetixV2, dYdX, Morror, Universal Market Access (UMA), Injective, and BarnBridge.

The projects I listed previously typically fall under the categorical heading of a DEX. To provide a little color and backdrop on the origin of DEXs, they exist as a system of exchange operation that serves the DeFi (Decentralized Finance) community, which is an esoterically created community group (i.e., something that is understood or intended to be understood by only a few people, especially those with specialized knowledge or interest) within the L2|L3 distributed network ledger technologies stack.

While there isn't one definitive person who "coined" the term DEX or decentralized exchange, the concept and its evolution are linked to the deployment of the Ethereum developer enterprise platform and emerged alongside Ethereum's L2 developer intrigue that pulled in many from the web developer community. And so began a significant deployment of L2 contracts of new digital exchange structures outside of the centralized exchanges that had become significant influences as intermediaries in the exchange of digital assets.

The term DeFi (short for decentralized finance) was coined in an August 2018 Telegram chat among Ethereum developers and entrepreneurs, including Inje Yeo of Set Protocol, Blake Henderson of 0x, and Brendan Forster of Dharma, as they discussed a new movement of open financial applications built on Ethereum. While the term and broader concept of DeFi emerged in 2018, the underlying projects that would eventually form the basis of DeFi had their roots in Ethereum launched in 2015 as centralized projects. Around 2016–2017, platforms like IDEX, EtherDelta, and ForkDelta began operating, representing the first generation of these types of exchanges. DEXs were needed by the community in order to operate outside the regimented structure of CEXs.

The early centralized bitcoin exchanges were the first to be launched and BitcoinMarket.com was deployed in 2010. It was founded by Dustin Dollar under the pseudonym of "dwdollar," in the same vein as the lead Bitcoin payment network developer, but without the anonymity, proposed the concept on Bicointalk web forum (founded by Nakamoto), which was a site for developers and advanced Bitcoin users in the Bitcoin community to share ideas. I collected dozens of images from that forum as I was actively gathering data to support my hypothesis that Bitcoin was not "funny money," as it was often described, to supervisors and counsel within the federal government. A rather unorthodox launch for a centralized exchange was Mt. Gox. Originally launched in 2010 as Mt. Gox (Magic: The Gathering Online Exchange) and founded by Jed McCaleband as a platform for trading cards, it was sold to Mark Karpeles in 2011 and quickly pivoted by converting it into a Bitcoin exchange.

The growth of centralized exchanges began to increase in 2011 and into 2012 with the founding of Kraken in 2011; it didn't launch until 2013, founded by Jesse Powell (a consultant for Mt. Gox with prior experience at Lewt MMORPG gaming), Thanh Luu (previously a software engineer at Citrix Systems), and Michael Gronager (previously managing international research infrastructure projects and later a cofounder of Chainalysis). In 2012, Frederick Ehrsam (a former foreign exchange trader at Goldman Sachs) and Brian Armstrong (a former Airbnb engineer) cofounded Coinbase. It is reported that the two met on the Bitcoin subreddit forum. The name Coinbase comes from the term "coinbase transaction," which is the first transaction in a block displaying the address that the block subsidy is issued to. And there were many more CEX launches in the coming years that culminated in the development and adoption of a new exchange format that came about with the rise of the Ethereum developer enterprise platform in 2015. In 2016, existing P2P OTC (over-the-counter) platforms were under attack by regulators around the globe and were losing market share to the massive infrastructure being created through investor cash coming into CEXs that were taking over the exchange system. One of the early P2P exchanges like VirWoX started in 2007, that had adapted from only existing as an exchange of virtual currencies and gaming assets (not connected to digital assets in distributed network ledger) in MMORPG and VR, began to include Bitcoin, a distributed network ledger asset, on its exchange platform. But that all ended in 2019 under significant regulatory authority to cease operations. Other early P2P OTC Bitcoin exchanges were LocalBitcoins, LocalCoinSwap, OTCBTC, and many others. But that is all in the past, so let's return to the present.

The primary reason for going through the history of exchange structures relating to distributed network ledger assets is that there is a trending change in how tokenized RWAs will be exchanged and traded. The tokenization hype in light of the reality of settlement is posing a barrier to development in this next generation marketplace. Even though RWA tokenization is being called the next trillion-dollar market in finance in equities, dept, and private equity by BlackRock, JPMorgan, and other major financial institutions, there is still a settlement issue. And while the L2 of the distributed network ledger technologies stack provides tokenization accessibility, it doesn't solve institutional settlement problems.

RWAs are being tokenized on multiple L2 platforms and exchanges, which include permissionless as well as proprietary permissioned infrastructure. This creates fragmented liquidity pools and inefficient settlement processes, and for institutional use cases, this tends to be a deal breaker. But it never fails as I conduct ongoing research on architectural engineering and economic application developments in rapidly evolving technologies like AI, quantum cryptography and computing, XR, and distributed network ledger technologies and begin to inform internal stakeholders about these developments, some new development gets introduced. So, after I completed the explanation on the current structures and economic state discussing the lack of integration in the exchange structure within the distributed network ledger exchange framework, Binance announced on March 30, 2025 that its platform is debuting a new infrastructure component that allows its customers to exchange the cryptographic keys custodied in Binance wallets (a CEX) to execute exchanges on DEXs, which removes the complex process of needing to send asset keys through vulnerable bridging contracts or execute key transfers to a DEX wallet. This definitely has the ability to change the landscape of what I previously wrote about fragmentation in the digital asset token contract mint and exchange system; however, until I have had the opportunity to conduct research and analysis around the architectural structure to determine compliance and cybersecurity vulnerabilities, it should be approached with caution. So, as a professor in this technology space, I am constantly emphasizing and cautioning students about thinking they know everything. Because, just about the time you think you know everything about something and self-impose the title "expert" upon yourself, the technology changes. And it is with this example of technology constantly and rapidly changing, I extend this cautionary warning to professionals that interact with technology because I encounter so many entrepreneurs, attorneys, bankers, podcasters, bloggers, and so on who always claim to be experts but are only spreading misinformation about something they read from some other source—i.e., most legitimate sources define an expert in technology as a person who has a thorough understanding of the underlying principles, technologies, and methodologies with the capacity to provide original contributions to their area of technology expertise. If more people calling themselves an expert in a technology followed this definition, there would be far fewer fake "experts" spreading misinformation and a more factually based analysis about currently hyped technologies.

In these exchange structures in various groupings that have been developed and introduced over the past 15 years, there have been (and continue to be) ethical issues, misrepresentations, and a serious lack of transparency intrinsic in third-party intermediary platforms. As I've articulated in other chapters, it is worth expanding on the reference to "decentralized" in the context of DEX and DeFi. It is because these platforms are clearly owned and controlled by the developers who architected and built the L2 contract and L3 application web interface, if there is an L3 interface. Additionally, the developers/founders/cofounders also benefit from the revenues generated, and many of these projects introduce a utility or governance contract token generated in association with the project that allows the developers/founder/cofounder the ability to further monetize and benefit from the revenues generated by the project.

I want to emphasize that there is absolutely nothing unethical about monetizing an idea and being enriched from revenues of a legitimate project, but marketing and promoting it under the guise of it being decentralized is where the harm is done. If one conducts a search for the definition of the term DEX, the most common output I received is "a platform where users can trade cryptocurrencies directly with each other without a central authority or intermediary." I trust by now that readers realize that developers act as intermediaries as they interact with the contract to increase or lower fees; developers integrate third-party oracles into the contract to obtain pricing information from external sources,[12] developers create foundations around the DEX project to give the appearance of decentralization but continue to exercise control over the contract and third-party interactions. The list goes on that clearly contradicts the principle of decentralization as measure by any reasonable standard. However, in presenting alternatives to a potential negative, as I have in previous chapters, these projects provide personal autonomy through peer-to-peer interaction as well as the much-needed democratization (i.e., the action of making something accessible to everyone) in respect to exchange markets that are often closed in the traditional marketplace—directly or indirectly. So, by simply replacing "decentralized" with "democratized," the result is an honest rendering of the term DEX as Democratized Exchange and an ethical representation of projects in the L2/L3 technology stack by providing access to everyone. I will also add a cautionary note about the DEX terminology related to L2 contracts that should not be confused with DEX, DEXed, or DEXing, which means to take dangerously large amounts of OTC cough suppressants containing dextromethorphan in an effort to get high.

It is important to grasp that a synthetic version of RWAs goes well beyond financial securities and fiat. Synthetic tokenization is a growing trend that is gaining traction in the commercial real estate market. And I will note that I have been involved with research organizations that

---

[12] NOTE: Oracles are often used by cybercriminals to execute pricing exploits within the contract.

have issued reports on the tokenization of the agricultural commodities market and carbon credit market. In 2024, I completed a research project supporting a study being conducted by a nuclear research arm of a firm where I provided technical expertise. I assisted them with the technology methods and benefits of tokenizing elements of spent and unspent nuclear waste, supporting national security on behalf of many countries with concerns of nuclear proliferation capabilities of rogue countries. Being able to tokenize nuclear material introduces a new level of global transparency into the use and disposition of nuclear material use and disposal, especially with the rise of interest in nuclear electric generation. And the concept of grid management and power distribution is the logical next step in the tokenizing units of power and distributed networks for grid distribution.

I want to make reference to my use of the phrase "asset class." It is for this reason that I have provided a taxonomical, topological, and typological categorization, to provide a framework to classify digital assets in logical categories that allows for a consistent and decipherable characterization of assets by risk and technology employed rather than just "crypto as an asset" class. In addition, it creates a backdrop to presenting a rousing sophistication and quantifiable truthfulness when discussing digital asset risk attributes in the DLT environment, which is currently lacking. My presentation of an advanced asset class categorization during one of my postdoctoral academic exercises a number of years ago is quite divergent and disruptive for the sector stakeholders that are holding to the colloquial misrepresentation of the term "crypto" or "cryptoverse" for these assets. But when brilliantly placing them into corresponding and logical classes, digital assets are provided with a context of respect for these digital assets that are born out of some very sophisticated convergent technologies. In simpler terms: Digital assets have risk classes, and what is frequently lumped into a characterless category of "crypto" or "cryptocurrency" is missing the underlying risk attributes that have no basis in cryptography. And the next section will add context to this.

Layer-2 Contract Meme Tokens and Layer-3 Project Development

Meme tokens, often incorrectly referred to as memecoins, are minted using token standards from various standards based on the network ledger on which the meme token is being minted. As most are minted on the Ethereum platform, the ERC-20 token standard, or any number of other ERC L2 token standards available, are effectively financializing social trends within the attention economy. The attention economy is a concept that refers to the economic and social value placed on people's attention and engagement in the context of information and media consumption by combining the viral nature of the internet culture and memes with an economic value mechanism. These meme tokens, often created as satire or leveraging the popularity of prominent figures or events, are created to monetize through community engagement and social media buzz rather than traditional economic fundamentals.

Various platforms have launching platforms to enable the average user to create a token and effectively financially benefit from the followers in a social community or currently trending status. While these tokens have long been considered to be lacking in any long-term value, they have, over time, proven to be sticky with respect to continuing community growth and growth of the various social trends.

With coins like Dogecoin and tokens like Shiba Inu holding a multi-billion USD market cap for many years now (and most recently with President Trump officially launching his own memetoken), the market has made it clear memecoins are not going away. We saw a similar trend in 2021 with NFTs. From this point once again, it will be interesting to see other creative ways in which industry innovates on these existing financialization mechanisms.

The digital asset space is poised for a transformative year in 2025, driven by these five key trends. As they unfold, the digital asset space will likely see increased regulation, innovation, and broader adoption, making 2025 a pivotal year for both industry participants and those looking to enter this space.

The "Degen Casino Model" or "PvP KOL degen casino" refers to a high-risk, speculative market ecology where a small percentage of users profit, while the vast majority lose money, often seen as a "best product-market fit" by some, despite the high risk. This is a trend that started a number of years ago on Ethereum's platform L2/L3 stack segment, and the trend, led by what I will simply refer to as unethical actors, is continuing to exploit the Layer-2 of many network ledger platforms. From a cybercrimes and fraud perspective, this is something that I have been raising the alarm about since early 2023, and until recently (2025), there has been no actual discussion in the developer space about curbing this trend, which has been escalating.

When I reference the involvement of developers in the "degen" L2 development movement as unethical actors, I believe I owe an explain for my reasoning behind issuing this label. This begins with the PvP KOL. In the area of token developers, KOL stands for "Key Opinion Leader" referring to their status as prominent figures who are respected for their influence in the community (this doesn't mean the influencer has any level of expertise in any area of technology that has enabled their rise to prominence). Many of the true experts are frequently silenced, cancelled, or censored. For curious readers, there is a surface internet website with the URL KOLmafia. KOLs are described on "InfluencerMarketingHub" for their marketing prowess: "KOL marketing only exists because many people trust key opinion leaders. KOLs make recommendations on their websites, video channels, or in their social statuses. These may be explicit, for example, when a KOL recommends a particular product or implicit, for instance, where people see a KOL using a product in action. People who respect the KOL trust them. They either believe their words when they make recommendations or their actions when they use a product."

Next is PvP, which is short for "Player-versus-Player." In the context of video games, PvP is about a type of multiplayer interactive competition or conflict gameplay where human players compete against each other rather than against the game's programmed environment, which sometimes includes AI controlling the direction of gameplay opponents. As such, PvP is distinguishable from Player-versus-Environment (PvE) and Player-versus-Computer (PvC).

To wrap up this this section on meme-token development is to highlight what is happening by way of an example. I am making no implications of nefarious activity, but it is a fascinating case study into the "degen casino model" movement in Layer-2 development platforms.

"Degen" is borrowed from gambling vernacular, where "degenerate" gamblers are known for their reckless betting habits. Within the traditional financial market, "Degen Trading" refers to a style of financial trading characterized by extremely high-risk and speculative strategies. This phrase has carried over into the Layer-2 digital asset trading markets, and this approach has gained notoriety for its potential to yield significant returns. Of course, it is accompanied by an unsavory reputation for a heightened risk of substantial losses. Combining the elements I laid out earlier, the "PvP KOL degen casino" model refers to a high-risk, speculative market ecology where a small percentage of users profit, while the vast majority lose money, often seen as a "best product-market fit" by some despite the high risk. In the end, the only consistent winners are the developers and KOLs because the L2 contract/L3 web interface project is promoted as decentralized where transactions take place on a transparent blockchain ledger. I trust it is now understood that these projects are under the central control of the developers (not decentralized) with no interest in providing decision-making privileges to users. And the transactions are typically obfuscated through Layer-2 contracts and are transmitted to the mainnet layer, which has a hash with no L1 transparency.

As an example of how complex many of these projects become for a professional unwind, I will walk through a degen project currently under the label of Degen Chain. It was originally launched in January 2024 as DEGEN, an ERC-20 meme token, used primarily within the Farcaster Degen channel to reward active participants. As a side note for those not familiar with Farcaster, it is a social media platform built on Ethereum and aims to empower users with control over their data and foster a more open community-driven social network, distinct from traditional platforms.

Recently, DEGEN has expanded its utility token infrastructure and launched the Degen Chain. And it is worth taking the time to break this down because a casual passing note of the Degan Chain development would be malpractice on my part as a Certified Fraud Examiner (CFE) to not explain the intricacies behind this platform.

Degen Chain is described by many articles as a Layer-3 (L3) blockchain and open-source decentralized social network. But to analyze the infrastructure of Degen Chain, it begins with the deployment of the project on Arbitrum Orbit, an L2 data chain development environment. Arbitrum Orbit is built as a child chain project on the Ethereum platform. I discussed child chains as alternative architectural designs for transaction scaling in an earlier chapter, so I am not going to pontificate on the nuances of child chains here. But the point is that child chain transactions are obfuscated when they are transmitted to the L1 mainnet, resulting in a significant lack of transparency. But Degen Chain infrastructure doesn't end there.

The transactions executed on Degen Chain, which is deployed on Arbitrum Orbit, are processed and settled on Coinbase's Base rollup application that further obfuscates the transaction data. The marketing and promotional information provided on Degen Chain touts that it is built on the Coinbase Base "blockchain"; however, the Coinbase Base utilizes the Optimism Superchain framework to construct a side chain (an L2 structure), all of which resides on the OP Stack, which is built on Ethereum's L2 operating as an L2 modular development platform for building rollups that aid in Ethereum transaction scaling. It is a lot more complex than what is realized, and unlike what the marketing and promotional information promises in calling Coinbase Base a "blockchain." While rollups and side chains utilize data blocking and hashing algorithms, they are Layer-2 constructs and rely on the distributed network ledger infrastructure of the Layer-1 mainnet that the Layer-2 is built on top of. So, the seemingly simplistic "blockchain" concept that everyone believes they grasp is yet another example on the lack of disclosure of the complex and reliant architectural frameworks that exist and are hidden through the use of oversimplistic terminology. This can be daunting for a professional trying to make decisions based on misleading web content. I outline rollup and side chain design in an earlier chapter, and it may warrant reviewing that portion as a review. But wait, there is more regarding Degen Chain.

Degen Chain utilizes AnyTrust for data availability. What does that mean in terms of data ledgers and data storage? AnyTrust is an Arbitrum application that is similar to a rollup in regard to data processing. However, a rollup and AnyTrust differ in that a rollup, after hashing a grouping of transaction data, submits the rollup hash to be included in the L1 mainnet ledger. But AnyTrust, on the flip side, stores and manages data through a permissioned set of parties responsible for enforcing data availability known as the Data Availability Committee (DAC), which does not provide the transaction data to the Ethereum platform transaction ledger. And while this provides a more fluid, faster data access and a lower transaction fee method of data interaction, all of the transaction data is off-ledger. These are integrated Layer-2 and off-ledger connected transaction interactions. But that is not the end. Degen deploys two types of Layer-2 bridging, shown on their bridge platform as the "Degen Chain Bridge" and "Relay Bridge," which is accessible at the time of writing through the Bridge Platform (https://bridge.degen.tips/).

Bridging for Degen Chain is accomplished using third-parties. One third-party used by Degen Chain is Decent (Nick Soman is founder and CEO). Decent is a no-code tool that employs simple APIs to build network transaction bridging. And not only is it an all-in-one developer platform for network transaction bridging, it enables transactions between L2 contracts and L3 DApp UIs. Decent aims to solve liquidity fragmentation issues in a simple, one-click UX (User Experience), which is exactly what Decent does for Degen Chain, and introduces another third-party application. Decent LayerZero (Bryan Pellegrino is cofounder and CEO) is an L2 contract that provides message verification and execution between contracts on behalf of supported networks to facilitate bridge swaps between assets.

But what about the Degen Chain Layer-3 web3.js interface? This is a valid question since Degen Chain is marketed as being designed with a Layer-3 blockchain architecture to facilitate movement of digital assets, support meme-token and community-driven projects, and fosters high-volume applications like gaming and distributed social media platforms across Web3 applications. I have no doubt that the reference to "Layer-3 blockchain" is to promote an idea of having some unique and advanced technology but is just more marketing hype. In fact, the only apparent technology connection that Degen Chain has in Layer-3 (i.e., the Application Layer of the Distributed Network Ledger Technology stack) is a third-party engagement with the BinaX UBT (Universal Token Bridge) that serves as a gateway between Layer-2 Decent with Layer-3 applications. And BinaX UTB integrates with Decent, mentioned previously, to bridge digital assets for swapping on the BinaX L3 application, which also interfaces with the LayerZero AMB (Arbitrary Message Bridge) that allows other bridges to access the Degen canonical bridge.

Lastly, Degen Chain can be accessed using a Degen Wallet. However, through another third-party engagement, Degen Chain can also be accessed through OKX Wallet that provides access to more than 85 different distributed network ledger platforms. This effectively provides another exchange point for conversion between digital assets.

And this is where fraud frequently begins—with the myth of "decentralized" L2 contracts. To make an important distinction, while the L2 contract platform is operating on top of an L1 supported distributed node network that in effect provides democratized access to L2 contracts, L2 contracts are not decentralized; in fact, they are highly centralized where the controlling individuals or entity can censor, divert, shut down operations, and take profit from the operations of the L2 contract. It is through this breakdown of the complex design framework of what happens in reality, as opposed to a simplistic naïve concept of a "self-executing" L2 contract "Web3" morphing of the internet that will bring the work into the age of the "metaverse." It is important that professionals grasp that there is a very complex structure with a frosting layer of hype linguistics to evade uncovering that the developers are using the same old HTTP/CSS web and internet TCP/IP infrastructures in the movement of digital assets that sometimes involves nefarious activities. In my experience in digital forensics and civil/criminal investigations, the hype and colloquial terms are often self-promoting and obfuscate the fact that what is advertised as "decentralized" is in fact highly centralized, but highly democratized to attract as many users as possible to increase the revenues from transaction fees—the monetization motive is built on democratization, not decentralization.

DeComm, DePIN, DeREN, DeWiFi, and DeVS

There is so much I want to get into about the developments in DeComm, DePIN, DeRen, DeVS, and other structures being built in this area of distributed network ledger and democratizing what has been centrally controlled for so long. However, there just isn't enough time and space to get deep into these areas, so my objective is to give a brief primer on a few of the more relevant structures currently under development.

Theres is an increasing trend in attempts to achieve decentralization through (1) deconcentration, (2) devolution, and (3) debureaucratization in the context and utilization of "distributed" network ledger technologies to remove intermediaries and organizational structures under the label of decentralization. This terminology would be accurate if in fact that is what these projects achieve; however, what these projects are achieving is democratization. That is a good thing and is exactly what distributed network ledger technologies are designed to do. I will note that the "de" in most of these structures as written in most articles is short for "decentralized" and should be interpreted as democratized because these initiatives are often far from decentralized. I trust by now that it is abundantly clear that research is required to determine if the infrastructure is truly decentralized or to determine what degree of centralization exists. I will note that these structures are doing an incredible service to democratize, through distributed network architectures, that for so long have been under the control of large conglomerates. But that doesn't make them separate from some centralized organizational structures that sustain the infrastructure of the network (i.e., not decentralized), as is the case with the Ethereum platform where the foundation, founders, and developers exercise extensive control over the maintenance and delivery of new features to the network participants. In other words, most of these projects are about as decentralized as Homeowner Associations (HOA) or Condominium Associations (COA) that are designed to provide decentralized management of communities to ensure community standards and maintain property values at their highest level under the decentralized participation and direction of owners living in the community. Following is a brief framework around several of these democratized infrastructure projects.

The majority of the infrastructure projects are now largely under the main category referred to as a DePIN (Democratized Physical Infrastructure Network). Unlike traditional centralized infrastructure services under the control of government or corporations, a DePIN project utilizes a distributed network ledger environment to remove intermediary serves and drive democratization with the goal of participants in the network being the contributors of underutilized physical infrastructure equipment, thus, disrupting the norm and removing the utility service provider from the equations. The term DePIN was coined by the digital asset analytics firm, Messari, in November 2022, following a poll on X (formerly Twitter).

A sibling of DePINs are DeRENs (Democtratized Resource Networks). Where DePINs focus on physical infrastructure, DeRENs focus on development of marketplaces, utilizing distribute network ledger technologies for the sale of resources that are consumable and fungible and used in a location-independent manner. There's no single person or group credited with coining that term DeREN, but the first use of the term DeREN as a specific area of focus emerged in November 2022 following Messari coining the term DePIN.

Projects that are often included under the category of DePIN or DeREN are Helium (provides distributed connectivity for IoT hotspot coverage), Render (provides distributed GPU capacity for task rendering), Storj and Filecoin (distributed data storage capacity), IoTeX (provides distributed IoT application development), Arkreen Network and Hivemapper (distributed network web interface to connect users of renewable energy resources), and Bittensor (facilitates distributed AI services) as just a few examples.

Quantum Cryptography & Quantum Entanglement Distributed Networks

I want to being by elaborating on the founding of quantum computing. The idea of quantum computing emerged in the early 1980s, with Paul Benioff's 1980 proposal of a quantum mechanical model of a Turing machine and Richard Feynman's 1982 suggestion that quantum computers could efficiently simulate quantum systems. However, David Deutsch is often referred to as the "father of quantum computing" for his significant contributions to the theoretical framework and principles of the field, including the development of the quantum Turing machine and the Deutsch-Jozsa algorithm and his 1985 paper titled "Quantum Theory, the Church-Turing Principle and the Universal Quantum Computer." But I would be remiss in mentioning that there were many key scientists, such as Max Planck, Albert Einstein, and Niels Bohr, who contributed to the development of quantum mechanics that later provide the principles for expansion in the development of quantum computing.

We have come a long way from the work of Dr. Shannon, the "Father of Mathematical Cryptography," and his notable work and papers published in the 1940s and 1950s introducing such concepts as block ciphers and computer communication networks (what we now call the internet). And by that measure, quantum computing is still in its infancy relatively speaking, but even in light of its relatively recent origin, quantum computing is again making notable leaps in our understanding of quantum states, entanglement, and qubit technology, which can be summed up into five distinct periods:

- The Theoretical Foundations of Quantum Computing (1900–1980)
- The Emergence of Quantum Computing (1980–1994)
- The Development of Quantum Algorithms (1994–2000)
- The Race to Build Quantum Computers (2000–2021)
- Ongoing Advancements (2021–present)

Most presentations on quantum computing and distributed network ledger technology that I am invited to attend are from the perspective of how quantum cryptography and distributed network ledger technology are intertwined and the potential threat that quantum computers pose to existing cryptographic algorithms used in DLT architecture. To be fair, there are some articles that I have read that move beyond the concerns of using Shor's algorithm to break current-day cryptography and discuss how quantum computing and "blockchain"—as a very limited view of distributed network ledger technologies—can work collaboratively, which is presented as a complimentary data security undertaking. But why limit quantum mechanics to a simple collaboration, which is not even a convergent relationship, when we can rethink the architectural engineering of distributed computing, distributed networking, and the concept of quantum assets—not existing as bit but as a quantum state? So, most people who discuss this topic are missing that quantum is actually the next revolutionary leap, not just an evolutionary step, in the future of digital assets and distributed quantum networks in the form of infinite quantum states and quantum entanglement, respectively.

And this brings the conversation into a current day technology perspective. Few are thinking or contemplating the demise of current digital asset technology and distributed network and ledger technology. Just as few today can reminisce about how cellular technology in phones has replaced the old switchboard party landline phones of the past, there is a rapidly approaching future where a revolutionary quantum networking environment will replace everything that people understand, or don't truly understand, about "blockchain" ledgers and distributed networks today. In observing behavior and conversation in what has become the traditional "crypto" technology that will vanish, this messaging is being lost on those promoting that the government hold 20-year Bitcoin reserve funds as a partial solution to financial issues because, in 20 years, all of that Bitcoin will likely be worthless due to quantum technology developments that are happening today.

For example, MIT researchers have developed a new interconnect device that can support scalable, "all-to-all" communication, such that all superconducting quantum processors in a network can communication directly with each other.

They created a network of two quantum processors and used their interconnect to send microwave photons back and forth on demand in a user-defined direction. Photons are particles of light that can carry quantum information. The device includes a superconducting wire, or waveguide, that shuttles photons between processors and can be routed as far as needed. The researchers can couple any number of modules to it, efficiently transmitting information between a scalable network of processors. They used this interconnect to demonstrate remote entanglement, a type of correlation between quantum processors that are not physically connected. Remote entanglement is a key step toward developing a powerful, distributed network across quantum processors.

Now, combine those developments with the MIT quantum network development with a 2010 research paper titled "Quantum Money from Knots." I will note that this paper was posted on Bitcointalk.org (the forum introduced by Nakamoto introduced earlier) in 2011 and described as a Bitcoin-ish like scheme. I will go on the record as noting that this paper is like the Jetson era technology when compared to Bitcoin architectural technologies.

This research paper by Edward Farhi, David Gosset, Avinatan Hassidim, Andrew Lutomirski, and Peter Shor lays the framework for a quantum currency unit created from a cryptographic protocol method in which a mint can produce a quantum state that no one else can copy, but anyone with a quantum computer can verify that the state came from the mint. They present a concrete quantum currency scheme based on superpositions of diagrams that encode oriented links with the same Alexander polynomial with the exception that the scheme will be secure against computationally bounded adversaries.

To grasp what this means at a basic level, I need to explain two principles: the Alexander polynomial and quantum states.

The Alexander polynomial is a knot invariant (in knot theory, knot invariants are characteristics of knots that don't change when the knot is deformed or manipulated, as long as the manipulations are continuous), which assigns a polynomial with integer coefficients to each knot type. James Waddell Alexander II discovered this, the first knot polynomial, in 1923. In 1969, John Conway showed that a version of this polynomial, now called the Alexander–Conway polynomial, could be computed using a skein relation (a mathematical tool use to study knots), although its significance was not realized until the discovery of the Jones polynomial in 1984.

Okay, now that the Alexander polynomial is probably as clear as mud to many readers, I'll move to quantum states.

In quantum computing, a two-qubit system can exist in four distinct states: $|00\rangle$, $|01\rangle$, $|10\rangle$, and $|11\rangle$, representing all possible combinations of the qubit states $|0\rangle$ and $|1\rangle$. The quantum currency scheme proposed in this paper has two components: quantum currency units and an algorithm M that verifies the quantum units. How this essentially works in an oversimplified explanation: a quantum currency unit consists of a serial number p (just like a USD serial number) that is authenticated as coming from the mint along with an associated quantum state $|\$_p\rangle$ on n qubits. The verification algorithm M takes as input a quantum state $|\varphi\rangle$ and a serial number q and then decides whether or not the pair $(q, |\varphi\rangle)$ is a legitimate quantum currency unit. If the unit is verified, then the verifier also returns the state $|\varphi\rangle$ undamaged so it can be used again. The authors formalize each of these requirements as outlined here:

1. There is a polynomial-time algorithm that produces both a quantum state $|\$p\rangle$ and an associated serial number p.
2. Running the verification algorithm M with inputs p and $|\$p\rangle$ returns "good money" and does not damage $|\$p\rangle$. Furthermore, anyone with access to a quantum computer (for example a merchant) can run the verification algorithm M.
3. Given one piece of quantum money $(p, |\$p\rangle)$, it is hard to generate a quantum state $|\psi\rangle$ on 2n qubits such that each part of $|\psi\rangle$ (along with the original serial number p) passes the verification algorithm.

This provides that the mint of a unit, using the same algorithm as the mint, from producing counterfeit unit quantum states is that the serial number needs to be authenticated that is produced at the time of the mint as a set of pairs $(p, |\$p\rangle)$.

In closing out this last chapter, it is exciting to present what I believe is the trend that is revolutionizing as well as antiquating everything that current adopters of digital assets know. Quantum distributed networks and quantum digital asset projects explore the intersection of quantum technologies, of quantum distributed systems and quantum state assets, focusing on secure and efficient solutions for the future. This includes quantum-resistant cryptography, quantum tokens, and quantum-enhanced asset management. And come to the understanding, everything that you thought you knew about this space is all about to change in the very near future.

Conclusion

In conclusion, I have been reluctant to write publicly about the technologies underpinning digital assets, and I have primarily gravitated toward classroom instruction. This is because of the rapid change in the technologies involved; I never wanted to put something in print that would be antiquated the day it would be submitted to a publisher. However, I have had a passion to share with a larger base of learners what is infrequently taught about the people who, over the centuries, have contributed to what became the Bitcoin payment ledger network that everyone has spent so much time in conspiracy theories and conjecture around a pseudonymous figure whose contribution was to take the technology puzzle pieces delivered by brilliant minds throughout history that made it possible for Nakamoto, and contributors, to deploy something nascent that is now being antiquated by a completely different group of brilliant minds—past and present. Take, for example, quantum computing that led to a 2010 paper on quantum currency, and quantum entanglement that is in the beginning phases of introducing the quantum internet.

I must confess, explaining quantum currency here has induced a flashback to 2008 when I was explaining the cryptographic algorithms discussed in the Bitcoin payment network white paper to people in the government who wanted to understand what Bitcoin is. And I trust that the information that I have provided in this book has given a small insight into what I observed and inspired me to begin studying the technology way back when the development of these technologies was introduced by David Chaum in the 1980s as he was developing digital currency cryptographic algorithms for currencies, optimization and privatization—and so much more. As time passed and I continued my education and research, I observed in the 2000s a development team under a pseudonym that was converging David Chaum's work in digital assets with Leslie Lamport's contributions of distributed networking and distributed computing. And what would Satoshi have done without the brilliant contributions from so many mathematicians and cryptographers over the centuries who developed encrypted data ledger technologies that gave us encrypted sequential linear and nonlinear block, directed acyclic graph, radix data storage that many understand with the simplistic contrived blockchain term? And there are so many other technological concepts and principles provided by predecessors who have brought us technical knowledge that we leverage today. I started using this line many years ago: "Those who do not know history have no perspective on the future."

However, with the contributions of technology by predecessors with the objective of enriching human knowledge bringing us the present state of technology, the depraved and morally weak minded in our global society have introduced new ways to misuse some very cool technology to execute some very nefarious activities. With the dawn of coins as alternative investments and the Degen meme-token explosion, it has introduced the ability for criminals to create scams using a different technology other than email, text, web, and more for cybercriminal nefarious creativity. One of the most widely known, largest, and longest running distributed ledger asset criminal scam investigations is the $4.5 billion OneCoin scam started in 2014 and propagated by cofounders Karl Sebatian Greenwood and Ruja Plamenova Ignatova. Greenwood was finally sentenced in 2023 to 20 years in prison imposed by the US District Judge Edgardo Ramos in the Southern District of New York. But still at large at the time of writing is cofounder Ignatova, who hasn't been seen since stepping off a Ryanair flight in Athens, Greece, in 2017. In 2024, the US Federal Bureau of Investigations (FBI) announced Ignatova is now subject to a global freeze on her assets. It is notable that OneCoin was only a concept and never existed as an actual asset distributed ledger network.

And as distribution ledger stack development has expanded from L1, many legacy technology structures have been integrated into the L2|L3 portion of the distributed network ledger stack (e.g., banking, securities exchange, lending, social media, Wi-Fi infrastructure), which has led to a move away from the originally designed transparency of L1. And now with the introduction of zero-knowledge proofs used to comingle L1 transaction data through an L2 contract with the objective of improving throughput, there has been an associated removal of transaction transparency resulting in data obfuscation, leading bad actors to remain hidden and disassociated from their nefarious actions.

To tie the good with the bad activities with a proposed solution to prevent a regulatory environment that simply labels it all bad and bans it, I return to some of what I wrote for this space about self-regulating. If self-regulation is not adopted, which already somewhat occurs at the project level, it will eventually lead to government regulating technology, which is what is currently taking place whether everyone realizes it or not.

As I reflect on my academic learning, I had professors that emphasized ethics in technology development. I will again articulate that developers, entrepreneurs, investors, and even users need to consider that what we do, or what we contribute to, needs to be done ethically, considering the social implications in introducing certain technologies and putting in safeguards to protect vulnerable members of society; ensuring that technology is accessible, to the greatest extent to the benefit of all; protecting the privacy of those who use the technology; and creating projects with security as a major component and not just a sidenote. Nothing will ever be perfect, but I grew up in an era of "peer review" before publishing research, technical journal articles, and even technology. Development communities need to prioritize these types of check-and-balance protocols in academia and industry and learn from each other in the process. *"Tell me and I forget, teach me and I may remember, involve me and I learn."*

— Benjamin Franklin

There is so much more that I would love to share, but my greatest encouragement is to never stop learning, and I depart with this closing quote: "We cannot solve our problems with the same thinking we used when we created them. Once you stop learning, you start dying."

—Albert Einstein

Index

Page numbers in *italics* denote figures.

A

account take-over (ATO), 143, 178
address, 97
airdrops, 114, 168
Alexander polynomial, 218
algorithm, definition of, 22
alternative ledger frameworks, 81–89, *86, 89*
AnyTrust, 212
app-chains, 87
Application-Specific Integrated Circuit
 (ASIC), 29, 169
Arbitrum, 211–212
array, 56
asset class, 208
attention economy, 209
augmented general intelligence (AGI), 104, 156
augmented narrow intelligence (ANI), 104,
 195, 201–202

B

bandwidth, 72, *72*, 156
bank run, 196
banks
 as currency creators, 197
 failures, 198–200
 synthetic fiat, 192
Berners-Lee, Timothy, 128
best product-market fit, 209, 211
Binance, 198–199, 206
bitcoin (BTC)
 centralized exchanges, 204–205
 distribution, 183, 185–186
 government ownership, 174–176,
  180–183, 217
 hoarding, 185
 introduction, 146–147
 liquidity, impacts of reduced, 181
 maximum minted supply, 183, 185–186
 reserve fund, 138–139, 175, 180–183, 217
 unrecoverable, 182–183
Bitcoin Improvement Proposal (BIP), 185–187
Bitcoin network
 atomic swaps, 109
 chain splits, 100
 convergence of technologies, 179
 decentralization, 168–169
 dependence on third parties, 161
 deployment (2009), 10, 13

digital asset convergence with DLT
     architecture, 146–147
ECDSA, 16
Ethereum platform distinct from, 24
flipping the off-switch on, 177, 179–180
gossip algorithm, 33
governance algorithms, 161
hard forks originating from, 99–101, 109, 188
lack of cryptography, 17
lack of governance framework, 184–185
Layer 2, 188–189
Merkle trees, 14–15
node network, 55, *189*
payment ledger as public data ledger, 46
as permissionless ledger network, 41, 46
profit motivation, 169–170
state channels, 110
Sybil attack on, 180
transaction fees, 184
UTXO spend method, 24
validation, 168–169
white paper, 11, 13–14, 54, 58, 91, 141,
     161, 164, 188
BitUSD, 190, 192
blockchain
  retiring of term, 56, 58–60, 81, 114
  use of term, 48, 52, 58, 59–60, 78, 91–93, 160
block cipher, 11–13, 59, 64–65, 216
block-DAG ledger architectural design,
     72–78, *74, 76*
block ledger, 58–65
  blocktree ledger, 60–61, *61*
  code, 63, *64*
  sequential linear block arrangement,
     60, *60*, 62–63
  sequential nonlinear block
     arrangement, 60–61, *61*
  visual representations, *60–61, 63*
blockless ledger architecture, 65–72,
     66–67, 69–71
blocktree (b-tree), 60–61, *61*
block validation, 15, 30, 168–169, 184
b-money, 140–141
bridge contract, 107, 118
bridge rollups, 116
bridges and bridging, 118–121, *119*
  channels, 110, 112
  for Degen Chain, 212–213
  exploits, 120
  general message passing (GMP) bridges, 120
  L2 bridges, 84–85, 118–121, *119*, 212
  overview, 118–121, *119*

permissioned and permissionless, 120
in relay-parachain model, 82–85
Buterin, Vitalik, 98, 103, 105
"Byzantine Generals Problem," 19, 31–32, 159

C

cars as architectures, *79*, 80
censorship, 163–164, 175, 179, 194
centralization, 165–166
CEX (centralized exchange), 204–206
chain-apps, 87
chain splits, 24, 99–100, 109, 188
Chaum, David, 13, 102, 131–132, 141–146,
     175, 179, 222
child chains, 114, 124–125, *127*, 127–128
ciphers, 11–13, 59, 64–65, 216
client, 27, 29–30, 55
client-server model, 55
coding language, in L2 contracts, 106–107
Coinbase, 179, 191, 199, 204–205, 211–212
collateralization, 194–198
collators, 84–85
collectible items, tokenization of, 187
commitment schemes, 126
communication protocol, 32–33
components, 25
connectors, 26
consensus
  concept introduction, 17–18
  definition, 19
  nodes underpinning the distributed ledger
     consensus system, 28
  protocols vs algorithms, 8–25
consensus algorithms, 18, 21–25, 34
consensus client, 30
consensus protocols, 18–21, 25
consensus rules, 19–21
contracts
  bridge, 107, 118
  HTLC, 109–110
  L1-to-L2, 107–110
  L2 (*see* L2 (Layer-2) contracts)
  smart, 102–104, 109
critical thinking, 153–156
crypto (term), inaccurate use of, 3–4, 17, 45,
     137–138, 140–141, 208
cryptographic hashing, 14–15
cryptographic proofs, 141–142, 178
cryptography
  absence from DLT digital assets, 140–141
  asymmetric, 14–15, 97, 100

Crypto War, 146, 178
Dining Cryptographers Problem, 145
quantum, 216
symmetric, 65
currency
characteristics, 135, 139
denationalization of, 174–175
digital, 137–146
fiat, 24, 136, 138–139, 182
history of United States dollar
(USD), 136–137
laundering, 178–179
money distinct from, 134
overview, 134–137
quantum, 5, 218–219, 221
types of physical items used as, 136
virtual, 149, 178–179
cyberattack, 180
cybercrime, in Second Life, 178
cybersecurity vulnerabilities, 2, 16, 84, 104,
124, 179, 206

D

DAG. *see* Directed Acyclic Graph
Dai, Wei, 140–141
DAO (Decentralized Autonomous
Organization), 168
data access, distributed ledger, 46
database management system (DBMS), 98
databases, 52, 98
data breaches, 142
data ledger
as distinct from database, 98
general description, 59
governance framework, 160
optimal distribution of, 161
data ledger structure
block ledger, 58–65, *60–61, 63–64*
blockless ledger, 65–72, *66–67, 69–71*
hybrid ledger, *72,* 72–78, *74–76, 78*
introduction, 56–58
data structures, 56–57
Decent, 212–213
decentralization
definition, 166
governance in, 164–171
lack of transference property, 170
misuse of term, 164–168
Nakamoto's attempt to achieve, 175
decentralized (term), misuse of,
55–56, 102, 108

DeFi (Decentralized Finance), 7, 203–204, 206
Degen Casino Model, 5, 209–210
Degen Chain, 211–213
democratization, 207, 213–215
beneficial aspects of, 163–164
definition of, 162
DePIN (Democratized Physical Infrastructure
Network), 215
DeREN (Democratized Reserve
Network), 215
governance in democratized systems, 161–164
depegging, 190, 194–195, 197, 200
DePIN (Democratized Physical Infrastructure
Network), 215
DeREN (Democratized Reserve
Network), 215
DEX (decentralized exchange), 203–207
digital asset. *see also* digital currency
convergence with DLT architecture, 146–147
"crypto" term association with, 140–141
definition, 147
DLT, 149–152
examples of, 147
government ownership, 174–177
key trends, 209
number in circulation, 132
taxonomy, 148–149, *149*
topology, 151, *151*
typology, *150,* 150–151
virtual, 149
digital asset reserve funds, 174–187
digital currency, 137–146
BitUSD, 190
central bank (CBDC), 138
Chaum's contributions to field,
131–132, 143–146
government control of, 138–139
list of prominent payment systems, 145–146
synthetic fiat, 139, 182, 188–201, 188–202
technology perspective on, 139–146
virtual currencies, 142–143
digital run, 196
digital signature algorithm (DSA), 15–17,
96–97, 101
Directed Acyclic Graph (DAG)
block-DAG hybrid model, 72–78, *74, 76*
defined, 65
family trees, 66–67, *67*
origin, 65–66
overview, 65–71, *67, 69*
Radix DLT, 71
vertex classifications, 68

distributed application (DApp) layer (L3),
    3, 128–130
distributed computing, 54–55
distributed ledger
  definition of, 98
  diversity of architectures, 36
  first, 13–14
  misuse of terms associated with, 40, 44–46
  sequential linear blocked data ledger, 48
distributed ledger architectural primitives
  block ciphers, 11–13
  consensus in DLT, 17–25
  Elliptic Curve Digital Signature Algorithm
    (ECDSA), 15–17
  first distributed ledger, 13–14
  historical perspective, 9–37
  Merkle trees, 14–15
Distributed Ledger Digital Asset
    Taxonomy model, 1
distributed ledger network design, 39–50
  architectural structure for, 62, 63
  federated network design, 47–50
  permissioned vs. permissionless design, 41–44
  privacy trust matrix, 47
  private vs. public network design, 44–47
distributed ledger stack, 91–130
  bridges, 118–121, 119
  child chains, 124–125, 127, 127–128
  introduction, 91–94, 94
  L1-to-L2 contracts, 107–110
  L2 contracts in general, 102–107
  Layer-0 (L0), 95–96
  Layer-1 (L1), 96–101
  Layer-2 (L2), 102
  Layer-3 (L3), 128–130
  oracles, 121–123
  rollups, 114–118, 115–117
  side chains, 124–127, 125
  state channels, 110–114, 113
distributed ledger technology (DLT)
  consensus in, 17–25
  as a convergence of several technologies, 53
  definitions for, 39–41, 52–53
  digital assets, 149–152
  intended design purpose, 146
  introduction of phrase, 52
  misuse of term, 52
  roots of, 52–53
distributed ledger technology (DLT) primitives
  data ledger structures, 56–80
  distributed computing, 54–55
  distributed networking, 55–56

distributed network, 55–56
  architecture, 25–37
  definition, 158
  governance in, 158–161
  measuring level of distribution, 159
  messaging protocols in, 31–37
  topology, 26–27
Distributed Network Secure Ledger
    Technologies (DNSLT), 53
distributed system, governance in, 158–161
DLT. see distributed ledger technology
Dogecoin, 24, 100, 209
double-spends, 16–17, 36

E
e-Cash, 131, 143–144, 146
ECDSA, 23–24, 97
Elliptic Curve Digital Signature Algorithm
    (ECDSA), 15–16, 23–24
entanglement, 5, 217–218, 221
ether (ETH), 99, 101, 103–106, 120, 126–127,
    141, 177, 192
Ethereum
  Avalanche-Ethereum bridge, 119
  clients and nodes, 30–31
  competitor platforms, 106–107
  distributed ledger architecture, 62–63
  founding, 101, 103
  Gossipsub algorithm, 33
  hard forks, 24, 31 105, 98–99
  L2 contracts, 103–106, 151
  peg zone, 88, 88
  Polygon side chain, 126–127
  relay-parachain model compared, 82
  rollup code, 115–116
  state channels, 110
  synthetic fiat token transactions, 191
  white paper, 98, 103, 141, 151
Ethereum Virtual Machine (EVM), 74, 106
ethics, 223
event blocks, 74–76
execution client, 30
exploits, 2–4, 8, 36, 104, 107, 120–121,
    123, 163, 179

F
family trees, 66–67, 67
fault tolerance, 21, 31–33, 62, 74, 163
federated network design, 47–50, 49
fiat currency, 24, 136, 138–139, 182

food safety, 170–171
forensic science, 2, 7, 22
fraud proofs, 115, 117
FTX, 198–199, 203

G
game theory, 34–36, 180
gaming, virtual currency in, 142–143, 178–179
gas fee, 7, 103–105
general message passing (GMP) bridges, 120
Gini coefficient, 159
gold, tokenized, 196
gossip protocol, 33, 69, 71
governance
  "binary code of governance" model, 157
  in decentralization, 164–171
  definitions, 157–158
  in democratized systems, 161–164
  in distributed systems, 158–161, 163
  self-regulatory organization (SRO), 167, 171
  tenets, 153–171
graphs, 57
guardrails, 3, 5, 36, 177, 193

H
Haber-Stornetta timestamp certificate
    ledger, 62
hard fork, 24, 31, 98–101, 105, 109, 168, 188
hashed timelock contracts (HTLC), 109–110
hash-lattice, 77, *78*
HashLock, 109–110
hash tables, 57
Hayek, Friedrich August von, 131, 174–175
heaps, 57
Hedera, 33, 77, 118
heuristics, 7, 22–24, 37, 68, 115, 124
HTML code, self-executing, 104
hub-zone model architecture, 86–89, *89*
hybrid ledger architecture,
    72, 72–78, *74–76, 78*
hybrid topology, 27
hyphen, use of, 57

I
IBM, 59, 70, 142
In Real-Life Assets (IRLA), 187–188
Inscription, 183–184
interchain, 87, 89
IOTA, 67–68
iterated product cipher, 11

K
knots, 218
KOL (Key Opinion Leader), 209–211

L
L0 (Layer-0), 81, 95–96
L1 (Layer-1), 96–101
L1-data link layer, TCP/IP, 96
L2 (Layer-2)
  bridges, 84–85, 118–121, *119*, 212
  child chain, 124–125, *127*, 127–128
  L1 design for demands of L2, 97–99
  side chain, 124–127, *125*
  state channels, 110–114, *113*
  token assets in circulation, 102
L2 (Layer-2) contracts
  coding language, 106
  Ethereum, 151
  exploit, 130
  in general, 102–107
  meme tokens, 208–211
  oracles, 121–123
  proxy, 115–116
  rollups, 114–118
L2-network layer, TCP/IP, 96
L3 (Layer-3)
  Degen Chain as, 211, 213
  distributed applications
      layer, 128–130
  project development,
      208–214
L3-transport layer, TCP/IP, 95
L4-application layer, TCP/IP, 95
Lamport, Leslie, 17–19, 32, 34, 71,
    157, 159, 222
latency, 72, *72*, 76, 99
linear sequencing block
    ledger, 59
linked lists, 56
liquidity, 181–182
Liskov, Barbara, 17–18
Litecoin, 24, 100, 109, 188
logical clock, 21, 71, 157

M
mainnet (main network)
    layer, 96–101
MasterCoin, 189–190
meme tokens, 208–211, 213
mempool, 74, *75*
Merkle trees, 14–15, 62, 115, *115*

mesh topology, 26
messaging algorithms, 31–33, 35,
    55, 62, 84, 93
miners, 31, 167, 169, 184
mining pools, 169
misinformation, 3–4, 6
mixes, 144–145
MMO (Massively Multiplayer
    Online), 178
Monero, 37, 46, 101, 140
money
  currency distinct from, 134
  defined, 132–133
  functions, 133–134, 135, *136*
  quantity theory of, 132
multi-tier model, 55

N
Nakamoto, Satoshi, 11, 13, 18, 54, 175, 179,
    186, 218, 221
NFT (non-fungible token), 187–188, 209
nodes
  archive, 30
  clients, 27, 29–30, 55
  defined, 28, 29
  distributed network topology, 26–33
  Ethereum, 30
  full, 30, 55
  light, 31, 55
  malicious, 159
  misconceptions concerning, 28
  network architecture, 28
  peer, 27
  server, 27, 55
  Sybil, 180
  typologies, 30–31
  validation, 74–76, 167–169,
    180, 184, 186
nominators, 84–85
nonlinear sequential block ledgers, 59
nuclear material, tokenization of, 208

O
off-ledger transactions, 111, 113
OneCoin, 67, 222
Onyx platform, 192–193
Optimism rollups, 116–117
oracles, 121–123
Ordinal, 183–184
oversimplification, 2, 18, 22, 56

P
parachains, 82–86, *86*
peer-to-peer (P2P) network, 16, 26–27,
    29–30, 55, 119
pegged assets, 189–192
pegged token, USD, 139, 189–190,
    194, 196, 200
peg zone, 87–88
permission, definition of, 41
permissioned bridge, 120
permissioned distributed ledger
    network, 41–44
  bank use of, 43–44
  closed as inaccurate description of, 44
  federated network design, 48–49
  multi-level permission authentication, 44
  privacy trust matrix, *47*
  relevance of, 193
  roles within, 43
  third-party actors, 44
permissionless, definition of, 41
permissionless bridge, 120
permissionless distributed ledger
    network, 41–44, *47*
permutations, in block ciphers, 11–12
photons, 217
PlayerAuctions, 108, 178
Polkadot, 83, 86, 106, 128
Polygon, 126–127
pools, 169
POS (point-of-service) terminals, 103
privacy
  Chaum's attempt at, 175
  zero-knowledge proofs (ZKP), 63
privacy trust matrix, *47*
"private" distributed ledgers, 44–47, *47*
private key, 15, 23, 97, 140
problem-solving, 153–154
programming language, 106
Proof-of-Stake (PoS), 18, 21, 23, 74, 190
Proof-of-Work (PoW), 18, 21, 23, 29, 100, 144
proxy contracts, 115–116
"public" distributed ledgers, 44–47
public key, 14–15, 97
PvP (Player-*versus*-Player), 210
PVP KOL degen casino, 209–211

Q
quantity theory of money (QTM), 132
quantum computing, 216–219
quantum cryptography, 216

quantum currency, 5, 218–219, 221
quantum states, 218–219

R

Radix DLT platform, 69–71, *70–71*
radix sort, 69–71, *70*
Real-World Assets (RWA), tokenization of, 187–191, 201, 203, 205, 207–208
relay-parachain model, 81–86, *86*
relay platforms, 82–86, *86*
reserve funds, digital asset, 174–187
risk
 from bridges, 120–121
 self-executing code, 104
rollups, 61–62, 114–118, *115–117*
root hash, *115*, 115–116

S

scams, 67, 222
Second Life, 178
securities, synthetic, 201–208
self-execution, 103–104, 167–168, 214
self-regulatory organization (SRO), 167, 171, 179, 200
semantics, 166
sequential linear block data ledger, 60, *60*, 62–63, 74
sequential nonlinear block ledger arrangement, 60–62, *61*
server, 27, 55
"Seven Bridges of Königsberg," 66, *66*
Shannon, Claude, 11–13, 59, 216
"shortest path wins" theory, 78–79
side chains, 114, 124–127, *125*
soft forks, 99, 168, 184
Solana, 102, 107, 118–120, 176, 182
Solidity, 106–107, 115–116, *116*
Sonic Labs, 73–76
sotashi (SAT), 184, 186–187
stablecoin, 190, 192–197
star node topology, 26
state channels, 110–114, *113*
state-of-states, 85
state variables, 97–98, 116
stream ciphers, 64–65
subgraphs, 119
substitution-permutation networks (SPNs), 12, 59
substitutions, in block ciphers, 11–12
Sybil Attack, 180
synthetic assets, 188

synthetic fiat, 139, 182, 188–202
 cautionary caveats involving, 194
 defined, 193
 growth in adoption, 191
 proposed legislation on stablecoins, 195–201
synthetic securities, 201–208
Szabo, Nick, 102–104

T

taxonomy
 definition, 147
 digital assets, 148–149, *149*
TCP/IP layer, 95–96
Tether, 182, 189–190, 199
theory of constraints (ToC), 79
third-party actors, 44
throughput, 72, *72*, 76
TimeLock, 110
timestamping, Haber-Stornetta, 14–16, 62
tokenization
 Real-World Assets (RWA), 187–191, 201, 203, 205, 207–208
 synthetic securities, 201–208
tokens
 meme, 208–211, 213, 222
 non-fungible token (NFT), 187–188, 209
 topology, 151, *151*
topology
 definition, 147
 distributed network, 26–27
 token, 151, *151*
transaction cost, 72, 76, 126
transaction fee, 7, 105–106, 169, 184, 212
transactions per second (TPS), 59, 61, 63, 67
 Bitcoin, 100
 Ethereum, 99
 Radix DLT, 71
 Sonic Labs' hybrid Block-DAG architecture, 76
 state channels, 111
transitive closure, 78
transparency
 barriers in permissioned systems, 41
 federated distributed ledger networks, 49
 inaccurate use of term, 102, 140–141
 loss in transaction activity, 2
 in a permissionless network, 41
trees, 56–57. *see also* Merkle trees
tumblers, 145
typology
 definition, 147
 digital assets, *150*, 150–151

U

Unspent Transaction Output (UTXO),
   23–24, 97, 139
USDC, 173, 176, 182, 191, 194, 199, 202
USD pegged token, 139, 189–192,
   194, 196, 200
UST, 194, 197

V

validation
  ASIC devices, 29
  block-by-block, 30
  DAG, 69
  event blocks, 74–76
  of state changes, 111
validation nodes, 167–169, 180, 184
validators
  action approvals, 118
  Bitcoin, 184, 186
  in hub-zone architecture, 89
  in hybrid ledger architecture, 75–76
  miners, 184
  in relay-parachain model, 83–85
  roles, 43
  zone, 89
virtual assets, 149
virtual currency, 142–143, 149, 178–179

W

wallet, 42, 63, 96, 120, 183
web3 concept, 128–129
white paper, 19–21. *see also specific platforms*
Willett, J.R., 188–190
Wood, Gavin, 83, 98, 101, 103, 106, 128–129

Z

zero-knowledge proof (ZKP), 63, 117, 223
ZK rollups, 116–118
zones, 87–89, *88*